Lifescripts

Lifescripts

What to Say to Get What You Want
in Life's Toughest Situations
Completely Revised and Updated

Stephen M. Pollan
Mark Levine

WILEY
John Wiley & Sons, Inc.

Published by John Wiley & Sons, Inc., Hoboken, New Jersey
Published simultaneously in Canada

Limit of Liability/Disclaimer of Warranty: While the publisher and the author have used their
best efforts in preparing this book, they make no representations or warranties with respect
to the accuracy or completeness of the contents of this book and specifically disclaim any
implied warranties of merchantability or fitness for a particular purpose. No warranty may be
created or extended by sales representatives or written sales materials. The advice and strate-
gies contained herein may not be suitable for your situation. You should consult with a professional where appropriate. Neither the publisher nor the author shall be liable for any loss
of profit or any other commercial damages, including but not limited to special, incidental,
consequential, or other damages.

For general information about our other products and services, please contact our Customer
Care Department within the United States at (800) 762-2974, outside the United States at
(317) 572-3993 or fax (317) 572-4002.

Wiley also publishes its books in a variety of electronic formats. Some content that appears in
print may not be available in electronic books. For more information about Wiley products,
visit our web site at www.wiley.com.

ISBN: 0-471-63101-9 (trade edition)
ISBN: 0-471-64376-9 (special edition with CD)

Printed in the United States of America
10   9   8   7   6   5   4   3

PART II: LIFESCRIPTS FOR DEALING WITH SUBORDINATES

PART III: LIFESCRIPTS FOR DEALING WITH OFFICE POLITICS

PART IV: LIFESCRIPTS FOR DEALING WITH CLIENTS, CUSTOMERS, AND VENDORS

The Continuing Power of *Lifescripts*

When *Lifescripts* was originally published in 1996, we were living and working in a different world. There was no such thing as an information technology department. Human resources was still called personnel. People worried more about scheduling their vacation than about securing their job.

Lifescripts made the revolutionary suggestion that difficult workplace dialogues should be preplanned—that you should carefully prepare for your conversations with your superiors, peers, subordinates, clients, and vendors.

When we first suggested a book that mapped out entire conversations for people, we were met with a great deal of skepticism. Some people thought it was a gimmick or something that would be peculiar to my own highly personal consulting practice and would never work for "average" people. Many people thought it was somehow immoral to plan out conversations to this degree. Others felt it was an admission of a personal failing to turn to a book for help in having a dialogue. But our agent, Stuart Krichevsky, and Natalie Chapman, then an editor at Macmillan and now at John Wiley & Sons, had the confidence and foresight to see that the idea of preparing for tough dialogues was not only ethical, but had universal appeal.

Since the first edition appeared, *Lifescripts* has taken on a life of its own, becoming a cottage industry. We put together a team of experts to produce specialized volumes, focusing on the unique needs of employees, managers, and entrepreneurs. These experts included Michael Caplan, Jonathon Epps, Andrew Frothingham, Deirdre Martin, William Martin, Nick Morrow, Allison Noel, Aldo Pascarella, and Roni Beth Tower. The psychotherapist and author Erik Kolbell helped us expand the *Lifescripts* concept to dialogues with family and friends in a subsequent volume.

In 2002, Tom Miller of John Wiley & Sons suggested that we update *Lifescripts* for the new world of the twenty-first century. This revision contains 109 lifescripts, about half of which were not in the original edition. The lifescripts that appeared previously have all been edited and updated to account for changes in jargon and workplace culture.

One of the great lessons we've learned since the first edition was published is that while individual lifescripts may over time become dated, the lifescript concept remains vital.

If we plan out our interpersonal exchanges—whether they involve our subordinates or our customers—not only will they be easier to deal with, but, more often than not, they'll turn out the way we want. With a lifescript, either directly in front of you or just in your head, you'll never be surprised. You'll have a plan that leads inexorably to your goal, regardless of what obstacle is thrown in your way. You'll have an answer to every question, a comeback to every crack, and a defense for every attack.

HOW TO USE LIFESCRIPTS

In the following pages we offer lifescripts for 109 of the most perplexing and problematic workplace dialogues you might face in the course of your business life.

Each lifescript begins with a general discussion of the overall *strategy* you should use in the dialogue, usually highlighting what your goal should be. Then we briefly describe the *attitude* you should adopt—for example, righteous indignation or contrition. We touch on what kinds of *preparation* you need before using the script—perhaps some research or the drafting of a memo. Next we offer tips on *timing*—whether it's better to have this conversation during the work week or on the weekend, for instance. Then we touch on what your *behavior* should be. This could involve body language or whether to sit or stand during the conversation. On the next page we present the lifescript itself in flowchart form. We offer icebreakers, pitches, possible responses, counters, and retorts. Obviously, each lifescript is different because each conversation takes a different form.

After the flowchart we offer some ideas for *adaptations*—other situations where, with some minor modifications, you could use the same lifescript. Finally, we've provided a few *key points* for each lifescript. You can use these as crib notes for your dialogue.

These lifescripts are written so they can be used verbatim. We've picked the words very carefully, and each has been chosen for a reason. However, we think it's best if you take the words we offer and play around with them until they sound like your own. That's because everyone has different diction and sentence structure. There's nothing wrong with sounding prepared—as long as you sound like yourself.

With 109 scripts and possible adaptations more than doubling that number, we think this book offers help in nearly every common workplace situation. However, we're sure there are some important situations we've left out either because we couldn't think of them or because they're unique to you and the circumstances of your work life.

In order to help you prepare your own personalized lifescripts, here is a brief course in the five rules behind these lifescripts.

Rule 1: Take Control of the Situation

If you gain nothing else from this book, let it be an understanding of this rule. The single most important element in getting these conversations to turn out the way you want is to take control of them. It doesn't mean that you monopolize the conversation or bully the other person. It simply means that through your choice of words and reactions, you frame and steer it in the direction you want it to go.

In many cases that means you make the first move, and by so doing, you force the other person to respond. In other situations it means responding in such a way that the other person is forced into retorts that you're already prepared to address. Unlike most icebreakers, ours aren't written just to make the person delivering them more comfortable. They're written to force the other party into a position where he or she has a limited number of options. That way you can prepare responses to each of those limited options.

Rule 2: Say What You Want

We're continually amazed at the inability of most people to come out and say exactly what they want. Whether it's because we don't want to be viewed as demanding or we're afraid of being turned down, most of us beat around the bush, imply, and drop hints, rather than come right out and say what's on our mind.

In almost every lifescript we've included direct, specific requests. You can't rely on other people to infer what you're after or to pick up on your hints. And besides, if you don't come right out and ask directly, you're giving the other party a chance to sidestep the whole issue. Make him respond directly. It's easier to deal with an outright rejection than you might imagine.

Rule 3: Show Your Power Before You Use It

Subtle demonstrations of power are often just as effective as the outright use of that power. For instance, if you're a restaurant patron you have two powers: your ability to make a scene and your willingness to pay your bill. By calling over a waiter or maître d' and whispering that you're unhappy with your meal and would like another, you demonstrate that you're aware of your power to make a scene but are holding it in check until they've had a chance to respond. If you actually raise your voice and make a scene immediately you have far less power, since you've used up half your ammunition.

Other ways of displaying your power include saying things like, "I'm a longtime customer and would like to continue our relationship," or "The last thing I want to do is hire someone else to finish this project." In both cases you're showing an awareness of your power but a willingness not to use it. That's far more likely to work that an outright threat. Though if push comes to shove, you may have to make such a threat.

Rule 4: Absorb or Deflect Anger

That doesn't mean you should get angry, however. Displays of anger can be just as self-defeating as gratuitous exercises of power. The actual message you may be sending is, "I don't have any real power so all I can do is make noise." Therefore, hold your temper unless your anger serves a real purpose.

Similarly, when you're met with anger, the best response is to disarm the other party by either absorbing it or deflecting it. You absorb anger by acknowledging it and refusing to respond in kind. ("I can understand your being angry. I would be, too.") You deflect anger by suggesting it's an odd reaction and must therefore be based on something other than your request. ("I don't understand why you're getting angry at me. Have I done something else to bother you?")

Rule 5: Have the Last Word

In almost every situation it's to your advantage to have the last word in a dialogue. That means either expressing thanks for getting what you wanted, asking for reconsideration of a rejection, pushing for another meeting, or saying that you'll call back if you couldn't get a definite answer. Having the last word does two things: It makes sure you retain the control over the dialogue that you seized when you broke the ice, and it allows you to close the conversation on advantageous terms.

The only exceptions to having the last word are in situations where it's important for you to give the other party a chance to "save face." In effect, by giving them the last word you're letting them think they're still in control, even though they're not.

A Final Thought

In a few of the lifescripts you'll notice lines such as, "I've already notified the boss about this," which effectively disarm threats from the other party. We're assuming that you're actually going to do what the lifescript says—in this case, speak to your superior before the meeting. Of course that doesn't mean you have to in order to use the line. That's something you'll have to decide for yourself. But if we can offer one more word of advice in parting it's this: the most effective lifescripts are truthful.

I

Lifescripts

for Dealing with Superiors

Asking for a
Salary Increase

1

STRATEGY

While it has never been tougher to get a raise than today, it's still possible. The key is to realize there are only three acceptable reasons anymore: your contributions to the company's bottom line have increased dramatically, your responsibilities have outgrown your job description, or (for professionals and upper-level managers) your income hasn't kept pace with your professional growth. Using and documenting one of these arguments, and forcing your superior to fall back on a poverty excuse, will at least result in your obtaining further nonfinancial compensation or a deferred promise. And sometimes, that's the best you can hope for.

TACTICS

- **Attitude:** Remember that your salary has nothing to do with your value as a human being. It is solely a reflection of what your superior or company is willing to pay for your services. It's an entirely economic issue.
- **Preparation:** It's essential to have irrefutable documentation that backs up whichever of the three arguments you're using. When it comes to documenting industrywide salary ranges, draw on trade magazine surveys, headhunters, and professional associations. All your information should be included in a memo, with appropriate attachments, that outlines your argument.
- **Timing:** The best times to ask are shortly after a positive evaluation, upon successful completion of an important project, or after receiving some third-party recognition, such as an award. Avoid Mondays and Fridays entirely. Ask for an appointment either before business hours or just after lunch. The former will offer fewer interruptions; the latter will find the other party more relaxed.

1. Asking for a Salary Increase

Icebreaker: I'd like to thank you for the opportunity you and the company have given me. I recognize that you've been very influential in my growth and advancement. However, I have a problem that I need your help with.

Pitch #1: What has happened is that I've been concentrating solely on my professional growth and haven't been paying any attention to my stream of income. So I've done some research and found my peers in the industry are earning on average 15 percent more than my current compensation. I've drafted this memo that shows what I've found. It's logical for my compensation to keep pace with my growth. To do that, I'll need an increase of [state increase].

Pitch #2: I think my salary no longer reflects my contribution to the company. In the past year I've helped the company save a great deal of money [or] bring in added revenue [or] trim quite a bit from the cost of operations. I've done some research and I've found that a salary of [state salary] would more accurately reflect my value. I've prepared a brief memo outlining my accomplishments and my request.

Pitch #3: I think my salary no longer matches my job responsibilities. During the past year I've moved from being an order taker to helping supervise the evening sales staff and helping draft the new selling scripts. I've done some research and I think a salary of [state salary] would more accurately reflect my responsibilities. I've prepared a brief memo outlining my increased responsibilities and my request.

Facts are wrong: *I can't believe you're underpaid. Let me take a look at your numbers. These figures come from companies larger than ours. If you check with companies the same size as ours you'll find you're making exactly what you should.*

Not enough time: *I won't argue your point. You've done an excellent job. But you simply haven't been here long enough [or] it simply hasn't been long enough since your last increase for you to merit a raise.*

Don't have the money: *I agree you've been doing a wonderful job. But, as you know, business has been slow. The company simply doesn't have the money for raises right now [or] it doesn't have that kind of money right now.*

Wouldn't be fair: *I agree with you completely. We're very happy with your work. But we have a policy of . . . How can I pay you more than Jean Smith, for instance, when she has worked here two years longer than you have?*

Solicit other sources: I don't want what I'm not entitled to. If my research is incomplete I'll be happy to do some more and come back to you with it, let's say, in two weeks. What companies would you consider comparable to ours?

Time is unfair measure: I really don't think you can fairly measure my contribution to the company by the amount of time I've been here *[or]* by how long it has been since my last raise. Let me go over the contributions I've outlined in my memo.

Expand the discussion: I understand. You can't do the impossible. But perhaps we can agree to an increase that would take effect, let's say, in six months. Meanwhile, there are some non-financial areas I need to speak with you about. For instance, I'd like another five vacation days . . .

Seniority is unfair measure: I've always assumed that excellent performance and taking on added responsibility would be rewarded in this company. I don't think it's fair to deny rewarding me for my contributions because of my lack of seniority. Let me go over the contributions I've outlined in my memo.

Won't offer sources: *I'd have to think about it. I'm really not sure. But I am sure you're not underpaid.*

Offers other sources: *Why don't you try looking at Smith & Jones and Pinnacle. They're both about our size. When you get numbers from them we'll talk again.*

Agrees to expand: *I can't guarantee the money will be there in another six months either. We'll have to see. But the added vacation days shouldn't be a problem.*

Refuses to expand: *I don't think either will be possible. The money may not be there in another six months, and adding to your vacation would be contrary to company policy. You'll have to wait.*

Seize initiative: I'll look into it further and take the companies you suggested into account. Then, I'll come back to you with more results. Meanwhile, let's nail down that meeting. How about two weeks from today?

Ask for another meeting: I understand. But I need to leave here with a definite date for our next discussion. How about four months from today? Also, I'd appreciate your double checking about those vacation days. *[Start looking for another job.]*

- **Behavior:** It's completely up to you to blow your own horn, so avoid humility and subservience. Don't project guilt—you're asking for what you deserve. This forthright attitude will come through if you maintain direct eye contact whenever listening or speaking. Only break eye contact when you're thinking. Avoid nodding reflexively. Your agreement is powerful, especially in this situation. Let the other party fill in gaps in the conversation. Chattiness will imply insecurity. Speak only when necessary and you'll convey strength and confidence.

ADAPTATIONS

This script can be modified to:

- Obtain consideration for a promotion to another department or get a title changed.
- Get your employer to pay for continuing education.

KEY POINTS

- Begin by stressing you love your job or company but have a problem you need help with.
- Your argument is that your compensation doesn't match either your growth, contribution, or responsibilities.
- If your numbers are called into question, ask where you can get "correct" numbers. If none are offered, suggest some of your own and ask for a follow-up meeting.
- If the other party says insufficient time has passed from some other event, say time isn't relevant to your growth, contribution, or responsibilities.
- If fairness to others is cited, say that compensation based solely on seniority is also unfair.
- If the other party pleads poverty, ask for nonfinancial compensation and/or a future agreement.
- If you're stonewalled, force a future meeting and start looking for another job.

Asking for a Promotion

STRATEGY

Asking for a promotion is even more difficult than asking for a raise. That's because you have to demonstrate not only that you have the skills to handle the new position but also that leaving your current job won't hurt either your boss or the company. The secret is to prepare two plans of action: one for the new position and one for your current job. Don't fall back on seniority or hierarchy to make your case—they don't hold water in today's business world. Focus on your proven ability to do the job and emphasize that you're ready to move up. One other essential: make sure to present your case as soon as possible, preferably before an outside search has begun.

TACTICS

- **Attitude:** Look at this not as something you're owed for past service but as an opportunity you've shown you're ready for. There are no entitlements in today's workplace.
- **Preparation:** Draft two formal memos—one outlining what you'd do in the first ninety days in the new job and another explaining how you'd assist whoever takes over your current position. In addition, have in mind potential replacements for your position.
- **Timing:** It is absolutely essential to stake your claim to the job as soon as you hear it's available. Consider dropping hints and spreading the word informally if you can do it without looking pushy. The more time that passes, the less your chances of landing the job.
- **Behavior:** Accept compliments and constructive criticism gracefully, but don't hesitate to argue around these points by directing the conversation to your strengths rather than your weaknesses.

2. Asking for a Promotion

Icebreaker and pitch: I understand Keith is leaving. I'm hoping that you'll seriously consider me for his job. Since he and I have worked so closely together over the past year, I'm very familiar with the department and what's required. And when I've filled in for Keith, I think I've shown that I can manage the staff effectively.

You're not ready: *You've shown tremendous growth over the past year, but you don't have enough experience yet with customer service or with managing a staff to take on a job like Keith's.*

Have inside knowledge: I may not have been at it a long time, but I think I've shown a real flair for customer service. Even more important, I know how this department works, inside and out. You won't get that kind of experience if you go outside.

Need you where you are: *You've been doing an outstanding job in your position—that's exactly why I can't afford to move you right now. I need you where you are.*

Will help train: Thank you. I appreciate your confidence in me. But I'd be happy to work closely with my replacement until she's completely familiar with my system. In fact, I can suggest people in my department who would be great for the job.

Going outside: *I appreciate your interest in the position, but we've decided that we need a completely fresh approach. That's why we're looking outside the company for a replacement.*

Have fresh approach: I think I can offer a fresh approach—and at a much lower cost than if you go outside the company. I have a lot of ideas that I think could really reenergize the staff. And after four years in my current job I'm eager for a new challenge.

No more money: *You understand that if I do put you in the position, I probably won't be able to give you a salary increase.*

I'm flexible: I'm most interested in my prospects over the long term. I'd be willing to take a little bit less right now than the job normally pays if we can accelerate the timetable for my next raise—provided you're satisfied with my work.

Let me think about it: *I can't make you any promises, but I'll think about what you said and get back to you.*

Offer memo: Thank you. Making this move is just as important to me as joining the company was. I'll put my ideas for the department in a memo and have it on your desk tomorrow.

ADAPTATIONS

This script can be modified to:

- Request a transfer.
- Move ahead in a political or social organization.
- Broadcast your ambitions and willingness for more responsibility.

KEY POINTS

- Acknowledge that you've heard there's an opening, state your qualifications, and directly ask to be considered for the job.
- Respond to arguments for going outside by demonstrating how you can bring a fresh approach . . . at a lower cost.
- Don't let your success be used against you. Offer to work closely with your own replacement.
- Claims that you don't have sufficient seniority can be met by showing how your time, while short, has been intensive and exactly what is necessary to do the job.
- Be prepared to forgo a raise—at least until you've proven yourself.
- Have a memo ready outlining your plans.

Asking for Emergency Leave

STRATEGY

Unless yours is a company with an established procedure for emergency leaves, you'll need to ask your superior directly for time off. Be forewarned that some superiors, despite their protestations, will be much more concerned with the effect your absence will have on the bottom line than your personal problem. The secret to this dialogue is to make it clear you've no choice but to take the time off; however, your workload can be adequately handled either by others or through your remaining in constant touch with the office. While you may be able to fend off attempts to turn your emergency leave into your vacation, when push comes to shove, you'll have to accept that unless your superior is both powerful and gracious, you may have to forgo salary while you're away. Your goal here is to get the time off and, if at all possible, to keep your vacation.

TACTICS

- **Attitude:** In your heart of hearts you must feel this is a true emergency—otherwise you won't convey the necessary sense of urgency to carry the day. You must be able to say honestly you've no choice.
- **Preparation:** Before having this conversation, make sure that you have plans—including detailed memos—in place to handle any workplace problems that could arise and that your current projects are all in good shape.
- **Timing:** To the extent possible, have this conversation as early in the day and as early in the workweek as you can. Try contacting your staff or whoever will be filling in for you before working hours so contingency plans are already in place when it comes time to meet the boss.
- **Behavior:** The more concerned and determined you are to take a leave of absence, and the more willing you are to do whatever needs to be done to get the time off, the smoother this dialogue will go.

3. Asking for Emergency Leave

Icebreaker: I have a family problem and I need an emergency leave of absence. I'll need to be away for two weeks.

Ask for details: *Slow down. First tell me what's wrong. What happened?*

Explain situation: My uncle passed away unexpectedly and his affairs are in a shambles. He has no children and there's no one else in the family with the ability to handle it. I've already spoken to my assistant, Pat, about all pending matters. All our projects are in good shape, and I'll be in touch daily by telephone, fax, and e-mail.

Use your vacation time: *Well, you do have one week of vacation coming to you, although I'd prefer having had notice about when you'd be taking it. As for the second week, we'll work it out . . . maybe we can take it out from next year's vacation.*

Gives grudging approval: *Well, as long as you're right and things are under control and you'll be in touch, I don't have a problem with it. Just try to be back as soon as possible.*

Not a vacation: I'd really rather not lose my vacation time for a family emergency. After all, it's not like I won't be working; and I will be in constant touch with the office. I was hoping the company wouldn't penalize me for the death of my uncle.

Won't take authority: *I can't make a decision like that on my own. Whether or not you'll be working, you won't be here. And if you're not here and you're not on vacation, I can't pay you . . . at least not without approval from upstairs.*

Offer to go upstairs: I'd appreciate it then if you'd go upstairs and tell them I really have no choice. If you'd prefer, I'll approach them directly, but I'd appreciate it if you back me up.

Okay, but no pay: *Okay, as long as you keep on top of things, I think we'll be able to give you an unpaid leave of absence. Just try to get back here as soon as possible.*

Accept conditions: I really have no choice in this matter. I'll be back as soon as I can.

ADAPTATIONS

This script can be modified to:

- Get partial time off to go to school.
- Get an extended leave of absence to wind up family business.
- Get a medical leave for elective surgery.

KEY POINTS

- Present your request for time off prior to divulging the details of the emergency. This forces your boss to ask what's wrong, hopefully setting a humane tone for the meeting.
- Stress that all your work is under control and that you'll be available should any problems arise.
- Fend off any attempt to take away vacation time by suggesting that it would constitute unfair punishment for something that's beyond your control.
- If your boss claims she's powerless, offer to take your case to the higher-ups, but ask for her support.
- If you're forced to go without pay, demonstrate the urgency of the matter by accepting the condition.

Asking Your Superior for Maternity Leave

4

STRATEGY

This dialogue isn't about what your superior is saying but what she's not saying. While she will congratulate you, what she really wants to know is how long you'll be gone and how your departure will affect the company. Your boss may be worried you'll never return from leave. Your goal is protecting your job while you're gone. Though in most cases your position will be protected—that's the law—lots of things can happen while you are on leave, particularly if you're in a competitive industry or company. You've worked hard, and taking maternity leave should not diminish your status in the company. Address your superior's fears and concerns, and you'll be able to protect your standing in the company.

TACTICS

- **Attitude:** Display concern. Your superior will be worried about the effect of your absence. If you share her concern, it will make the situation easier to negotiate.
- **Timing:** Set an appointment early in the week to speak with your superior in private. Make sure she hears about your pregnancy from you and not through the grapevine. Naturally, you cannot set an exact date for your leave, but the more advance notice you can give, the better.
- **Preparation:** Speak subtly with coworkers who have taken leave and check the company's policies prior to your meeting. Review your current workload and create a strategy for sharing your responsibilities with other employees.
- **Behavior:** Although you're conveying good news, your superior may view it as bad. Don't smile and celebrate during the meeting; you should be serious and concerned about the company. Your superior will appreciate your unselfish approach to the situation.

4. Asking Your Superior for Maternity Leave

Icebreaker: Thanks for meeting with me. My job is very important to me and for that reason I wanted you to be the first in the office to know I'm pregnant. I'd like to talk to you about taking maternity leave.

Friendly: *That's great news. When are you due?*

Practical: *Congratulations. When are you planning to take leave? We'll need to talk about what to do with your work.*

All-business: *Oh, I see. We'll miss you. Perhaps you and I should discuss hiring your replacement [or] dividing up your work?*

Skeptical: *Oh, how nice for you. Now, is this really a request for temporary leave? A lot of mothers say they're going to come back but never really do. If that's the case, I'd like to know now.*

Stay focused: Thank you. It's not for another five months. What I'd really like to discuss is how I can best help the company remain productive while I'm on leave.

Unveil plan: I'm glad you mentioned that because I would like to help the company prepare for my leave.

No replacement: You certainly won't need to hire a replacement. The company should be able to compensate for my temporary absence by hiring a temp [or] dividing up my work.

Leave is temporary: Oh, I'm coming back. I'd like to discuss how I can help contribute to the company while on leave.

Open-minded: *Well, the company policy is to provide six weeks of maternity leave . . . but if you need more time I'm happy to consider it.*

Pandering: *Let us worry about finding someone to do your work. You should be thinking about your baby. Your work will still be here when you get back.*

Inflexible: *The company offers six weeks of leave. We've always brought in outside help and divided up the individual's work among others.*

Get follow-up: If it's all right with you, I'd like to schedule a meeting for a couple of weeks prior to my due date to discuss the specifics of my leave.

ADAPTATIONS

The script can be modified to:

- Request leave to care for an elderly parent.
- Request leave to care for a sick child.

KEY POINTS

- Dismiss any notion that you won't return or need to be replaced.
- Show concern for the effect your leave will have on the company.
- Emphasize the importance of your job and your commitment to your career.

Asking Your Superior for Paternity Leave

5

STRATEGY

The problem with requesting paternity leave is that history isn't on your side. While you've just as much legal right to parental leave as a mother, society in general, and employers in particular, don't view things that way. Women are expected to place their family first. Men are not. Your goal here is to get sufficient leave without weakening your position in the company. Customarily, companies offer shorter paternity leave than maternity leave, and that can actually work in your favor. Still, your superior may accuse you of leaving at a crucial time, since there's never a good time to take leave. To mitigate objections, suggest working part-time at home and calling the office daily. Stress that you don't see this as a vacation, and show your superior that you want to continue to contribute to the company. Offer to work with other coworkers who will share your assignments during the leave, but be certain that such arrangements are temporary. Volunteer to come to the office one day over the weekend. Whatever you can do to meet your superior halfway will ultimately be appreciated and smooth the effects of your paternity leave.

TACTICS

- **Attitude:** Be flexible but not a pushover. You're entitled to this leave; just negotiate a mutually beneficial agreement and your superior will be satisfied.
- **Timing:** Request leave well before your wife's due date. The more advance warning, the less your superior can protest. Try to approach him after you have successfully completed a project or done something beneficial for the company.
- **Preparation:** Check around the office to see if any other fathers have taken leave. Find out how they were treated and check your employee handbook regarding the terms of the leave. Have specific ideas about staying in touch with the company.

5. Asking Your Superior for Paternity Leave

Icebreaker: As you may know, my wife is pregnant. She's due in about two months, and I'd like to speak to you about my paternity leave. My wife is going to take her leave first, so I'll be beginning my leave in four months.

Angry: *That's right around the Fall Show! That would be a terrible time to take off. We can't afford to lose any time on our fall projects.*

Threatening: *I can't stop you from taking leave, but I'll have to reassign your work.*

Delay: *Can't you postpone your leave until the winter? Maybe your wife can get an extension. You know how important the fall season is to us.*

Worried: *Naturally, you can take leave. I'm just concerned about the impact your absence will have on the company.*

Team player: Oh, I don't plan on leaving work completely. I want to arrange a part-time schedule with you. If I work from my home and come in on weekends, I don't think the office will suffer.

Keep your work: I don't think reassigning my work will be necessary. I can still contribute by working part-time from my home and coming in on weekends. I'm committed to my job and won't be losing touch with the office.

Can't delay: My wife will already have expended her leave, so I'm afraid I can't postpone mine, but I would like to work part-time from home and come in on weekends. That way I can continue to contribute on a daily basis.

Share concern: I'm concerned myself. That's why I'd like to work part-time from my home and come in on weekends. I'm sure that will ease the impact of my absence.

Bad example: *If I don't at least hire a temporary replacement for you or divide up your responsibilities, I'll be setting a new precedent. I'm afraid I just can't do that.*

Unrealistic: *Believe me, parenthood isn't as easy as you think. I've been there. If you're taking leave to care for a newborn, you're not going to find time to work.*

Just leave: *I think you should just take the regular three weeks full-time leave. A part-time or home-based employee will just be a distraction to everyone else.*

Positive example: I understand your position, but if we set up an effective strategy for continuing to work while on leave, it can only be a positive precedent, not a negative one.

Well planned: I really have thought this plan through. My in-laws have volunteered to watch the baby while I dedicate a few hours a day to work. With their help, I can be productive working at home.

Address this fear: I agree it would be a slight adjustment, but I think it's worth a try. Even part-time I can still be productive for the company.

Rejects offer: *You can take your leave, but we'll be dividing up your work [or] hiring a temp to help fill in for you.*

Maybe: *Let me think about your idea and get back to you.*

Follow-up: Let's schedule another meeting in a month. We can iron out the specifics then.

Agrees: *Okay, you convinced me. I appreciate your dedication. I'm willing to give your plan a try.*

- **Behavior:** Be ready to compromise on terms but not on timing. You must be granted the leave, it's just a question of the effects it has on your career. Be firm but open-minded.

ADAPTATIONS

This script can be modified to:

- Request leave to care for an ill family member.
- Request time off after elective surgery.

KEY POINTS

- Emphasize the importance of your career.
- Do not accept any delays. Tell your superior when you're taking the leave, not the other way around.
- Point out the positive effects of your plan. Convince your superior he would be setting a fine example by granting you part-time leave at home.
- No matter what the outcome, schedule a meeting to discuss your leave again in a month. If your superior disagrees with your plan, use this follow-up meeting to try again.

Asking Your Superior for an Increased Budget

6

STRATEGY

Asking for an increased budget is the ultimate uphill battle in today's lean business environment. Still, it can be done—as long as you frame it properly. The secret is to present the budget increase as a proactive effort to take advantage of an already existing opportunity, resulting in an improvement to the company's bottom line. That means it will boost revenues more than it will increase costs. It cannot be seen as a reaction to prior cuts, an attempt for more personal power, a totally new concept, an effort to save time, or a drain on the company's coffers. Be aware that asking for an increased budget carries risks, whether you get it or not. If you achieve your goal, you'll be under increased scrutiny. If you don't achieve it, you may be marked as being out of step.

TACTICS

- **Attitude:** Whatever the real circumstances underlying your request, the attitude you bring to the meeting must be one of excitement and hope, rather than despair and exasperation.
- **Preparation:** Develop an ironclad business plan that documents how your proposed change will positively affect the bottom line. Make sure there are no loopholes or question marks. In addition, have a host of fall-back positions ready in case you're unable to overcome your superior's objections.
- **Timing:** Don't wait for budget time to present your plan. If you do, it will simply be seen as an effort to grab a bigger piece of the pie or to maintain what you've already got. Present your plan as soon as you've got all your documentation ready.
- **Behavior:** Act the same as in every other planning meeting you have with your superior. Remember: you're not asking for more money—you're demonstrating an opportunity to make more money and urging the company to take advantage of it. Refrain from suggesting cuts elsewhere, even if you're pushed. That will color your proposal as political.

6. Asking Your Superior for an Increased Budget

Icebreaker: Thanks for seeing me. I think I've figured out a way for us to dramatically increase the net revenue generated by my department.

Pitch: By adding a sales position dedicated to classified sales, my figures show we can increase gross revenue by more than 40 percent with only a 10 percent increase in overhead. That translates into a substantial boost in our profitability. Take a look at this.

Attacks you: *Aren't you talking about something you should have done yourself? [or] Aren't you just trying to add to your power base?*

Too long-term: *Maybe you're right. But it looks like it could take a couple of years for it to pay off. We're not in the position to make any long-term investments right now.*

Don't have money: *You might be right. But we just don't have the money to gamble on something like this right now.*

Against grain: *Haven't you been reading the papers? The last thing anyone is doing these days is adding staff [or] increasing budgets. It's out of the question.*

Company's first: I'm surprised. The company has always been what's most important to me. I thought you wanted suggestions. If you think I'm doing this for myself you're mistaken.

Do it halfway: I've thought of that. There are a couple of ways we could get instant results. We could hire a part-timer or we could start off with a temp.

Cut to add: I think we can eliminate the risk by temporarily cutting back 10 percent on our T&E budget. That way the new move will pay off from day one.

An opportunity: I'm aware this is against the grain, but everyone's also saying take advantage of openings. I don't think we want to spite ourselves just because of a trend.

Open to idea: *All right, let's go over what you have in mind.*

Still against idea: *I'm sorry. I just can't bring that kind of suggestion upstairs.*

Outline plan: I've prepared this memo. In it I've got a two-year, monthly profit and loss for the change I'm suggesting. I've validated all the assumptions. I'd like you to look at it. Of course, I'm willing to make any modifications you'd suggest before kicking it upstairs.

Ask for reconsideration: Let me leave this memo with you. In it I've got a two-year, monthly profit and loss for the change I'm suggesting. I've validated all the assumptions. Just take a look at it. I think you'll reconsider when you see the numbers. I'll get back to you tomorrow.

See script 28: "Going over Your Superior's Head"

ADAPTATIONS

This script can be modified to:

- Ask for an assistant.
- Ask for a new piece of equipment.

KEY POINTS

- Frame your proposal as "an opportunity," explain that you've just "uncovered" it, and stress, as early in the conversation as possible, that it will boost net revenues.
- If your superior attacks you and suggests the proposal is self-serving, act surprised and hurt, but not angry, and stress that you've always put the company first.
- If your superior objects to even a short-term negative impact on the bottom line, provide temporary options that will offer instant positive results.
- If your superior objects to any additional outlay, suggest temporary shifts in your own operations to compensate.
- If your superior says your idea is counter to current trends, show how it's really in line with today's business philosophy.
- If your superior remains hesitant, ask her to think about it and reconsider. Meanwhile, consider going over her head.

Breaking Bad News to a Superior

7

STRATEGY

This is one of the most stressful and difficult dialogues you could have with a superior. Not only are you somewhat embarrassed by the failure—whether it was your fault or not—but you're also worried the setback could affect your standing in the organization. The key to fulfilling your obligations and minimizing any potential damage to you is to turn this meeting as quickly as possible into a discussion about what to do now, rather than a postmortem of what went wrong. The secrets of doing that are to make sure the news comes from you so you can control the spin; demonstrate that the situation was beyond your control, or accept the responsibility; and present a plan of action that mitigates the damage.

TACTICS

- **Attitude:** Approach this as an opportunity to prove you're resourceful and can take charge in a crisis. Be willing to accept the responsibility for what has happened but not necessarily the blame. Finally, realize that your superior's anger may not be with you but with the situation.

- **Preparation:** Have an explanation for why the problem has occurred. If there were any hints of trouble be ready to explain what you did in response. Most importantly, have a detailed written proposal that suggests a course of action.

- **Timing:** While you shouldn't burst into a closed-door meeting and blurt out the news, you must bring this to your superior's attention as soon as you can. It's essential the news come from you first.

- **Behavior:** Don't show contrition unless you were actually to blame. However, do show concern, not for yourself but for the company. Use every possible chance to move beyond what happened to what to do now. Don't shy away from playing to your superior's ego but try to be subtle. Sucking up won't take the place of accepting responsibility, but it can help deflect free-floating anger.

7. Breaking Bad News to a Superior

Icebreaker: I have some bad news. Although I think we'll be okay in the long run, Jane from Acme just called to tell me they're moving to the L&H Agency.

Demonstrate you're blameless: She emphasized that they've had no problem with our work—it was strictly a dollars-and-cents move. You were right when you said they were looking for million-dollar results on a hundred-dollar budget.

Acknowledge some responsibility: They'd raised some concerns about our approach, but I was addressing them. They just jumped the gun on me. You were right when you warned me that Acme is very impatient for results.

Calm response: *They're one of our biggest accounts. They've been with us for five years. What happened?*

Disbelieving response: *Acme has been with us for five years. Now they walk out with no warning and you think your handling of the account had nothing to do with it?*

Angry response: *I can't believe you screwed this up. I don't know what I was thinking when I let you take over Acme. Do you know how much this will cost us?*

Threatening response: *If I can't trust you to handle Acme, maybe you can't handle Apex either. And with this happening I wouldn't count on a raise any time soon.*

Take charge: I think the economy was the straw that broke the camel's back. Even though we did everything possible, I take full responsibility for what happened—and for replacing the lost revenue. I've come up with a plan I think will work.

Absorb anger: I understand your anger; I'm upset, too, even though I believe we were on the right track. I know how important this account is to us, and I've come up with a plan that I think can replace, maybe even top, what we earn on the Acme account.

Political response: *First, think about how we're going to break the news to the people upstairs. They're going to want heads to roll.*

Skeptical response: *I'd like to hear it, although I don't see how we can replace a client of such long standing that easily.*

Receptive response: *I'm open to suggestions. We certainly can't afford to lose that amount of revenue.*

Present the plan: I've drawn up this list of possible replacements for Acme, all of which should bring in at least as much business as they have, possibly more. That should reassure the folks upstairs about the way we're handling the situation. But I don't think we should give up on Acme just yet. I know we can get them to meet with us. And I think with you there, we'd have a great chance to win them back.

ADAPTATIONS

This script can be modified to:

- Break bad news to parents, friends, spouses, teachers, etc.
- Deliver negative financial news to an investor or partner.

KEY POINTS

- Be direct, but try to offer some hope as soon as possible.
- Immediately either demonstrate you're blameless or acknowledge your responsibility.
- If your superior takes the news well, or still questions your account, restate your position and move right on to your plan of action.
- If your superior gets angry or threatens you, try to get on her side by saying you're angry, too, and then move on to what you think should be done now.
- Whatever the initial response to your plan, reaffirm your belief that it will work, add some flattery, and offer whatever help you can in overcoming the problem.

Maximizing a Performance Review

8

STRATEGY

The key to getting the most from a positive performance review, or to minimize the damage from a negative one, is to subtly take charge of the conversation by preempting the reviewer. If you expect a positive review, immediately launch into the new challenges you'd like to take on. If you expect a negative review, immediately describe your plan to improve. The idea is to get off negative issues as quickly as possible and turn the meeting into a positive and constructive discussion of your plan. If you don't succeed in taking control, push for a subsequent meeting and try again.

TACTICS

- **Attitude:** Look on this as a chance to take charge of your future, rather than a postmortem on your past.
- **Preparation:** Conduct a thorough self-analysis to determine whether your review will be primarily positive or negative. Then, develop a plan to either take advantage of the positive review or correct past mistakes and shortcomings.
- **Timing:** While you'll have little control over when this meeting takes place, be ready to postpone it should anything problematic occur during the conversation. For example, if you're in your superior's office discussing your performance and she gets a call that the company's largest customer has gone bankrupt, immediately suggest an adjournment.
- **Behavior:** When receiving constructive criticism or compliments, it's important to acknowledge them with more than just physical gestures. Rather than just nodding, say you understand. Take your superior's suggestions, put them in your own words, and repeat them. Offer sincere thanks for any input, positive or negative.

8. Maximizing a Performance Review

Icebreaker: I really enjoy my work, so I'm glad to have this opportunity to talk with you.

Expect positive review: I believe I've met most of last year's goals—I've brought in new clients and revamped our marketing strategy. So I've developed some new goals I'd like to shoot for.

Expect negative review: I know that I've had some difficulties this year and that some clients have complained. I've thought a lot about what happened and why and about how I can improve.

Gives up control: *I've been very happy with your work, and I'm pleased that you took those goals so seriously. What do you have in mind for next year?*

Retains control: *In general, you've done a very good job this year, but there are a few areas I think you need to work on. [Explains specifics.]*

Retains control: *I have gotten negative feedback, and that has added to my own concerns. Let me tell you what I see as the major problems. [Explains specifics.]*

Gives up control: *I haven't been pleased with your performance, and I'm glad that you realize that. Now tell me what you plan to do to turn things around.*

Your pitch: I've enjoyed working in marketing, but I think I'd be more useful if I had financial expertise. So I'd like to take on budgeting.

Lead-in to pitch: *[After hearing specifics.]* I appreciate your suggestions, and I'll work hard on them. I'd also like to get your feedback on my idea.

Lead-in to defense: *[After hearing specifics.]* I understand completely, and I'll get right on it. In fact, I've already started to address some problems.

Defense: I think I was so focused on drumming up new business that I neglected some of our existing clients. So I've started taking clients out and mending fences.

Accepts pitch: *That's a great idea. Why don't you start by tackling ways to cut costs in your own department?*

Rejects pitch: *I'm not sure you're ready for the added responsibilities. I'd like you to focus on marketing a while longer.*

Rejects defense: *You'll have to do a lot more than make nice with a few clients to get back on track.*

Accepts defense: *I'm glad you've started to work on these problems. If you follow through, things should work out.*

Push for another meeting: I understand, and I'll give it my best. But can we schedule another meeting three months from now, when we could talk again about other ways I can contribute?

Push for another meeting: I understand, and I'll start working on the problems right away. Could you review my performance again in, say, three months, and let me know if I'm on the right track?

ADAPTATIONS

This script can be modified to:

- Counter a problem that may arise when you're discussing a proposed raise or promotion.
- Use as a segue into a discussion of a raise or promotion.
- Handle a nonwork-related problem.

KEY POINTS

- Stress how much you love your job and that you've looked forward to this meeting—whether or not it's true.
- If you expect a positive review, immediately launch into what you'd like to do in the coming year in order to set up raise or promotion discussions.
- If you expect a negative review, admit your problems and immediately launch into your plan for self-improvement.
- If your superior doesn't let you take charge of the conversation, segue into your plan after absorbing her comments.
- If your superior doesn't accept your plan, ask for another meeting at which you can try to take charge once again.

Asking for a
Salary Advance

9

STRATEGY

Believe it or not, this is one of the most dangerous scripts in this book. While getting an advance on your salary may, in the short term, get you out of financial trouble, it carries a great many long-term risks. In order to maximize your chances for getting the advance, you're going to have to push your superior right to the edge—and then back off if necessary. That could change what has been a good relationship between you and your superior into an uncomfortable one. It could also change your superior's perception of you from a rising star to just your average Joe or Jane. Therefore, consider asking for an advance only as a last resort.

TACTICS

- **Attitude:** Realize you're asking for something out of the ordinary but that you're really asking only for what already belongs to you. You're not a beggar or a borrower, but you are possibly asking to be treated like one.

- **Preparation:** Make sure that you've exhausted all your other options before going to your superior and that the reason you need the money doesn't reflect an inability to manage your life or your finances. The best, in fact the only good, reason is that something unforeseen and beyond your control occurred to someone other than you.

- **Timing:** Lay the groundwork for the request by seeing your superior before business hours and asking for an appointment to discuss a personal matter. That conveys urgency but reassures your supervisor that it has nothing to do with business.

- **Behavior:** Stress that you're not asking for a loan. Instead, refer to this as a "draw" or an "advance" on future salary. Don't plead or beg, but showing some anxiety is okay—particularly if it's anxiety over what your superior will think of you.

9. Asking for a Salary Advance

Preliminary icebreaker: Excuse me, Marcus, I need to speak with you sometime today about a personal matter. Would 2:00 P.M. be okay?

Later that day

Icebreaker: Thanks for seeing me. I need your help concerning an unforeseen financial responsibility. My aunt passed away last night, and since she left no money and there's no one else, I'm going to have to pick up the costs of the funeral and burial.

Pitch: My problem is that I'm not in a financial position to pay these costs right now. What I'd like is an advance on my future salary. I want to make it clear I'm not asking for a loan from you or the company.

No way: *I'm sorry about your aunt. However, the company has a policy against lending money to employees.*

Okay: *I'm sorry about your aunt. The company isn't crazy about issuing advances, but I think I can swing it. How much do you need?*

Sneaky no: *I'm sorry about your aunt. We're not a bank, but I'd like to help. Why don't you call Robert Smith at our bank about a loan? I'll put in a good word for you.*

Restate pitch: I think you're missing my point. I feel very uncomfortable about borrowing. I'd rather use what amounts to my own money.

State plan: I'll need $2,000. The funeral will cost $3,500, but I have $1,500 in my emergency fund. I'd like to pay back ten percent, or $200, every month for ten months. That way I'll be able to keep up with my bills.

Bookkeeping problems: *I can't blame you for wanting to keep up with your bills, but the company may have a problem if this goes beyond the end of the fiscal year—that's in six months.*

Off the books: I can understand that. I can take a cash advance on a credit card and clear the matter up at the end of the fiscal year as long as I know we can reissue the funds again at the beginning of the next year.

Restate pitch: I guess I haven't explained myself well. I don't like the idea of a loan either. I want to try to do this out of my own assets.

Agrees: *That sounds okay. I'll speak with Julie in bookkeeping and ask her to cut the check and make the arrangements.*

Still no: *I'm sorry. The company can't be put in the position of helping employees when they have a financial problem.*

Final no: *I'm sorry, but there's nothing we can do for you.*

Restate case: This isn't a case of me having a financial problem. I couldn't anticipate this expense. It doesn't reflect an inability to manage my life. I'm not doing this for myself. And I'm just asking to draw on my own assets.

Back off: I guess I made a mistake. I'm sorry for bothering you about this, but if you should reconsider, please call me.

ADAPTATIONS

This script can be modified to:

- Ask forbearance from a major creditor.
- Ask for more after already receiving a major financial favor.

KEY POINTS

- As early as possible, say you need an advance, not a loan, to help someone else, preferably a family member, out of an unforeseen and unavoidable problem.
- Make the point that this is actually drawing on your own assets.
- Reiterate your points until you feel your superior truly understands the situation and either relents or refuses outright to help.
- If your superior expresses bookkeeping concerns, offer to do whatever it takes to overcome the problem.
- If your superior refuses to help, back down, apologize for bothering him with a nonbusiness matter, but leave room for him to come back if he changes his mind.

Justifying an Expense Report

10

STRATEGY

You need to tread very carefully if one of your expense reports is questioned by a superior. You can assume that if you're called into a face-to-face meeting the problem isn't one of documentation—that could be handled with a telephone call or a visit from an administrative assistant or bookkeeper. Therefore, this meeting is calling into question either your judgment or your honesty. It's even possible there's a hidden agenda—perhaps your superior is building a case for termination or a negative review. Whatever the situation, your goal is to immediately admit to the error, but turn it into one of omission rather than commission. Your mistake was not catching the error yourself or not preparing your superior for the unusual charge.

TACTICS

- **Attitude:** Take this as a very serious probe, even if it's for a small amount. You need to clearly demonstrate that this in no way reflects on your honesty or judgment.
- **Preparation:** Unless you're given advance notice of a problem with your report, you'll have little or no time to prepare for this specific meeting. Instead, make it your business always to double- and triple-check your expense reports prior to submission and *never* to knowingly pad them.
- **Timing:** You'll also have no control over the timing of this meeting. The only element of timing you can control is to have an immediate answer ready for any questions: Either the questionable expense was a mistake or you forgot to provide advance warning.
- **Behavior:** Even though this may be a probe of your personal integrity, don't become defensive. And never, ever argue—no matter what the amount involved—the risk is too great. Anger is a defense mechanism. It could be seen as an admission of guilt and could turn the meeting into a fight rather than a conversation. Instead, be forthright, sincere, and, if need be, apologetic.

10. Justifying an Expense Report

Opener: *I have a problem with your expense report for last week's trip to Las Vegas.*

Express puzzled concern: Is there a problem with my documentation?

Personal, not business: *No, your documentation is fine. The problem is you've got about $100 here for in-room movies. It's not our obligation to pay for your entertainment when you're not out with clients.*

It was a mistake: I'm sorry. I didn't realize that was on the bill. Normally I [*or*] my secretary audit[s] the bills before submitting them, but I used the rapid checkout and didn't have a chance this time. I never intended for the company to have to pay those charges. I'll take care of it right away. It won't happen again.

You spent too much: *No, your documentation is fine. The problem is how much you spent. Don't you think $600 for a dinner for four is way out of line?*

Not your choice: You're absolutely right . . . but I left the choice of restaurants up to them. Since I initiated the dinner, and they're such good clients, I felt I had no choice but to pick up the check. If you look at past reports, you'll see I usually take clients to Joe's, where the prices are more reasonable. I really felt dreadful for the company. I'm sorry—I should have attached a note explaining the situation.

Questions explanation: *That sounds like a reasonable explanation. But what if I hadn't gone over your bill so closely—what would've happened then?*

Reaffirm honesty: The minute I saw the mistake I would've reimbursed the company for the personal charges, whether or not they were discovered.

Wants more notice: *I understand. In the future, just remember I have to send these upstairs. I need some warning if there's anything unusual so I can offer my own explanation.*

Express thanks: Thanks for being so understanding. I appreciate it. It won't happen again.

ADAPTATIONS

This script can be modified to:

- Explain a financial surprise to a spouse or partner.
- Explain an error in an employment, loan, or credit application.

KEY POINTS

- Even though you know it's not likely, ask if the problem is with your documentation. This shows you're feeling no guilt and were unaware of any potential problems.
- If you're accused of requesting reimbursement for personal expenses, immediately explain that the inclusion of the charges on your report was a mistake.
- If you're accused of spending too much, show how the cost was beyond your control and admit that it was a mistake not to provide forewarning of the unusually large charge.
- If your explanation is questioned, reaffirm your honesty as strongly as possible.
- Always express your thanks and stress the mistake won't happen again.

Refusing an Assignment

11

STRATEGY

The problem with refusing an assignment is that there's no way to come out of it without some kind of loss. If you say it's a bad idea, you insult your superior who came up with it. If you say you don't have the time, your superior will think you're lazy. And if you say you don't have the skill to do it, your superior may lower her estimation of your abilities. Your goal should be to minimize the damage.

TACTICS

- **Attitude:** Realize that since you can't refuse outright or say it's a bad idea, you'll have to accept some damage to your image in order to get out of the assignment.
- **Preparation:** If you're going to claim lack of skill, have the name of someone else who has the skill. If you're asking for priorities to be set, prepare a complete list of the projects you're working on and the dates they're due.
- **Timing:** Never accept or decline an assignment immediately. Instead, say it's an interesting idea and you'd like some time to study it and prepare questions. Then, wait for your superior to bring it up again.
- **Behavior:** Express your disappointment at not being able to take on this wonderful assignment and your willingness, in fact eagerness, to take on others in the future. Everything should be put in terms of what's best for the company.

11. Refusing an Assignment

The idea: *I was listening to the radio last night, and I heard a story on a company that's selling compact discs in vending machines. I suddenly realized we could do the same thing with our books. We could put vending machines selling our line of books almost everywhere. Think of it! People could buy books at gas stations, at Laundromats, at banks. I think this could revolutionize the way we do business. I want you to get on this right away. I need you to draft a report outlining how we can institute a vending-machine effort by this time next year. If this works out the way I hope, you could be in charge of our entire vending-machine effort. What do you think of that?*

Ask for time: I think you've come up with a fascinating idea, and I'm flattered you've brought it to me. I'll look into it right away, formulate some questions, and get back to you early next week. Thanks for thinking of me.

One week later

Icebreaker: I've finished reviewing the assignment we discussed last week. You were right to be excited. I think it's an extremely interesting idea. Ironically, that's why I'm not sure I'd be the best person for the job.

Pitch #1: This project is potentially extremely important, so I need to put my personal interests aside. While I think I'm our best financial *[or other discipline]* person, Meadow is our best marketer *[or other discipline]*. As much as I'd like to take it on, I think she's the most qualified person for this assignment.

Pitch #2: This project is so important it should be someone's top priority. As you know, I'm already devoting all my extra time to preparing the annual report. I'd love to tackle this project, but I would need you to help me reset my priorities and figure out a schedule.

Agrees to someone else: *You're right. I need the best for this assignment. I appreciate your honesty. Can you ask Meadow to come see me?*

Still wants you: *I don't think you want to turn this assignment down. It's very important to me and the company. I really want you to do it. How about it? Will you take it on?*

Won't set priority: *I thought you knew that to succeed in this company you've got to juggle more than one ball. I want you to do this and finish the annual report.*

Sets priority: *You're right. I forgot you're still working on the annual report. I suppose I'll have to give this new job to someone else or put it on hold until you get the annual report done.*

Reinforce your expertise: *Sure. I hate to pass this one up, but the company's interests do come first. I'll speak with Meadow and let her know that I'll be available if she needs my help with the financial projections [or your area of expertise].*

Suggest committee formation: *I appreciate the faith you have in me. Rest assured I'll give it 110 percent. Since it's so important to the company to do it efficiently, I'll need to set up a team of our best people and bring all our resources to bear on it.*

Discuss future plans: *I'll be finished with the annual report and can take this on in about two weeks. I don't like to turn you down on an assignment—especially such a great opportunity—but if it's urgent, I'd suggest assigning it to Meadow—she's an excellent marketer [or other discipline].*

Demands you go solo: *By all means reach out for whatever help you need. But remember, it's your assignment. You're in charge. And you're responsible for its success or failure.*

Agrees to committee: *That's an excellent idea. This is an important project and I want our best people working on it.*

Accept with protective memo: *I won't let the company down. I'll draft a memo that outlines the project, notes the high priority you've placed on it, and explains you've put me in charge of executing your idea.*

Accept with outlining memo: *We can do it. We've got a great team here. I'll draft a memo outlining how we're going to tackle the project and circulate it among the team.*

ADAPTATIONS

This script can be modified to:

- Counter a request by a family member, friend, or officer of a club or organization.

- Counter a request coming from your superior's supervisor.

KEY POINTS

- Express gratitude for being considered, say the idea is interesting, and ask for time to study it and formulate questions.

- Stress that the project is so important that it should either be done by an expert or be a top priority. Then say you're not an expert (but someone else is) or that you need help in setting priorities.

- If your suggestion of someone else is taken, reinforce your own expertise and future availability.

- If no priority is set or the assignment isn't shifted to someone else, ask to form a special ad hoc committee in order to dilute the potential fallout.

- If attempts at diluting responsibility fail, prepare a protective memo that subtly makes it clear the whole thing was your superior's idea.

Asking for a Deadline Extension

12

STRATEGY

The secret to asking for a deadline extension is to make it clear that your only problem is time; nothing else is wrong. Rather than coming in to your superior with an apology and series of reasons why you're not going to be able to meet the established deadline, steer the discussion as quickly as possible to solutions. The schedule established was clearly unworkable, and now you need help in coming up with ways to deal with the situation. Offer alternatives, but make it clear that delivery as intended is impossible.

TACTICS

- **Attitude:** This is a time neither to fall on your own sword nor to assign blame to others. It's not important who or what is to blame. What's important is deciding the next step. The more you adopt this attitude, the more likely your superior will as well.

- **Preparation:** Don't waste time determining why you won't be able to deliver on time—invariably it's because the schedule was overly optimistic; there's nothing you can do about it now. Instead, come up with as many alternative solutions as you can. There are usually three variations: getting more time, hiring outside help to deliver on time, or submitting a draft on the due date with the final product to follow later. Be prepared to advocate one alternative over the others in case your superior is unwilling to take responsibility.

- **Timing:** It's essential you have this conversation as soon as you realize you're not going to meet your deadline. Procrastination can only hurt you since you don't know if there are other issues involved. The sooner you realize the deadline is unworkable and convey that to your superior, the better. The longer you wait, the more this will look like a failing on your part.

12. Asking for a Deadline Extension

Icebreaker: We need to talk about the Jackson project. It can't be completed in the thirty days we have available. I need your help in coming up with a solution.

Calm but curious: *What went wrong?*

Nervous: *Time is of the essence. I've committed us to that delivery date.*

Angry: *I should have known better than to rely on you for something this important.*

Disappointed: *I relied on your promises. This is a real letdown.*

Was simply unworkable: In retrospect it's clear our original timetable simply wasn't workable. But I think I have some workable solutions.

Don't panic: I don't think we need to panic. I think I have some workable solutions.

Absorb anger: Your anger is understandable, but let's focus on solving the problem. I think I have some workable solutions.

Absorb disappointment: I understand and share your disappointment. But I think I have some workable solutions.

Present plans: I think we have three options. The first, but most costly, option is to bring in an outside team of temps to work over the next four weekends. Obviously I'd be willing to come in and supervise them. The second option is to get a fifteen-day extension from the client. The third option is to submit an outline and first draft of the project to the client as soon as possible; solicit their comments and suggestions, saying their happiness is very important to us; and ask for additional time to incorporate those ideas into the finished project.

Still hesitant: *That's all very well, but you've left us in an awkward position with the client, not being able to deliver on time.*

Gives a cushion: *Okay. I'll take care of the client. You take another fifteen days. Just make sure you deliver a first-class product.*

Needs time to choose: *Good thinking. Those are three viable options. Let me give it some thought and get back to you on which way we'll go.*

Suggest your choice: I've been thinking about that, too. I've put together an outline and a first draft. I think you'll agree it's an excellent start. I think that once we incorporate your changes, we may be able to show this to them and mitigate the damage.

Express admiration: The way you've handled this situation just reaffirms my admiration for your management skills. Thanks for your help.

- **Behavior:** Remain objective and rational. Don't let anger put you on the defensive or fear get the better of you. You, your superior, the project, and the company will all be best served by your continuing to steer the conversation around to solutions rather than postmortems.

ADAPTATIONS

This script can be modified to:

- Mollify a client or customer.
- Ask a client or customer for more time.

KEY POINTS

- Present the failure to meet the deadline as a given and go directly to offering alternative solutions.
- If you're asked for a reason, just say the schedule was unworkable and launch into your suggestions.
- If your superior expresses anxiety, anger, or disappointment, say these feelings are understandable, but immediately shift the topic to solutions.
- Solutions generally involve either getting more time, bringing in outside help, or presenting an outline on time with the finished product to follow later.
- If your superior seems unwilling to select from your set of solutions, be prepared to advocate one approach.

Asking for Relief from an Assignment

13

STRATEGY

Trying to get relief from assignments that you either don't have the skill to accomplish or don't have the time to do well is an extremely delicate procedure—one that should never be entered into except when you have no other choice. Unless handled well, this could dramatically alter your superior's opinion of you for the worse. That's why it's essential you make sure you have a bona fide reason for the relief—saying you don't have the time simply won't do. The only way to come out of this with minimal damage to your reputation is to frame it as an objective problem for the company. It's not that "you" don't have the time, it's that the project can't be done well in the time allowed or that your department doesn't have the skills necessary to do the job correctly. Expect resistance since such a reshuffling is going to cost the company money one way or another. The only way to counter bottom-line objections is to note that the alternatives are increased liability or decreased quality—both likely to be unacceptable. Deflect any personal attacks by saying you place the company's interests before your own. By the way, if your superior thinks you're bluffing, refuses your request, and says the increased liability or decreased quality is acceptable, prepare a memo for your files describing the meeting.

TACTICS

- **Attitude:** Realize this should be used only as a last resort to avoid disaster. At best it will hurt your reputation temporarily. At worst the damage will be permanent.
- **Preparation:** Determine whether the problem lies with your lack of skill or is specific to this project.
- **Timing:** Don't delay. While this won't be a pleasant meeting, it needs to take place as soon as possible.

13. Asking for Relief from an Assignment

Icebreaker: Thanks for meeting with me, Kristine. I think we need do to some minor reengineering and I need to run the situation by you.

Lack skills pitch: As you know, for the past year my department has had the responsibility for municipal credit analysis in addition to our normal corporate analysis function. According to the projections we just got from the head office, next year the company will be doing several billion dollars' worth of municipal refinancings. We won't be able to handle the credit function effectively. I think we need to form a separate municipal credit group.

Project problem pitch: I've just completed a thorough analysis of the Johnson project and, needless to say, I'm very excited about it. I know how important timing is to them, and the last thing I want us to do is jeopardize the project by having to go back and get an extension from them. Even though it's against my own interests, I'd like to suggest we give the project to Peggy's department. I've checked, and she and her team have the time to meet the client's schedule.

Doing a fine job: *Your department has been doing a fine job since you took this function over. Besides, if we have to form another group, it's going to be costly for the company.*

Don't disappoint me: *You know I'm counting on you. I gave this project to your team for a reason. I hate to bring in new bodies at this stage. Don't disappoint me.*

Potential liability: We've been able to do the job so far because the volume has been light. While I'm confident we can do the job on an occasional basis, we're functionally not able to handle the kind of volume that's being projected. We just don't have the skills. While forming another group may generate some initial costs, that's preferable to exposing the company to potential liability.

Sacrificing quality: That's exactly the point. We don't want to disappoint you or the client. There's no question we could get the job done by the deadline they've set . . . but it would be at the risk of sacrificing quality. And the last thing I would ever do is jeopardize the quality of the company's products.

Still a risk: *There's also risk involved in forming a new group [or] bringing in a new team that isn't familiar with the project.*

I'll help: I realize that, but I think I can mitigate that risk by making myself and my team available to the new group [or] providing any help or guidance that's needed.

Your first "can't": *You know, this is the first time I've ever heard you say you "can't" get the job done.*

Not a "can't"—a "won't": It's not that we can't get the job done, it's that we won't knowingly expose the company to potential liability [or] sacrifice the quality of the company's products.

- **Behavior:** One way or another you're going to have to eat some crow, so be humble from the beginning. Accepting criticism or hearing that you've disappointed a number of people is the price you'll have to pay for getting relief.

ADAPTATIONS

This script can be modified to:

- Get out of something you volunteered to do for the company, a friend, or a relative.
- Get out of an office in an organization or association.

KEY POINTS

- Present this as a problem brought on by your inherent lack of skill or the unique circumstances of the project.
- If your past ability to perform is cited, stress the differences of this situation and the potential liabilities.
- If your superior says she's disappointed, note that it's more important the client isn't disappointed.
- If your superior implies her opinion of you has dropped, state that the company's reputation is more important to you than your own.
- If she remains hesitant, offer to be of whatever assistance you can, short of carrying the ball yourself.

Asking Your Superior for Help with Your Workload

14

STRATEGY

This delicate dialogue must be handled with care. Ask your superior for assistance and she may think you're an underachiever or a lazy employee. Even if you've taken on or accepted too much work, your superior may not recognize this. That's why you should only use this dialogue as a last resort, after all else has failed. That being said, the secret to this conversation is guiding the dialogue toward a solution. Don't let your superior turn the meeting into a review of your employment history. Remind her that you're doing good work, but there's just too much for one person. The fact that you recognize the work overload and are attempting to solve the problem is a sign of strength. It's entirely possible your superior is not aware of the enormous workload and may sympathize with your predicament. However, you should be ready to deflect anger or disappointment. This meeting should appear to be about your concern for the company and the quality of your work. If you're unable to keep pace with an unreasonable workload, the company will ultimately suffer. Don't be passive and throw yourself on the mercy of your superior. Explore options and have possible alternatives prepared to discuss with your superior during the meeting. Show her you're eager to solve the problem early so the company isn't adversely affected.

TACTICS

- **Attitude:** Be concerned but not intimidated. Be decisive. Act positively, deflect anger, and discuss solutions. You're seeking a solution, not an excuse.
- **Timing:** Speak with your superior the moment you realize there's too much work to handle. Procrastinating will make the situation worse. The moment your superior has any free time, you must pull her aside and alert her to your quandary.
- **Preparation:** Prepare a memo outlining your solution, and present the plan to your superior during the meeting so she can comment immediately.

55

14. Asking Your Superior for Help with Your Workload

Icebreaker: I need your help in solving a potential problem. I've taken a close look at my workload and realize my enthusiasm has gotten the better of me. I've accepted too many assignments to keep up my usual high standards. I'm hoping we can discuss some possible solutions or alternatives.

Angry: *This is the last thing I need. I can't believe this. How far behind are you?*

Disappointed: *This is going to set us back. We don't have time for this. I was really counting on you.*

Threatening: *Perhaps someone else would be able to handle your workload. Maybe I should give Nelson a try.*

Calm: *What do you think went wrong? You've always been a hard worker.*

Deflect anger: I'm not behind yet, but if things don't change, I will fall behind. Maybe you could help me identify the most important project I'm working on now so that I can complete my work on a priority basis.

Deflect disappointment: I agree that we can't waste time, but I don't think this is a setback. What I need is a little guidance. Perhaps you could set priorities for each project. That way my coworkers and I will be able to dedicate our time to the right assignment.

Respond to threat: I considered that, but I think Nelson will run into the same problem I have—it's just too much work for one person to handle. If you could assign each project a priority rating, then I can work on each task in the order of importance.

Explain: I'm simply about to become overloaded. There's just more work here than there are hours in a day. If you evaluate each project on a priority basis, I could work through each assignment and not fall behind the deadlines.

Disagrees: *Look, you have to be multifaceted to work in this department. I can't hold your hand and point you in the right direction every day. You need to take some responsibility for your work.*

Disagrees somewhat: *It's just not that simple. Each project has subtle levels of importance. You have to work on multiple projects every day. Even if one project is on the front burner, others cannot be ignored.*

Agrees somewhat: *I see your point, but it would be difficult to set priorities for each project. It might be tough to realign the department on a priority basis.*

Agrees: *I think you're right. We need to get everyone on the same page. I didn't realize the confusion created by multiple deadlines. If the department understands the importance of each project, do you think that will solve your overloading problem?*

Stress your point: I understand your position, but if we can set priorities, then everyone will be working at full capacity. I fear that I may not be the only employee who is overloaded. Eventually, the company is going to lose work, quality, and money.

Sell the idea: I'm not suggesting we ignore any projects, but I think we can focus on the most important projects, and no one person will be overwhelmed. If everyone cooperates, we can save time and money.

Convince boss: If everyone pitches in, it won't be too difficult. If you list the most important projects, then I can make sure I'm spending my hours on the correct project. The payoff is that assigning work on a priority basis will save time and money.

Express thanks: Yes, absolutely. I knew coming to you would solve the problem. With your approval, I'll organize a meeting Monday morning to discuss the projects you think we should be concentrating on.

Final no: *I just think you need to apply yourself. If you can't handle the work, I'll give it to someone else. All our projects are of equal importance, and we can't neglect any assignments. Now, what should we do about your situation?*

Retreat and suggest compromise: If Nelson and I could share the June report, then we can balance the workload. By combining our efforts, we can finish the report on time.

- **Behavior:** Be direct and swift. Don't just throw up your hands and cry for help. Be active in the solution process. Remain calm, even if threatened, and present a positive solution that will benefit you and the company.

ADAPTATIONS

This script can be modified to:

- Ask a business partner to help you during a busy time.

KEY POINTS

- Remind your superior that you're not an underachiever—there's just too much work for one person.
- Emphasize you're concerned about the quality of your work and the success of the company.
- Don't tuck your tail between your legs and beg for help. Be proactive in the solution process.
- If your superior won't budge, suggest a specific alternative to lighten your workload.

Asking Your Superior for a Bigger or More Private Workspace

15

STRATEGY

With the increasing reliance of management on small cubicle work-spaces, getting a bigger or private workspace is entirely reliant on convincing your superior that it will make you a more efficient worker. No superior is interested in vanity, ego, or a personal desire for a nice view, unless it affects his own vanity, ego, or desire. Consider that your superior cannot give you something that doesn't exist, so start by checking around the office to make sure there's a better space available. By having specific spaces in mind, you can force your superior to comment on them, rather than on your request in general. Your conversation must be about how a better space will maximize your work output. Explain that being crammed into a tiny space doesn't allow enough room for your files and documents, or for you to meet privately with clients or peers, or even to work efficiently. Tell your superior how much time is wasted in trying to maneuver and work in the small office, when the sensible answer would be to provide you with more space. Point out that you're not seeking a raise or promotion, just enough room to do your job. Deflect accusations that you're not utilizing your current space by assuring your superior you've tried every alternative but are limited by the lack of room. After discussing the problems of a smaller space, explain how much more productive you'll be in a larger space. Describe how an improved space will allow you to work effectively, how much time will be saved in a practical and efficient space, and how you'll be able to meet with clients and coworkers. Your superior may suggest that giving you a better work-space will create jealousy among your peers. Steer him away from a dialogue about everyone else's feelings and back to a discussion about your specific situation. It's essential to illustrate how your workspace may soon negatively affect your job performance. Center the dialogue on the quality of your work, and your superior will understand the importance of moving you.

15. Asking Your Superior for a Bigger or More Private Workspace

Icebreaker: I need to discuss a problem that I fear is affecting the quality of my work. I've grown out of my workspace. The lack of space for my files *[or]* the inability to meet with clients *[or]* the lack for space for a staff meeting is preventing me from working at maximum efficiency. It's getting increasingly frustrating, and I'd like to move to a larger *[or]* more private space.

Angry: *What have you done to deserve a better office? I think you're overestimating your importance.*

Patronizing: *It would be nice if we all had better spaces. I'd like a better office, too. I'm afraid, however, there's just nowhere for you to move.*

Delays: *Maybe, down the road, we can move you to a better space. But for now you'll just have to make do with what you've got.*

Reasonable: *Really? I had no idea you had a problem. Tell me how moving to a better space would help your work.*

Stay calm: I've tried to work in my space, but that will soon become almost impossible. A larger space down the hall has just opened up. I've taken a look at it and I know I'll be able to work more effectively in there.

Inform him: Actually, when Warner leaves the company, his space down the hall is going to be vacant. His office would give me the space I need to get my job done.

No delay: I'm afraid the longer we wait, the more my work will suffer. A space down the hall has just become available. In that office, I know I'd be able to work more productively.

Present case: I'll be able to organize and prioritize my work better *[or]* I'll be able to meet with clients more frequently *[or]* I'll be able to conduct staff meetings to keep on top of projects *[or]* I'll have enough space to house all the documents I need. Fighting with a lack of space is wasting valuable time that I'd rather devote to work.

No movement: *In the past, office upgrades have been done on a seniority or merit basis. If I make an exception for you, everyone will want a new office.*

Delays: *Is there a space open? Well, I still think we should hold off for a while. Other spaces will become available in the future. Just be patient and wait your turn.*

Confused: *I still don't understand what's wrong with the space you have now. You'll just have to make more room for yourself. Be a little creative.*

Agrees: *Okay. I see your point. I don't see any reason why you shouldn't move. Let me talk to the people upstairs and get the okay from them.*

Convince him: I understand your position and past company policy, but I need the larger space for the benefit of my work, not my increased comfort. Because of that, I was hoping you'd consider my situation a priority.

No delay: I don't want to appear impatient, but I think this situation is reaching critical mass. If we wait any longer, my productivity may decline.

Not enough space: Believe me, I've tried many different ways of organizing the space and my work, but it's simply too small. There's just not enough room for my needs.

No: *Listen, you're not in line for a better office, and I can't make an exception for you. You have to manage in your current space.*

Maybe: *Okay. To be fair, I'll have to wait and see who else is going to request the new space. At the end of this week, I'll review all the requests and give it to the most deserving individual.*

Retreat and regroup: I understand. I'll do the best I can with the space I have, and I'll look into other ways of making the space more workable. Perhaps we can meet again when the next larger space comes open. Thanks for meeting with me.

Follow up: Okay. That sounds fair. I'm going to write a quick memo outlining the reasons I need a larger space. I'll drop it off later today so you can look at it prior to making your decision. Thanks for discussing the matter with me.

TACTICS

- **Attitude:** Be confident and concerned. Remind your superior this request is about your job performance, not your personal comfort. You're only concerned about the quality of your work.
- **Timing:** Approach your superior as soon as you discover a desirable space. Stake your claim immediately. Open offices are like vacuums; they demand to be filled. If you hesitate, one of your coworkers will be the one moving.
- **Preparation:** Search around the office and have specific spaces in mind prior to your meeting. Have examples of how your smaller space is negatively affecting your work and how a larger space will improve it.
- **Behavior:** Act worried. After all, if you don't get a larger space, your work will suffer. Your superior will recognize dedication and reward it.

ADAPTATIONS

This script can be modified to:

- Ask to share an office with a different person.
- Ask to move because of a problem coworker.

KEY POINTS

- Scout out available spaces within your company.
- Stress that moving to a larger space is about work quality, not personal comfort or ego.
- Try to get an answer about moving soon—don't let your superior delay the situation.
- If he tells you he'll think about it and get back to you, prepare a memo so your points stay fresh in his mind.
- If he says no, don't panic. Tell him you'd like to be considered for the next open space.

Asking Your Superior for Additional Responsibilities

16

STRATEGY

Approach this meeting like a job interview. Being eager is one thing, but being prepared is another. Work extra hard the weeks before this meeting. Demonstrate you can easily handle your current assignments. Recognize that asking for additional responsibilities will trigger a discussion of your employment history. Your superior will refer to every failure, no matter how insignificant. Be ready to respond with information about all your successes too and to answer questions about past assignments. Still, try not to dwell on small episodes. Instead, make your superior focus on the big picture. Overall, you've done a good job and deserve more responsibility. Explain that you're happy with your job but discouraged by the lack of challenges. Tell your superior that expanding your role will save the company time and money. Present specific ideas for expanding your responsibilities. Refer to ongoing projects and display your knowledge of company policies and procedures. You have to prove your familiarity with the company and be interested in the work. If she denies your request initially, don't panic. Calmly defend your work record and, if necessary, compromise. You can suggest working as an assistant on a new project. This will expand your work portfolio and satisfy your superior as you ease into more responsibilities. Another tactic is offering to take work on a trial basis. Suggest a month of new responsibilities, after which you and your superior can meet to discuss your performance and progress. Identify your superior's particular concern and address it head on—you'll be rewarded with more to do.

TACTICS

- **Attitude:** Be confident and enthusiastic. You're displaying a strong work ethic, something an employer loves to see. Make your superior understand your need for more responsibility.

16. Asking Your Superior for Additional Responsibilities

Icebreaker and pitch: I really enjoy my job and feel I've learned a lot working here. I believe I've shown a firm grasp of my assignments and dedication to my job. With that in mind, I'd like to take on more responsibilities, branch out, and contribute more. I'm comfortable with my workload and will have no problem taking on more work.

Not ready: *You fell pretty far behind on the spring report, remember? I think you need to work on certain skills before we entrust you with extra responsibilities.*

Big picture: I realize I was behind on the spring report, but I worked hard and did make the deadline. Overall, I think my record speaks for itself. I'm dedicated to my job. I'd really like to become more involved.

Delay: *I think you're getting a little bit ahead of yourself. You're doing a good job, but I think you need more experience in your current role. Just be patient.*

Now: I understand what you're saying, but I'm ready for a new challenge. I'd like the opportunity to prove how much more I can do. I just want to help the company and contribute to its success.

Wait your turn: *We have a full staff on every project. I know it seems like you've been working on the same type of assignments for a while, but you're too valuable to be moved. I need everyone to be a team player.*

Make room: I won't abandon my current responsibilities. I just want to expand my role. Being involved on the fall update would allow me to be part of a large project, meet tough deadlines, and broaden my skills as an employee.

Yes: *I'm glad you came to me. It's good to see someone taking an aggressive interest in work. What kind of responsibilities were you thinking about?*

Plan: I'd like an expanded role on the fall update. There are some available assignments I can handle. Given the opportunity, I can help ensure we deliver the update on time.

Disagrees: *I appreciated your hard work, but you still fell behind. If you give a full effort over the next quarter, we can discuss giving you extra work. Until then you need to prove yourself to me.*

Too risky: *I'm not sure I can risk spreading you too thin. If we assign you extra work, your current assignment may suffer. It's just not the time for us to be taking chances.*

Maybe: *Well, I'm not sure how comfortable I am giving you more work. It may confuse your priorities and cause more problems than it solves.*

Okay: *It's true we need an extra hand on the fall update. It would be a big help, but do you have enough time for all that work? I don't want you biting off more than you can chew.*

You're ready: *I've given this serious thought, and I'm certain I can handle more work. I've researched the goals of the fall update and know exactly where I can contribute. I hope you'll give me a chance to pitch in and help the company.*

Alternative: What about assigning work on a trial basis? You can give me a couple of extra assignments and let me give it my best shot. After a month, you and I can meet again and evaluate my performance.

Compromise: Well, I know Laura has her hands full with marketing. What if I help her out a few hours a week? It wouldn't be a full-time commitment, but I would still be contributing and expanding my role.

Agrees: *That sounds like a reasonable solution. We'll try your suggestion and see how it works out. You'll be responsible for your old and new assignments. If I see a decline in work quality, I'll have to withdraw your new responsibilities.*

Yes: *All right, you convinced me. We'll meet next week and talk about your role on the fall update. You've been doing good work—I'll expect more of the same.*

No: *I admire your desire to help, but I think it's just too soon for you to take on more work. Maybe down the road we can discuss it, but for now I have to say no.*

Reschedule: Perhaps we can meet again in a couple of months to discuss this further. It would give me a goal to work toward. If it's all right with you, I'll schedule another meeting with your assistant.

Express gratitude: Thank you for the opportunity and your confidence in me. I look forward to our meeting and starting work on the fall update.

- **Timing:** Schedule this meeting following some type of personal success. Your superior will have your most recent work in mind during the conversation, so it's important this meeting follow a job well done.

- **Preparation:** Try to learn everything and anything you can about the company. Show off your knowledge during the meeting. Your goal is to impress your superior with your interest in the company's projects.

- **Behavior:** Stay calm no matter what negatives from your past are dredged up. Steer your superior toward a discussion of job performance. When speaking, don't be afraid to show your passion for your job.

ADAPTATIONS

This script can be modified to:

- Request work with a new client or customer.
- Offer your services for an experimental or new project.

KEY POINTS

- If your work record is questioned, calmly defend your actions and quickly refocus the conversation on your entire employment history.
- Express a strong desire to expand your work horizons and help the company.
- Have in mind a specific assignment or project on which you'd like to work.
- If you meet resistance, suggest a compromise or alternative.
- If your superior refuses, schedule a follow-up meeting and try again.

Asking Someone to Become Your Mentor

17

STRATEGY

For mentor relationships to truly be of value, the protégé needs to select the mentor, looking for someone who's currently doing what the protégé would like to do in the future. However, it's human nature to want to pick your own protégé. That makes this dialogue a little tough. What makes it even harder is that a protégé really isn't offering anything in exchange for the mentor's guidance. That's why a key to winning someone over is flattery. Be wary of someone who readily accepts your request. She's probably the type who collects followers in an effort to boost her ego. She's likely not to offer you anything of real value. The best mentor is someone who doesn't have the time for such activities and doesn't need the ego boost.

TACTICS

- **Attitude:** Realize that you're asking someone to do something entirely altruistic. You are basically in the position of a supplicant. You don't need to fall to your knees and beg, but you have to be willing to put your own ego aside for the duration of this conversation.
- **Preparation:** Look for someone who's in the position you want to grow into or who has the reputation you would like to have in the future. Develop a brief description of that position or reputation and use it in your pitch.
- **Timing:** Set up this initial meeting for a time that's most convenient for your mentor candidate. That hints at your willingness to be flexible.
- **Behavior:** The keys are to act humble, offer some subtle flattery, and remain persistent. In effect, you're looking to flatter the person into taking you on as a protégé. Even if you're greeted with an outright "no," ask for reconsideration before looking for another potential mentor.

17. Asking Someone to Become Your Mentor

Icebreaker: Thanks for taking the time to meet with me. I've been giving a great deal of thought to my career for the past few months, and I'd like to get your help.

Pitch: I want to become an account executive who's known for creativity and originality, while also being someone who isn't afraid to stand up for what she believes is in the client's best interests. I don't know of anyone who exemplifies that more than you. I was hoping you'd be able to spare a few moments of your time on a regular basis to meet with me and help me make sure I'm going in the right direction.

Time constraints:
I appreciate the compliment, but I simply don't have the time to mentor anyone.

Self-deprecating: *I'm flattered, but I doubt I'm the right person for you. After all, things have changed a lot since I was an account executive.*

Suspicious: *I'm not sure I understand what you're looking for. Are you asking me to put in a good word with your boss about a raise or something?*

Already committed: *Thanks for the compliment, but I'm already working with Nancy. I don't have the time to mentor anyone else.*

Beg for moments: I'm not surprised. I know how busy you must be. The last thing I'd want to do is interfere with your schedule. I'd be happy with a just a few moments now and then. And I'm perfectly willing to work them around whatever time problems you might have.

Admire modesty: One of the things I admire most about you is your modesty. I don't think there's anyone in this industry whose advice and guidance could be more insightful and helpful. I wish you'd reconsider.

Allay fears: I'm sorry. I guess I didn't make myself clear. I wasn't talking about company politics. I was just hoping you could offer me general career guidance from time to time—serve as a mentor.

Offer to wait: I was afraid that might be the case. Nancy's very lucky to have your help. I know it's a lot to ask, but do you think you could also meet with me now and then, even if it's on a less regular basis and for less time?

Not interested: *I'm sorry. I'm really not interested in mentoring anyone [else] right now. I've just got too much of my own to do.*

Grudging acceptance: *Okay, but it really will have to be for only a few minutes a month at my convenience.*

Please reconsider: I understand. Thanks for meeting with me anyway. Would you mind if I give you a call back in a couple of weeks to see if you've reconsidered?

Express thanks: Thanks so much. I really appreciate your letting me draw on your knowledge and experience. Can we schedule our first meeting today?

ADAPTATIONS

This script can be modified to:

- Gather information for a career change.
- Get an informational interview.
- Conduct reconnaissance on a company for any reason.

KEY POINTS

- Realize you're a supplicant and act accordingly.
- Explain why you've chosen to approach this person.
- If you're greeted with suspicions, allay them by making your request clearer.
- If the person acts humble, take it as an invitation for flattery.
- If she claims time constraints or a previous commitment, stress your flexibility and meager needs.
- If she still refuses, subtly ask her to reconsider.

Asking for a Lateral Reassignment

18

STRATEGY

While employees are being told to broaden their skills base and experience to get ahead in today's workplace, it can be extremely difficult, even potentially risky. Not only will you need to go over your immediate superior's head—unless you're already heading up a department—but you may also need to risk your career in order to get the company to take a chance on someone they perceive to lack experience.

TACTICS

- **Attitude:** Once you've decided you need to transfer to move ahead, you must determine whether you're willing to risk your job to make the move. If you're not, either wait until you feel more daring or concentrate on finding a new job outside the company.

- **Preparation:** Make sure you're prepared to show that you do have experience in the area—even if it's in the past and hasn't been tested in the workplace. In addition, if you know there's an important project coming up soon, and you're committed to getting this position, work up a well-organized, comprehensive memo outlining your preliminary ideas for how to handle it. That may persuade the company to give you a shot.

- **Timing:** It's essential you make this approach as soon as you learn there's an opening. By offering yourself for the job before a search is launched, you can offer cost savings. In addition, you'll be judged independently on your past positive performance rather than be compared to more experienced candidates.

- **Behavior:** Be confident and determined but understanding of the company's needs. Frame your growth in terms of how it will benefit the company. And by the way, don't even consider asking for a salary increase. Wait until you've succeeded in the new position before discussing salary.

18. Asking for a Lateral Reassignment

Phase I: Approaching your immediate superior

Icebreaker #1: I'd like to ask you for some career advice. I've heard there's an opening in the public relations department, and while I'm very happy here in direct marketing, I think I can become more valuable to the company by broadening my skill base. First, I'd like your permission to speak with Barbara. And second, I was hoping you could advise me how best to approach her.

Grudging help: *I'd hate to see you go, but I won't stand in the way of your improving your career and helping the company. We'll miss you if you get the spot. Let me think about it and get back to you with some ideas.*

Doesn't want to help: *I can't deny I'm disappointed. I certainly don't want to stand in your way, but I really need you here. I'd only be hurting myself if I helped you transfer. I'd rather you don't apply for the job. You have a future here, you know.*

Express thanks: Thanks so much for your support. I knew I could count on your help—you've always been a wonderful mentor to me.

Sorry, but I must: Thanks for the compliments. I'm sorry you can't back me up on this, but I really need to give this a shot. I think the best way to protect my future is to expand my skills.

Phase II: Approaching your superior's supervisor

Icebreaker #2: Thanks for meeting with me, Barbara. I wanted to speak with you about my professional growth in the company. You've always said that to the extent we're valuable to the company, we'll move up, and I think the opening in public relations offers me a chance to increase my value. I really think by transferring over I could increase my contribution to the company.

Doesn't want to lose you: *Everyone has been telling me you're doing an excellent job in direct marketing. I don't want to lose your efforts there.*

My deputy's ready: Not to be immodest, but I know I'm doing a fine job in direct marketing. But so is my assistant, Heather. I really think she's ready to take my place. I don't think there'd be any drop-off in productivity.

No experience: *I'm sorry, but we're looking for someone with experience. And from what I recall you don't have a PR background.*

But I do: Though I haven't worked in PR I do have a background in it. It was one of my main areas of study in business school, and since I've always been fascinated by it, I've kept up with the changes and developments in the field even while I was in direct marketing.

Wants fresh approach: *I'm sorry, but we're looking to bring someone in from outside the company. We've decided we need a fresh approach.*

Have fresh approach: I can understand you wanting a fresh approach, and coming from outside the department I think I can bring that to the job. That would also save the company the expense of having to look outside for candidates.

No time to learn: *You've made some good points, but we really can't risk having someone learn on the job. We need to hit the ground running with our campaign for the spring. Maybe after a year you'd be up to it, but we need results in two months.*

Ask for future consideration: While I think I could hit the ground running, I can understand your concerns. I'd appreciate it, however, if you could keep me in mind for any future openings in public relations. As I've said, I want to increase my value to the company by broadening my skills and experience.

Offer to accept risk: I thought that might be the case. That's why I took the time to prepare this memo outlining some ideas I have for the spring campaign. I'm not asking for a total commitment. Read my ideas, and if you think they've got some merit, just give me sixty days to get results. If you're not satisfied at that point, you can replace me.

ADAPTATIONS

This script can be modified to:

- Switch specialties at an academic or media employer.
- Get a similar type of position at a different type of firm.

KEY POINTS

- Ask for your immediate superior's help in furthering your career, but be willing to go it alone if need be.
- Present your transfer as a way to increase your contribution to the company.
- Stress that your transfer won't hurt the department you're coming from.
- Offer whatever experience you can to counter the "no experience" excuse.
- Explain that coming from outside the department you can offer as fresh an approach as someone who comes from outside the company—and at the same time save the company money.
- If immediate success is important, either back off and ask for future consideration or be ready to stake your future on producing results right away.

Warning Your Superior of Potential Client Problems

19

STRATEGY

Be cautious when delivering the news of a potential client problem. You need to tell your superior you have a feeling, call it intuition, that Acme, Inc. may be preparing to pull its business. The fear is your superior will react poorly and blame the messenger. Deliver the news and assume control of the meeting right away. If your superior has a chance to vent anger, lay blame, or panic, the possibility of accomplishing something productive will be lost. Concentrate on moving the conversation forward and searching for a solution to the client problems. If you can demonstrate calm under fire, your superior will think of you as a valuable employee. This is your chance to help the company avoid losing a client and make an effective impression. Devise a plan of action to share with your superior during this potential crisis. Before he has time to point fingers, you can steer him toward a discussion about how to deal with the problem. Get him involved in the discussion, seek his opinions, and force him to comment on your thoughts and ideas for handling the client. Don't discuss who's at fault, but subtly prove you're not to blame for this situation. You're trying to help the company avoid a problem, not throwing yourself at the mercy of your superior. By meeting with your superior, you're taking a proactive stance and thus protecting yourself from future recrimination. If Acme pulls its business without any warning, you will be held accountable. If you warn your superior of the potentially volatile situation, you will be recognized as a team player who is watching out for the well-being of the company.

TACTICS

- **Attitude:** Be quick and decisive. Seize control of the dialogue and make your superior search for a solution. Force a discussion of potential defenses and countermaneuvers to the client problem.

19. Warning Your Superior of Potential Client Problems

Icebreaker: Thanks for meeting with me on short notice. I have a feeling that Acme may be preparing to pull its business. No one has said anything directly, but I have a strong sense that something is wrong. Just to be on the safe side, I think we should discuss possible plans of action.

Remains calm: *Can you tell me why you have this feeling? If we can identify the problem, we'll have a better chance of rectifying the situation.*

Gets angry: *How the heck did this happen? What did your team do? Acme is an important client, and we can't afford to lose it. If we do, heads are going to roll.*

Panics: *If we lose Acme, we're in a heap of trouble. We need its business. What are we going to do about this? What did the partners tell you? What did they say?*

You're paranoid: *I think you may be overreacting. You say you only have a sense. If the partners haven't said anything to indicate they're unhappy, then I don't think we should lose sleep over this.*

Explain: As I said, it's nothing concrete, just a feeling. Still, I think we should prepare ourselves. I propose we meet with the partners at Acme. We can tell them we just want to review our working relationship.

Cautious, not paranoid: I think it would be a big mistake to ignore this problem. It can't hurt to meet with the partners at Acme. At the very least, they will appreciate our personal attention and it will solidify our working relationship.

Soothe panic: If we react swiftly, we may not lose its business. We need to re-evaluate our working relationship and address any problems. If we arrange a meeting with the partners at Acme, I think we can clear the air and get to the bottom of this.

Redirect anger: I believe something is wrong at Acme. We need to find out what the problem is and address it head on. I propose we arrange a meeting with the partners at Acme to address any issues.

Still angry: *Maybe if we knew who the heck screwed up or at least what's wrong we could fix the problem. What are we supposed to do? Sit down with the people from Acme and say we have a feeling something is wrong?*

Wants elaboration: *What would the meeting you propose accomplish? We can't exactly sit down and ask what's wrong. We could end up looking foolish.*

Not convinced: *I still don't see a problem. Let's wait a couple of weeks and see what happens. If you get any concrete evidence that Acme is going to pull its business, we could talk again. Until then, let's stick to business as usual.*

Solve the problem: We can tell them the meeting is about reviewing our working relationship. If they feel something is wrong, they're more likely to air their concerns in this forum. We'll be demonstrating our dedication to their business and seeking the solution to their problem.

Disagrees: *I don't think a meeting is necessary. We may give them a sense of power in our relationship. We don't want to show too much of our hand. Let's just play along for a while and see what happens. If you hear anything, let me know.*

Protect yourself: I understand your position. Just as a precaution, I'm going to prepare a brief memo outlining the possible reactions to an Acme pullout. I'll write the memo in my free time. Thanks for taking the time to meet with me.

Agrees: *All right, I guess I can't see a down side. You'll coordinate with our group and theirs. Find a good time for a brief meeting; I want you to personally arrange everything.*

Express thanks: I'll handle all the arrangements. I'm sure this meeting will heal any wounds with Acme. Thanks for hearing me out and addressing this situation.

- **Timing:** Meet with your superior soon after you sense there's a problem, but don't race into a meeting half-cocked. Have the meeting as soon as you have control of your emotions and feel able to explain the situation in a clear and coherent fashion.
- **Preparation:** Organize your thoughts and prepare notes about the problem. Try to rehearse a quick and effective speech to begin the meeting. Formulate ideas for dealing with the situation and be ready to share your thoughts during the meeting.
- **Behavior:** Be confident. You are racing to the rescue of the company. Move the conversation swiftly and remind your superior that the most important thing to do is address the situation.

ADAPTATIONS

This script can be modified to:

- Protect yourself from a destructive peer.

KEY POINTS

- Guide the conversation toward a solution. Don't let it degenerate into a finger-pointing melee.
- Don't accept blame for the situation. You have a feeling, but it's not your fault.
- Suggest meeting with the client and try to get them to air any grievances. Even if they don't have a problem, the meeting will be a boost to your working relationship.
- If your superior doesn't heed your warning, offer to prepare a memo outlining possible reactions to a client pullout. This will further protect you from recriminations.

Warning Your Superior of Potential Vendor Problems

20

STRATEGY

If you learn a vendor your company relies on may be about to run into trouble either with its own operation or in servicing your company, you need to alert your superior. However, you'll first need to take certain things into consideration. What's the likelihood that vendor service will be interrupted and how long will it be for that to happen? What are the alternative sources for the goods or services, and what are their relative strengths and weaknesses? Does the problem have to do with the workings of your own company or its relationship with the vendor? The reason for all this preliminary thought is that you want to provide some advice on a potential course of action. However, remember that the problems you foresee may not arise. If your company goes through a costly or time-consuming shift that wasn't necessary, you'll be blamed—just as if you hadn't noticed the problem at all.

TACTICS

- **Attitude:** You've noticed something that may be harmful, but because you've noticed it early, the company has the opportunity to proceed with caution. That means not rushing to judgment or taking action, although the more people you make aware of the problem the better.

- **Preparation:** Thoroughly analyze the problem and the potential solutions, coming up with a list of alternative responses, both now and in the future. Choose one response because you may be asked for a specific recommendation.

- **Timing:** Time may not be of the essence, but the longer you delay, the less of an advantage your foresight will seem. Present the problem as soon as you've gathered all your facts and have formulated your own opinions. Don't schedule an emergency meeting or interrupt regular business—just ask for the next available time slot.

20. Warning Your Superior of Potential Vendor Problems

Opening: I think we might run into trouble with All Corp.

Wants info: *Why?*

State problem: I've learned that it has just signed on to service our main competitor.

Emphasize time: I agree, but I think we've got time. We don't want to do anything prematurely, but we should keep an eye on the situation and think about our alternatives.

Sees potential problem: *That could be disastrous.*

Doesn't see problem: So? It doesn't have an exclusive deal with us. Why would that be a problem?

Asks for opinion: *What do you think we should do?*

State theory: Well, our competitor can offer them twice the volume we can, so I'm worried our shipments will be given a lower priority and perhaps even delivered late.

Not worried: *I don't think that's going to happen. You're worrying too much.*

Drop it: Okay. I hope you're right. I just wanted to let you know about my fears. I'll keep an eye on the situation and let you know if anything changes.

Suggest immediate change: I think we need to shift vendors immediately before our competitor blows us out of the water.

Has problem with list: *What about Consolidated? It isn't on your list.*

Suggest other vendors: I've done a preliminary survey of other potential vendors; here's a list. As you can see, one is the cheapest, one is the most reliable, and one is affordable and reliable but probably too small for our purposes.

Suggest waiting: I think we should sit tight for now, but keep an eye on the situation. If it looks like problems might develop, we should consider shifting vendors.

Suggest internal changes: I think that if we shift our own policy from shipping at the end of the week to shipping early in the week, we can get a jump on our competitors and guarantee we won't become a secondary priority.

Suggest approaching vendor: I think we should approach All Corp. and tell them our fears and let them know that if there's a problem, we'll have to shift vendors.

Disagrees with approach: *If we do that, they'll just yes us to death regardless of the truth.*

Agrees to approach: *Good idea. Call them today and set up a meeting.*

Agree to amend list: You're right. I thought it was too large for us, but I'll add it to the list.

Agrees to wait: *Okay, let's sit tight and see what develops.*

Disagrees with waiting: *No. We've got the jump on them. Waiting will only hurt us. Let's make the shift now.*

Agrees to internal changes: *Good idea. Let's make the shift this month.*

Disagrees with internal changes: *If we did that, we'd lose the weekend and would have to change our "delivery in three business days" claim. We can't do that.*

Let's shift: Then let's make the shift ASAP.

- **Behavior:** While this isn't good news, the fact that you saw the potential for it happening before it did gives your company a competitive advantage. Don't gloat, but don't shy away from credit. Try to walk the middle ground between alternatives unless the evidence clearly points to one solution or unless you're forced to choose.

ADAPTATIONS

This script can be modified to:

- Warn a superior about a potential personnel problem.
- Warn a superior about a potential client problem.

KEY POINTS

- Be prepared to present alternative responses to the problem.
- Recognize that time is an ally that shouldn't be ignored or relied on.
- Don't discount the possibility that the problem won't arise.
- Emphasize the advantage of taking the time to make the right choice, placing an even greater value on the time you've provided the company.

Asking Your Superior for More Staff

21

STRATEGY

If you're in charge of a department that needs more staff yet you know your company either cannot or will not hire more people, you'll need to convince your superior to let you poach staff from other departments. Not only do you need to make a strong argument for why you can't get by with the staff you have, but you also have to justify how the department you're poaching from can get by without them. Make your reasons and rationales as factual as possible and as closely tied to the specific individuals involved as possible. Emphasize the benefits to the company as a whole. Realize this could be perceived as a power play by your boss and will be resented by the manager of the department from which you're poaching. That's why your reasons for the shifts must be beyond reproach.

TACTICS

- **Attitude:** Your department is doing well but could be doing even better. What you are proposing will boost profits, not only for your department but for the whole company. It's an idea that makes the most sense under the current staff restrictions.

- **Preparation:** Figure out who you can poach and from where. Develop a rationale for the shift. Decide whether you want this to be temporary or permanent, realizing that temporary shifts will be much easier to achieve.

- **Timing:** This is a tough call. The need for the added bodies must be near enough to be apparent, but the more time you allow for the shift, the more apt you are to get it. You'll need to use your judgment.

- **Behavior:** Be upbeat and positive. You've come up with a proposal that makes more money for the company and that benefits everyone. Don't be defensive—this isn't a power play. Be flexible and open to suggestions: your goal is to improve your department's efficiency so any steps made in that direction are positive.

21. Asking Your Superior for More Staff

Icebreaker: I've been trying to figure out how to increase my department's and the company's bottom line, and I've come up with a solution that won't cost the company anything.

Bites: *I'm all ears.*

Pitch: I'd like you to shift Oscar and Hector from the Midwest department to my department.

What about other departments?: *Everyone is understaffed right now, including the Midwest. If I let you poach people, I'll just be robbing Peter to pay Paul.*

Why do you need them?: *I don't see how two more staffers will help your department. You've got enough staff right now.*

Sets bad precedent: *If I let you get away with that, everyone will be poaching from everyone else—it will be open season to steal from other departments.*

Questions individual choices: *Do Oscar and Hector know enough about the Eastern accounts to make a difference?*

Questions individuals' morale: *Are you sure Oscar and Hector are going to be happy moving from Cincinnati to Boston?*

Other department justification: The Midwest is down 25 percent this year; I'm up 25 percent. They don't have enough work for all their salespeople; I've got more than my staff can handle.

Justify own need: Our business is up more than 25 percent this year, and we were understaffed before the increase. I can't keep up the level of customer service that's led to this increase without more salespeople.

Not bad precedent: Not necessarily. If the reason for the shift were made clear, it would just demonstrate that the company is flexible enough to allocate its resources wherever they're needed.

Individuals' qualifications: Oscar spent two years as a sale assistant in the Eastern department, and Hector handled the Eastern region for Acme before he came here to work for us.

Individuals' motivation: After they see the opportunity to make more money out here in the East, I'm sure they'll have their bags packed.

Questions motives: *Are you sure this isn't just a power play [or] some kind of vendetta you have against Bernard out in the Midwest?*

Asks for time: *Okay, you make a good case. Let me think about it and get back to you.*

Denies request: *Your argument is a good one . . . but not good enough. I can't justify it.*

Agrees instantly: *You know, I've been thinking the same thing. I don't see why not. Let's do it.*

Focus on goal: My goal is, has always been, and will always be to boost the company's bottom line. I think this is the best way to do it. If sending two of my people to Bernard in the Midwest made sense, I'd be the first to suggest it.

Press for decision: The sooner we get them over here and working, the sooner the profits will start climbing.

Ask for compromise: Well, what if you let one of them transfer [or] let me have them for one quarter so you can see the results?

Express thanks: Thanks for hearing me out.

ADAPTATIONS

This script can be modified to:

- Respond to a superior's request to improve your department's productivity.
- Request a greater share of supplies or resources for your department.

KEY POINTS

- Be prepared to justify your request as far as your department, the other department, the company, and the individuals are concerned.
- Be prepared to negotiate for a partial shift.
- Emphasize the positive impact on the company, not your department.
- Prepare to defuse any charges of power grabbing.

Advocating a Subordinate's Raise Request to Human Resources

22

STRATEGY

No one enjoys receiving a mere cost-of-living increase, especially if she has received positive performance reviews but is underpaid. While you can empathize with employees who experience this, you need to be selective about whom you will advocate for. This is a high-risk, low-reward effort that is only justified if you're sure you will lose a valued staffer and will end up paying more for a replacement than you would to retain her. The best approach is to make your case to HR and get their approval or at least acquiescence in going over their heads. This isn't a wasted effort, since you're respecting the company's procedures and hierarchy, and getting practice making your case.

TACTICS

- **Attitude:** This is a dramatic effort to make for an employee. Make sure she is worth the risk.
- **Preparation:** Ensure that she is indeed underpaid compared to her peers and that the company will in fact spend more in replacing her than in keeping her.
- **Timing:** If possible, do this before the next round of pay raises is issued.
- **Behavior:** Show respect for HR in word and in deed, making it clear that if they are powerless, you're asking them not to block your approach to their superiors.

22. Advocating a Subordinate's Raise Request to Human Resources

Icebreaker and pitch: I know we have a policy of maintaining salary parity, but I have a significant problem in my department and I need your advice and help with it. Deb Parker says that she has a problem with only getting a cost-of-living raise. I told her that this was the company policy this year, but she noted that she'd received excellent reviews two years in a row without an increase in pay grade and remains dramatically underpaid compared to her peers at other companies in the industry. I've checked her numbers and she is indeed underpaid.

Parity is primary: *We simply can't go down this road with every person in the company. Our policy is that no one can be treated differently. Everyone is getting a 2 percent cost-of-living increase and that's all.*

Send her to us: *If you'd like, we'll speak with her. Perhaps that will take some of the pressure off you. We'll explain that rules are rules.*

Will cost us: I hear what you're saying. The problem is that she is an outstanding employee who is indeed being underpaid. If we don't give her something more than this cost-of-living increase, I'm fairly sure she'll start looking for another job. To replace her, we will need to pay at least 15 to 20 percent more than she is currently earning. In addition, we'll have the costs of recruiting and hiring. I think we're shooting ourselves in the foot by not giving her a larger increase.

No power: *Your argument is a good one. But we simply don't have the power to make these kinds of exceptions. I'm sorry.*

Going upstairs: In that case, I'll need to plead my case directly to the VP. Would you mind if I explain that I'm speaking with her based on your suggestion?

Your responsibility: *It's your right to speak directly with her. You can tell her we said we that couldn't help you.*

Express gratitude: Thanks. I appreciate your hearing me out.

ADAPTATIONS

This script can be modified to:

- Advocate a subordinate's transfer request to human resources.
- Advocate a subordinate's promotion request to human resources.

KEY POINTS

- Frame the issue as your problem, and potentially the company's problem, not just the employee's problem.
- The only real argument is that denying the raise will actually cost the company more than agreeing to the raise.
- Realize that you'll inevitably need to take your case to the higher-ups.
- Express gratitude for having your argument heard.

Setting Recruiting Goals with Human Resources

23

STRATEGY

Despite all the exhortations to think creatively, most businesses still make decisions and judgments based on what was done before. Nowhere is that more obvious than in filling staff openings. Job descriptions are often outdated and treated like sacred texts. Since they're most often drafted and approved by HR people and administrators with little direct connection to the job, they rarely reflect changes in the job. To set recruiting goals that more accurately reflect your needs, you'll need to put your specific expertise up against the general expertise of HR. The only winning argument you can make is that your point boosts the company's bottom line. That may be enough to get HR to relent. If not, you'll need to go over their heads.

TACTICS

- **Attitude:** You're not quarreling with their judgment. You're simply pointing out that you have a unique need of which only you are aware.
- **Preparation:** Have as much proof as you can muster that the recruiting goal you're advocating would sooner or later boost the company's bottom line.
- **Timing:** Make the approach as soon as you realize that your input on the recruiting goals will be either nonexistent or minimal.
- **Behavior:** Be respectful but firm. This is a discussion between two professional people with nonopposing needs: You both want what is best for the company; you just disagree over what that is.

23. Setting Recruiting Goals with Human Resources

Icebreaker and pitch: I have a real need that will require setting some unusual recruiting goals for the opening in our department. You're the only one with the expertise and experience to help me out. Thirty percent of our customers are from French-speaking countries, and most of our sales push for the coming year is in France, Belgium, and Quebec. While the position we're looking to fill is technically just a sales assistant, I think it's vital that we hire someone who speaks French so he or she can serve as a fluent telephone communicator and translator on sales calls.

We're the experts: *We've thoroughly reviewed your needs and have come up with a job profile for the opening. You really should just leave it to us.*

Too costly: *While I'm sure hiring a French speaker would be great for you, it would cost the company too much. We've allocated $18,000 for the starting salary for this position, and we're not willing to spend any more to hire someone with language skills.*

Real need: You're absolutely right. I have no quarrel with your expertise. It's just that I have a real and pressing need brought on by the very specific circumstances of my department, an area in which I'm the expert.

Short-term thinking: You're probably right that hiring a French speaker would cost us more than what you've allocated. But that's only in the short term. In the coming years we'll need to hire temporary help both here and while on our sales calls. In the long term we'll save money if we hire an in-house French speaker. Besides, I think it could help us gain goodwill and boost revenue as well.

Not our call: *Those kind of short-term versus long-term evaluations aren't yours or ours to make. We've been given a budget and we intend to stick with it. You should do the same.*

Going upstairs: In that case I'll be going upstairs to make my arguments and talk to the higher-ups about changing the budget. I'll get back to you.

Gives in: *You've made some good points. Let me go back and redraft the ad copy and do some research on what the new skill package will cost us. I think we can probably make it work.*

Express gratitude: I really appreciate your help and your willingness to listen to my needs.

ADAPTATIONS

This script can be modified to:

- Argue that a position should be filled with a full-time rather than a part-time worker.

KEY POINTS

- Bow to HR's expertise on general personnel issues.
- Stress your expertise on your department's specific needs.
- Argue that savings would only be short term.
- Express your willingness to go over HR's heads if need be.

Protecting a
Subordinate from
a Possible Layoff

24

STRATEGY

Sometimes company-wide personnel policies can have unintended consequences. For instance, orders can go out to lay off the most recently hired employees to trim costs. If that new person happens to be your most productive person, the company would be making a huge mistake. Human resources, which probably played a major role in developing the termination policy, will always focus on the big picture and push for a standardized policy. Your goal is to get past HR and get to upper management, which should care more about the bottom line than about uniformity. To do that you'll need to make it clear to HR that you are advocating an exception, not for the employee or yourself but for the company.

TACTICS

- **Attitude:** Accept the validity of the policy and HR's role in the process, but don't accept that either of these factors makes the layoff inevitable.
- **Preparation:** Draft a memo that lays out the grounds for your chosen argument. Even if it's based only on your observations and analysis, having it in writing will make it more powerful.
- **Timing:** Make your approach as soon as you realize that one of your key people will be affected by the proposed layoffs. It's best if you can say that you, rather than the affected employee, initiated the approach.
- **Behavior:** Acknowledge HR's role in the process and show that you respect their position. But at the same time demonstrate that your highest loyalty is to the company and that you will do what you think is in its best interests. Accept responsibility willingly.

24. Protecting a Subordinate from a Possible Layoff

Icebreaker: Thanks for meeting with me today. I wanted to speak with you about Jim Johnson. Based on my understanding of the company's plans, I think he's a layoff candidate. It's my own fault for not raising this issue earlier. But I think letting Jim go would be a mistake for the company.

Chain reaction: He's a very valuable member of our team, and his loss would have a terrible impact on the department's morale. I'm afraid there would be a chain reaction with other team members fearing for their own jobs and a resulting drop in productivity.

Bottom-line hit: Despite his relatively junior status he's our top-performing salesperson. Losing him would have a direct and immediate effect on our bottom line and would far outweigh any cost savings from eliminating his salary.

Fairness is essential: *We can't make any exceptions. The only fair way to cut staff is by making the layoffs based on an objective fact like seniority. Bringing any other factors into play leaves the company open to potential problems.*

Powerless: *I'm afraid both you and I are powerless to protect Jim. These staffing decisions have been made by the people upstairs and there's nothing either of us can do about it.*

Debates argument: *I sympathize with you, but in my experience no one employee is indispensable. The actual impact on morale and on productivity is never as great as the affected manager initially fears. Trust me.*

Exceptional case: I realize that you have a great deal of experience with these situations, but I think this is an extra-ordinary circumstance. The loss of our top-producing salesperson will have a devastating impact on the bottom line.

Take it upstairs: I understand that your hands are tied. I guess what I need to do is to go directly to the people upstairs and make my case to them.

Real outweighs potential: I understand the importance of fairness, but I think this is an extraordinary circumstance. I don't think the company should directly hurt the bottom line in an effort to ward off potential problems that may never arise.

You're responsible: *We simply can't assume responsibility for making an exception to the company's policy. Of course you're well within your rights to approach the people upstairs about this issue.*

Accept responsibility: I understand that, and I'll tell the people upstairs that it's my butt on the line. Thanks for your time.

ADAPTATIONS

This script can be modified to:

- Ask a parent to make an exception to family tradition in dealing with a child or grandchild.

KEY POINTS

- Be respectful of HR's power but determined in your approach.
- Stress unintended circumstances that will result from the policy.
- If fairness is cited, say the bottom line is more important.
- If your argument isn't accepted, stick to your guns.
- If superiors are blamed, say you'll approach them directly.

25

Defending a Subordinate against Criticism from Human Resources

STRATEGY

Strict enforcement of company rules and regulations can often cause problems in a department. Efforts by HR or upper management to make an example of an employee could hurt morale and productivity. In such cases it's a manager's role to intercede on behalf of a staffperson. Rather than trying to debate or contradict HR, offer mitigating information. If you're unable to derail the disciplinary action and keep the matter in-house, push for your comments to be a part of the record. Respect HR's role, but in return ask that they respect your role in the process as well.

TACTICS

- **Attitude:** Never frame situations like this as personal matters. You're doing this in order to maintain staff morale and productivity.
- **Preparation:** Make sure you know all the facts and any mitigating factors. Place all your data and arguments in a cogent memo and have it with you when you meet with HR.
- **Timing:** Have this conversation as soon as you hear of the disciplinary matter and have had a chance to do your preparation.
- **Behavior:** Be respectful but persistent. You're not just defending your staffer, you're defending your prerogatives as a manager.

25. Defending a Subordinate against Criticism from Human Resources

Icebreaker: I just heard that Betty Baker received a reprimand for lateness. While I'm certainly not condoning that behavior, I think it's important we make note of the circumstances and her contributions to the company. Her infant child has been very ill, putting a great deal of strain on her family and, I'm sure, leading to the lateness. But her productivity while here has been as good as ever.

Not your business: *I can appreciate your coming in to defend your staffer. But repeated tardiness is a company-wide problem that we've been told to address by the people upstairs. It's an HR issue, not a departmental one.*

It's my job: Anything that threatens the morale and productivity of my department is my job. I'm the one who would be most affected by a tardiness problem, and I'm here to tell you that there has been no problem.

Backs off: *I'm glad you came in to speak with us. I admit I was surprised when I saw Betty's name on the list. Let me speak with the VP who has been pushing this issue and see if we can't make an exception in this case.*

Duly noted: *I'm glad you're willing to participate in the process. We'll be happy to let you add a letter to the file making the points you've just made to me. However, the disciplinary action needs to come first.*

Not a footnote: I'm sorry but I take this very seriously. I don't want my comments to be a footnote. A formal reprimand could hurt Betty's future with the company, and I don't want to see that happen. I think this is something I should handle inside the department.

Express gratitude: I'm glad to hear you say that. I knew that once you heard the facts we'd be able to work this out.

Put it in writing: *I hear your comments. Put them in writing and I'll present them to the VP who's pushing this issue.*

Present memo: I've already prepared a memo. Here it is. I'd be happy to make the case in person as well.

ADAPTATIONS

This script can be modified to:

- Defend a family member against overzealous criticism from an authority figure.

KEY POINTS

- Don't debate the facts. Just offer mitigating factors.
- Stress that this should be kept in-house.
- Insist on having your comments be part of the record.

Telling Your Superior Someone Else Took Credit for Your Idea

26

STRATEGY

It's essential to deal with idea theft right away. If you don't stop someone else from taking credit for your ideas, it will become a recurring pattern that derails your career. Confronting the thief in private might keep this from happening again but won't help you recover the lost credit. That will require bringing the issue to your superior. The only way to do this without seeming petty is to acknowledge that's how it may appear, but offer nobler, less selfish reasons as the real motivations. It matters less that you're actually believed than that it gives you a rationale to bring the facts to your superior's attention.

TACTICS

- **Attitude:** This isn't back-stabbing, it's self-defense. And the only way to recover from the damage is to bring it to your superior's attention.
- **Preparation:** Make sure you have a paper trail that proves that the idea was originally your own.
- **Timing:** Bring this up as soon as you learn the idea has been stolen. The sooner you raise the issue, the more honest you'll appear.
- **Behavior:** Be more concerned than angry. The more irate you appear, the more this will seem a personal matter. Shake your head rather than your fist, and shrug your shoulders instead of pounding a table.

26. Telling Your Superior Someone Else Took Credit for Your Idea

Icebreaker: I need to speak with you about something that's a bit uncomfortable.

Potential problem: I'm not here to cast aspersions. My only concern is the company's success. I think you need to be aware that Brian is taking credit for other people's ideas. The Southeast expansion plan, for instance, is an idea I came up with. I'm not here to claim credit for myself. I'm here to warn you that this isn't the first time and that the department's morale is suffering.

Being petty: *We're a team here. It doesn't matter where ideas originate, only that they work. I'm not interested in this kind of departmental bickering and politics.*

Success is essential: I want to be sure the Southeast expansion plan is done as well as it could be. I know Brian has portrayed the idea as his own, but actually I developed it. I'm really not interested in who takes credit for it. I wouldn't be bringing it up at all if I didn't think there were a few elements of the plan, crucial to its success, that he hasn't quite gotten down. I want you to know that I'm willing to do whatever it takes for it to succeed, even if I have to work on it behind the scenes.

Gets message: *I appreciate this is a difficult conversation for you. I also appreciate your putting the company first. I'll make a note of what you've told me [or] I'll make sure you're an ongoing part of the process.*

Got proof?: *Do you have any proof Brian stole your idea [or] has stolen ideas?*

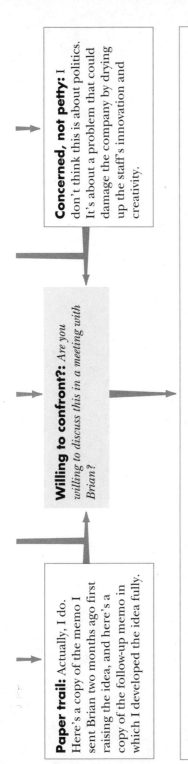

Paper trail: Actually, I do. Here's a copy of the memo I sent Brian two months ago first raising the idea, and here's a copy of the follow-up memo in which I developed the idea fully.

Willing to confront?: *Are you willing to discuss this in a meeting with Brian?*

Concerned, not petty: I don't think this is about politics. It's about a problem that could damage the company by drying up the staff's innovation and creativity.

Company first: Certainly, if you think that despite the embarrassment it would cause Brian, it's necessary for the company's health and success.

ADAPTATIONS

This script can be modified to:

- Protest another's undeserved award or honor.

KEY POINTS

- Bring up the matter with reluctance.
- Stress that you're more concerned for the company than you are angry with the thief.
- If asked for documentation, provide it.
- If accused of pettiness, expand on the nature of broader potential harm.
- If asked to repeat claims to a third party, agree.

Asking Your Superior to Stop Micromanaging

27

STRATEGY

A manager who can't or won't delegate will end up forcing out quality staff people. Her micromanaging will end up a self-fulfilling prophecy: the only staffers who stay will be those who aren't capable and who are happy to let someone else do their job. The best way to end such interference is to frame it as a personal, not business, problem. Question the manager's health, not her management style or effectiveness. If that doesn't work and the problem continues, you'll need a blunter approach. Again, don't get into the issue of effectiveness. Instead frame it as an economic issue: it will cost too much to replace those who quit. Having raised the issue twice, all you can then do is keep your fingers crossed . . . or start looking for a new job yourself.

TACTICS
- **Attitude:** This concerns the health of the manager and the health of the company, so it's both a delicate matter and an important one. It's your responsibility, as a friend and as a loyal employee, to address it.
- **Preparation:** Make sure this is indeed an ongoing problem and that there are definite rumblings among the rest of the staff. A one-time occurrence should just be shrugged off.
- **Timing:** Make your initial approach as soon as you learn that the micromanaging is causing a problem, and make your second approach as soon as there is a recurrence of the behavior. Hold both dialogues in private in your superior's office.
- **Behavior:** Be friendly and personal during the initial approach. If you need to have the conversation again, be more businesslike and formal.

27. Asking Your Superior to Stop Micromanaging

Icebreaker: Wendy, I hope you don't mind, but I'd like to speak with you as a friend, not as a subordinate. I'm concerned with how much stress you're putting yourself under. I'm worried about your health. I think you need to let some of the rest of us help carry the load.

Heard it before: *You sound just like my husband! He's been saying that to me for months now. Maybe you're right. I have been a little stressed out. Okay. I'll try to ease up a little and let you and the other assistant managers pick up the slack.*

It's up to me: *Thanks for being concerned, but there's no need for you to worry. I thrive on working hard. I know you can do your job well, but I can't count on everyone else doing things the way they need to be done. It's like that old saying: "If you want it done right, you need to do it yourself."*

Counterproductive: It's not just you I'm concerned with, Wendy. I think we're also starting to have some morale problems with the staff. I'm getting the sense that they think you're second-guessing them and micromanaging. Why not give them a chance to show you what they can do?

Agrees: *Okay. I'll try to ease up a bit and give them a chance.*

If it happens again

Blunt confrontation: Wendy, we need to talk. Your micromanaging hasn't let up, and I think it's leading to a crisis with the staff. Some key people are going to quit if you don't let go of the reins and let them do their work.

Angry: *Well, maybe they should quit. If they can't keep up or produce, we don't need them.*

Expensive: We're not talking about slackers, Wendy. We're talking about some of our best people who are about to look for another job. If we lose these staffers, it's going to cost us a great deal to replace them. I really think you need to ease up.

Agrees: *Okay. I'll try to ease up a bit and give them a chance.*

ADAPTATIONS

This script can be modified to:

- Suggest that a friend or family member is being overprotective of a child.

KEY POINTS

- Frame this first as a personal health issue; one friend concerned with another.
- Hold the conversation in private in the other party's workspace.
- If staff is criticized, defend them gently without starting a debate.
- If your first approach is ineffective, frame it as an economic crisis, not as an effectiveness issue.

28

Going over Your Superior's Head

STRATEGY

Taking a problem to your superior's supervisor is one of the biggest gambles in office politics. The payoff can be great, but you run the risk of becoming a pariah whose days in the company are numbered. That's why you should take this step only if you believe your future at the firm is at stake—because of a negative performance review, say, or because a vital project has been canceled. First, try to get permission for your end run. You may get the okay if you frame your request as a search for expert input. Even if your immediate superior objects, persevere. Asking to go over her head is as bad as actually doing it so you've nothing more to lose. When you do get upstairs, continue to frame your efforts as a search for advice. Resist the temptation to badmouth your superior. If you manage to win the top person over, you'll have gained a valuable ally—one who will most likely be able to protect you from recriminations. If you don't win Ms. Big to your side, start looking for another job.

TACTICS

- **Attitude:** Realize there's nothing your immediate superior can do to stop you, but you'd still like her permission.
- **Preparation:** Have your facts and arguments down cold—your future in the company will depend on your winning your superior's supervisor over to your side.
- **Timing:** While this should be done soon after either a negative review or the cancellation of an important project, your decision must be thought out, not reflexive. Give yourself at least a day or two to think things over.
- **Behavior:** Be forthright and determined. You must convey that you're bucking the system because of your extremely principled position and concern for justice.

28. Going over Your Superior's Head

Asking for permission

Project icebreaker #1: I understand your objections. Would you have a problem if I unofficially batted this around with Sharon? Maybe she can help us come up with a way to overcome your objections.

Personal icebreaker #1: Thank you for your time. I have one other request. I'd like permission to speak with Sharon about this issue.

No need: *I've already spoken to Sharon. She's in accord with me.*

New spin: I'd assumed you had, but I think I can put another spin on it that might change both of your minds.

No permission: *You can do whatever you want; but you don't have my permission.*

Won't help: *This is my decision to make. Speaking to Sharon won't change my mind.*

Still want to: That may be the case, but I don't want to do an end run. I'd like your permission to try.

Refuses: *I don't want you speaking to anyone else about this.*

Am I forbidden?: Are you saying if the issue comes up I should say you've forbidden me to discuss it?

Grudging permission: *If you want to waste your time, it's okay with me.*

Express thanks: Thank you. I appreciate it.

Explaining your actions

Project icebreaker 2: I've been having a dialogue with Kelly about a project I'd like to develop. We've had a difference of opinion about whether it's a good idea for us to pursue.

Personal icebreaker 2: I've been having a dialogue with Kelly about my performance. She has expressed some serious doubts about my ability to stay and thrive in the company, and I need to take these up with you.

Fishing for controversy: *Are you questioning Kelly's judgment?*

Backs your boss: *I'm not going to overrule her. I've got a lot of respect for her judgment.*

Company comes first: Absolutely not. I just don't want to see the company make a major mistake.

Me too: So do I. I'm not asking you to overrule her. I was hoping you would see something that the two of us have missed that could resolve this.

Wants to mediate: *Listen, shouldn't the three of us talk about this together?*

Okay . . . but: I have no problem with that . . . but she knows you and I are meeting to discuss it.

Agrees to intervene: *Okay. Tell me about the project.* [or] *Tell me about her comments to you.*

ADAPTATIONS

This script can be modified to:

- Appeal a loan rejection.
- Correct detrimental or incorrect information your superior has passed along to her superior.

KEY POINTS

- Frame your jumping the ladder as a search for expert advice.
- If your immediate superior objects, persist.
- Regardless of your immediate superior's conclusion, thank her.
- If your superior's supervisor wants to serve as mediator, explain that your immediate superior knows of this meeting.
- If your superior's supervisor fishes for controversy, stress that your concern is first and foremost for the company.
- If your superior's supervisor refuses to overrule a decision, stress you're looking for a potential compromise, not a reversal.

Complaining about an Immediate Superior's Behavior

29

STRATEGY

No one should have to put up with an insulting, abusive superior. If you've tried to speak to your immediate superior about his behavior and have gotten nowhere, the only solution is to make an end run and speak with his supervisor. Of course, this is one of the most dangerous political maneuvers you can make in an office environment. Not only could you appear to be a disloyal backstabber to your superior's supervisor, but it's possible your relationship with your immediate superior could get even worse if he learns of your actions. The best way to minimize the potential damage from such a conversation is to portray the situation as a rescue mission. Sure it's an end run, but it's not for your benefit, it's to help someone in trouble. This isn't about your problems with your superior's behavior—it's about *him* having a problem. Being an underling, you're probably in no position to have such a conversation with him. You're asking his supervisor to speak to him about a problem (his behavior) that's affecting the company. Framed this way, there's little a manager can do but intervene.

TACTICS

- **Attitude:** Don't feel guilty about this end run. You're helping out someone in trouble whose inappropriate behavior or actions could be self-destructive and could bring harm to the company.
- **Preparation:** Try to commit to memory a list of your superior's inappropriate behavior. *Do not* put this in writing, however. Presenting such a memo, or even just reading from it, would imply premeditation and would have the appearance of backstabbing.
- **Timing:** Do this either before or after normal business hours, if possible, reinforcing that it's a personal matter unfortunately affecting business.

29. Complaining about an Immediate Superior's Behavior

Icebreaker: As you know, I have a great deal of respect for Martin. I think he may have a serious problem, and although I'd like to help him on my own, I can't. That's why I'm here. I know how important he is to the company and that you respect him as well.

Concerned with hierarchy: *Does he know you've come to speak to me?*

Takes the bait: *Okay, tell me what's going on.*

Not about business: No, but that's because this isn't job related. It's not about the chain of command, it's about someone who I think has a problem and may be in trouble.

Explain situation: In the past few weeks he has had a number of temper tantrums, launched into rages, become irrational, and even acted insulting in front of third parties. All this has led me to believe something personal is bothering him.

Deal with it: *Listen, that's just Martin. I know he's a pain, but he's also the best salesperson in the industry. I know he flies off the handle, but he doesn't mean anything by it. You have to learn to let that kind of stuff go. Just do the best you can with him.*

Accepts responsibility: *Okay. Let me speak with him and see if there's something going on. Until then, just sit tight.*

Suspects intrigue: *Do you have another agenda here? You never got along with Martin. Is this really about politics in the department?*

Not political: This isn't a question of whether or not I like Martin. This is a question of a person I think is in trouble. I wouldn't step on someone when he's down. I think he really needs help . . . help I can't give him.

Reaffirm concern: I hope you'll be able to help him out. I truly am worried about him. If there's anything I can do, please let me know.

Last resort: I've been trying to do just that. You're my last resort. This is becoming a regular pattern. I'm worried about him. I've spoken to him about it and gotten nowhere. I can't do my job and be his therapist, too.

- **Behavior:** Be concerned, caring, and compassionate. Show that your number one concern is that your superior is hurting himself and the company.

ADAPTATIONS

This script can be modified to:

- Discuss a problem child with his or her parent.
- Complain about a municipal or governmental functionary.

KEY POINTS

- This is your superior's problem, not yours. You're here to help him.
- If the chain of command is cited, explain that this is a personal, not a business, issue.
- If the behavior is explained away or minimized, reiterate that this is a potentially self-destructive pattern that could damage the company as well.
- If your motives are called into question, stress that your concerns are for your superior and the company, not yourself.
- Reinforce your statements by expressing your willingness to help in any way you can.

Apologizing to Your Superior for Your Own Backstabbing

30

STRATEGY

If you've been badmouthing someone rather than complaining to the individual involved or your superior directly, and you suspect word may get back to your superior, you're best off heading in to apologize before you're called on the carpet. While your undignified and potentially fractious behavior may not be something you're eager to own up to, it's better to face it now than let it come back to haunt you. If you admit your own backstabbing, you'll not only undercut the seriousness of your behavior, but you'll indicate that you're aware of your mistake and that it won't happen again. Start by apologizing to the individual involved. Then offer your superior a solid reason for your behavior, even if it's just a matter of losing your temper. However, acknowledge that there's no excuse for backstabbing. You'll have simultaneously turned yourself in and given yourself a suspended sentence. You may actually come off gaining in your superior's eyes!

TACTICS

- **Attitude:** You are contrite. You've seen the error of your ways. You realize your behavior has had a potentially damaging impact, not only on the individual involved but on the company's esprit de corps. Still, you're positive you've cleared the matter up directly and have mended your working relationship. Don't be smug. Emphasize your determination not to repeat your mistake.

- **Preparation:** Assess the extent of the damage before going in to see your superior. How much does she know and how upset will she be? Have a reason (not an excuse) for your actions. Apologize to the individual involved beforehand.

- **Timing:** Do this as soon as you've realized the error of your ways and have had a chance to apologize to the injured party. If you wait for signs that your superior may find out, you'll be too late.

30. Apologizing to Your Superior for Your Own Backstabbing

Present the situation: This is somewhat awkward for me, but I want to apologize to you for some unprofessional behavior on my part.

Wants info: *What do you mean?*

Knows what you mean: *You mean your comments about Jason?*

Admit backstabbing: I said some pretty nasty things about Jason earlier this week.

State reason and apologize: I know it's no excuse, but I was upset we were running behind schedule, and I just exploded. I've apologized to Jason, and I just wanted you to know it won't happen again.

Lets you off easy: *Well, it sounds as if you handled everything well. Between you and me, I was upset about running late, too. Forget about it and get back to work.*

Takes you to task: *You're right on two counts: that's not an excuse and it better not happen again. I'm glad you've apologized to Jason and came to tell me about it. Now get back to work.*

Express thanks: Thanks for listening to me.

- **Behavior:** Nobody likes admitting errors, but be as natural as possible. Present what happened calmly and tell the truth. If it's awkward, say so. If you can't believe what you did, share that as well. Human beings make mistakes. The more human you come across, the more likely you'll be readily forgiven.

ADAPTATIONS

This script can be modified to:

- Apologize to a superior for poor judgment.

KEY POINTS

- Have a reason but acknowledge it's not an excuse.
- Be positive about your ability to continue working with the injured party.
- Be prepared either to be let off with a slap on the wrist or to be taken to task, depending on your superior's own past behavior.
- The more human you are in behavior, the more apt you are to be forgiven.

Giving Two Weeks' Notice to Your Superior

31

STRATEGY

Giving notice can be dangerous, even when you already have another job. It's conceivable an angry superior could fire you on the spot, forcing you to lose at least two weeks' pay. If you give too much notice, you could end up getting fired as soon as you've wrapped up your work or your replacement is selected. The solution is to give the two weeks that have become customary and to be prepared to deflect attempts to fire you. The best way to do that is to practice a subtle form of workplace extortion. Your obligation to conclude short-term projects and prepare memos on your long-term projects should be implicit with your being given two weeks to wrap things up. By the way, it makes sense to hold off actually preparing and presenting those memos as long as possible since they're your only leverage to ensure you get your final paycheck.

TACTICS

- **Attitude:** Be direct, businesslike, and confident. The only thing he can do to you is fire you—and you're leaving for another job anyway.
- **Preparation:** In this script it's actually more a matter of not preparing. State what you'll do during your two weeks as a lame duck, but don't actually do it until you've gotten his agreement that you'll be employed for those two weeks.
- **Timing:** Do this as soon as possible after learning you've been hired and have cleaned up your files. Do it as early in the day and as early in the week as possible so the company has a chance to react right away.
- **Behavior:** Remain calm, even in the face of anger or threats. Don't simply absorb abuse, however. Make it clear that your being fired will not only hurt the company and the staff, but it will send a clear message to other staffers that they should simply quit rather than give notice.

31. Giving Two Weeks' Notice to Your Superior

Icebreaker: I've received an irresistible job offer from Acme, Inc., which I've accepted effective two weeks from today. I've gone over everything that I'm working on here, and I believe that I'll be able to complete all of my short-term projects without incident or additional expense within two weeks. I'll prepare memos for those who take over my long-term projects.

Accepts inevitable: *I hate to see you go, but that's part of business. Just make sure you finish your projects and get those memos to me as soon as possible.*

Thanks: Thank you. I'll get those memos to you right away. Incidentally, working for you has been a wonderful experience for me and I'm grateful.

Not enough time: *Two weeks' notice is like quitting on the spot. If that's all you can give me, you might as well leave today.*

As much as possible: I honestly have considered your needs very carefully. As I said, I'll wrap up my short-term projects and prepare memos on my long-term assignments. I'll also do whatever I can to help you find a replacement for me. Finally, if necessary, I'll be available on weekends and evenings to help out my replacement, even after I make the shift. However, if you prefer that I leave today, I will.

Gets angry: *You ungrateful SOB. We don't need your help. Pack up your stuff and get out of here today. And don't even try to take any of our customers. I'm going to call security right now and have them watch while you empty out your desk.*

Giving notice a mistake?: Was it a mistake to give you notice? Would you have preferred that I just leave? Is that how you want this company to operate? It's your choice. I've told everyone in my department that I'm leaving and that I'll help them with the transition. But if you want me to leave today without helping them, and you want everyone in the company to see it's a mistake to give you any notice at all, that's fine, too.

Backs off . . . some: *No, you can spend the next two weeks tying up loose ends. I should have realized I couldn't count on you. Get me those memos as soon as possible.*

Backs off: *No, I was just worried about the workload. I'd appreciate your doing everything possible to get your work done. And get me those memos as soon as you can.*

ADAPTATIONS

This script can be modified to:

- Terminate a personal relationship.

KEY POINTS

- Be confident, direct, and determined. The die has been cast, so be forceful.
- If he gets angry and threatens to fire you, say that will hurt the company and give the wrong message to employees.
- If he says two weeks isn't enough, tell him you'll do everything possible to help, but insist it's the best you can do.
- Unless he accepts the situation gracefully, give him the last word—it will help assuage his bruised ego.

Recommending an Incentive Plan for Yourself

32

STRATEGY

In times of economic uncertainty the first thing companies do is refrain from offering salary increases. Trying to argue against such a policy is a mistake. It will only mark you as "not a team player." That doesn't mean you need to forgo income increases. A bonus plan based on improved performance and productivity is a perfectly logical alternative. The only real objections to such a plan would be the need for fairness and there not being a precedent for it. If your superior starts debating the details, you can start celebrating. He has accepted the concept and simply wants to cut the best deal he can.

TACTICS

- **Attitude:** Thinking you should be rewarded for improved performance isn't disloyal. There's a big difference between automatic increases and performance bonuses. Pushing for the latter is a sign of healthy self-esteem.
- **Preparation:** Write a clear, well-researched memo outlining your proposed incentive plan and bring it with you to your meeting. Have talking points for further presentations readily available as well.
- **Timing:** The best time to make this approach is after you've achieved a success that boosted the company's bottom line. Try to hold the dialogue before normal business hours.
- **Behavior:** Show equal concern for the company's financial health and your own. Be reasonable but assertive.

32. Recommending an Incentive Plan for Yourself

Icebreaker: Thanks for meeting with me this morning. I know the company isn't able to offer salary increases right now. I'm dedicated to this company, and even though I'm underpaid, I'm willing to help it through this difficult time. I'm suggesting that in lieu of an increase the company pay me a year-end bonus of 10 percent of the sales I book over last year's total sales.

Open to idea: *I'm glad you're willing to sacrifice for the company. Your idea of a performance bonus is an interesting one. I've been thinking along those lines myself. But the 10 percent figure seems a bit high.*

Salami slice: What number do you think works better? How about 8 percent?

Unfair: *I'd be the first to go in and push for a raise for you. But I can't offer you an incentive plan such as you've suggested without offering it to everyone else.*

Company wide: If fairness and full disclosure are important issues, why not open up this kind of incentive plan to everyone in the company? The worst that could happen is that everyone boosts his production and profitability over last year.

Too innovative: *That's certainly a creative idea, but we've never done anything like that before. I don't know if now is the time for innovations.*

Now's the time: I realize that. But the company has never been in this situation before. If you don't mind my saying, there's probably no better time than now for innovative solutions to our problems.

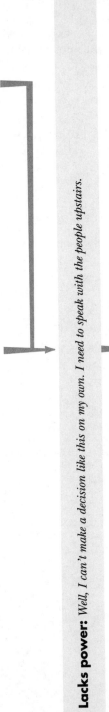

Lacks power: *Well, I can't make a decision like this on my own. I need to speak with the people upstairs.*

Offer help: I understand that. Here's a memo outlining my idea, which you're free to present.

ADAPTATIONS

This script can be modified to:

- Ask to be shifted from a straight salary to a salary plus commission or profit-sharing compensation plan.

KEY POINTS

- Show you accept the need for the company to adjust to economic circumstances.
- Present your incentive plan without excuses.
- Unique times call for unique solutions.
- Don't be afraid to advocate it as a companywide solution.

II

Lifescripts

*for Dealing with
Subordinates*

Criticizing a Subordinate's Work

33

STRATEGY

Delivering criticism requires a delicate touch. You need to present the problem strongly enough so the subordinate gets the message and hopefully changes his behavior but not so strongly that you undermine his confidence or create lingering resentment. The best way to accomplish this is to start with positive comments before delivering the criticism. If the information is received openly, reaffirm your confidence and set up a future meeting. If the subordinate disputes your perception or gets angry, give him a chance to get over reflexive defensiveness by offering specifics. If that doesn't calm him down, stop pulling your punches and make it clear his future depends on improved performance.

TACTICS

- **Attitude:** Think of yourself as a teacher or mentor, not a judge and jury. And be willing to absorb a little anger without retaliating—it's not easy to take criticism submissively.
- **Preparation:** Make sure your list of criticisms is accurate and detailed—you don't want this to turn into a debate over facts. Have specific suggestions and advice ready to help the subordinate improve his performance.
- **Timing:** If this isn't a formal review, it should take place as soon as possible after a problem so it's fresh in everyone's mind. If you can, schedule it for early in the week so the subordinate has a chance to act on your advice right away and won't have to dwell on it over a weekend.
- **Behavior:** Lead off with positive comments so the meeting doesn't seem as if it's a one-sided attack. If the subordinate won't get past his initial anger or denial, forget subtlety and make it clear his future is at stake unless he cleans up his act.

33. Criticizing a Subordinate's Work

Icebreaker: I'm generally very pleased with your work—especially the way you're handling the arrangements for the winter festival. But there is one thing you need to work on. Maybe I haven't made it clear that you're also responsible for supervising all the cleaning personnel, but lately I've found the building a bit dirty.

Accepts criticism: *I'm really sorry. I didn't realize that I'd slipped up. I won't let it happen again.*

Denies problem: *Really? I've been very careful about checking on their work. I don't think there has been any letdown.*

Gets angry: *I've been working overtime to get everything set for the festival. I can't believe you're complaining about this, given all I've done lately.*

Chance to get past denial: Let me show you what I mean. Here are three empty cans I found in the hallway.

Chance to defuse anger: I'm surprised by your reaction—is there something else troubling you?

Gets past denial: *I guess you're right. I didn't realize that all the time I was spending on the festival was affecting my other work. I'll be more careful from now on.*

Still denies problem: *I can't believe that those cans weren't left after the event ended.*

Remains angry: *I think you're being very unfair. On the whole, my work has been excellent; you're just nitpicking. You've been overly critical of me from day one.*

Gets over anger: *I'm sorry that I got so defensive and snapped at you. It's just that I work very hard and really want to do the best job that I can.*

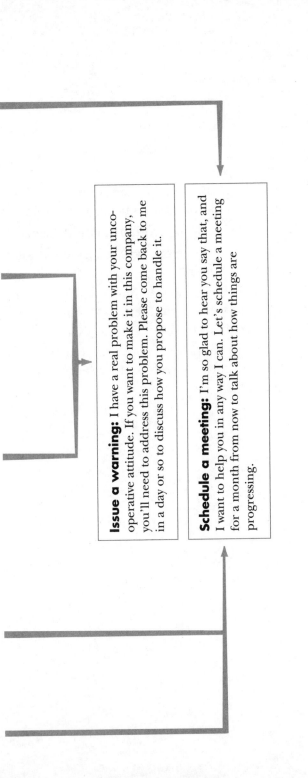

Issue a warning: I have a real problem with your uncooperative attitude. If you want to make it in this company, you'll need to address this problem. Please come back to me in a day or so to discuss how you propose to handle it.

Schedule a meeting: I'm so glad to hear you say that, and I want to help you in any way I can. Let's schedule a meeting for a month from now to talk about how things are progressing.

ADAPTATIONS

This script can be modified to:

- Review a student's poor performance.
- Discuss a partner's lack of effort.
- Speak with a volunteer about lethargic efforts.

KEY POINTS

- Soften initial criticism by suggesting that perhaps your instructions weren't clear or maybe the subordinate has been overworked.
- If your criticism is denied, offer specifics without getting defensive.
- If the subordinate responds with anger, show surprise and ask if there's something else troubling him.
- If the subordinate accepts the criticism immediately, or after having a chance to blow off some steam, reiterate your desire to help, and schedule a subsequent meeting.
- If the subordinate refuses to get past his anger or denial, say you have a problem with his attitude, warn him it must change, and demand immediate action.

Turning Down a Raise Request

34

STRATEGY

In many situations it's easy to turn down a raise request: if a person's performance hasn't been up to expectations, that's a justifiable reason to maintain his salary level; if a person bases his request on what others are making, it's easy to explain that everyone is treated as an individual. The difficult dialogue is when you have to deny a request from someone who, in fact, merits an increase but can't get one because of the company's financial situation. The secret here is to hammer home that he is a valued worker, making a legitimate request that simply can't be met right now because of the company's financial situation. Every rational person realizes you can't get water from a stone. Temper his justifiable disappointment by stressing that you will come back to him with a raise, based on the argument he made in his request, as soon as the financial picture brightens.

TACTICS

- **Attitude:** Accept that in tough economic times, the needs of the company must come first. Simply maintaining staff is often a sacrifice for struggling companies.
- **Preparation:** You'll have little opportunity to prepare unless you're given advance warning of what the meeting will be about. In that unlikely case, documentation of the company's financial problems could help ease the pain.
- **Timing:** You'll have little or no control over when this meeting takes place since it will be instigated by the subordinate. Once asked, don't delay or stall.
- **Behavior:** Be compassionate, caring, and understanding. There's no need to apologize, however. It's just a fact of life that when a company's business is off, its employees will have to forgo raises.

34. Turning Down a Raise Request

Opener: *I need to thank you for the opportunity you and the company have given me. I recognize that you've been very influential in my growth and advancement. However, I have a problem that I need your help with.*

Show concern: I think you know that I'm always here if you need my help. What's the problem and what can I do?

Professional growth:
What has happened is that I've been concentrating solely on my professional growth and haven't been paying any attention to my stream of income. I've done some research and found my peers are earning on average 15 percent more than my current compensation. I've drafted this memo. It's logical for my compensation to keep pace with my growth. To do that I'll need an increase of . . .

Contribution up: *I think my salary no longer reflects my contribution to the company. In the past year I've helped the company save a great deal of money [or] bring in added revenue [or] trim quite a bit from the cost of operations. I've done some research, and I've found that a salary of . . . would more accurately reflect my value. I've prepared a brief memo outlining my accomplishments and my request.*

Responsibilities up:
I think my salary no longer matches my job responsibilities. During the past year I've moved from being an order taker to helping supervise the evening staff and helping draft the new sales scripts. I've done some research, and I think a salary of . . . would more accurately reflect my responsibilities. I've prepared a brief memo outlining my increased responsibilities and my request.

Anniversary raise: *I've come to ask you for a raise of 10 percent. It's been a year since my last increase, and in the past the company has had a policy of giving annual raises on the anniversary of our hiring date.*

Universal response: Although you may not be aware of it, I've been watching you carefully, and I've tried to help nurture your development. The company would never consciously be unfair to you, and neither would I. The company has always done its level best, consistent with its obligations to the stockholders [or] owners. I want you to know that we love having you here. I'm aware of everything that you've said [and] I'm sure your memo makes your case persuasively. But raises are out of the question right now. You do have an excellent future with this company if you continue on this track, and we do appreciate all you've been doing.

That's no help: *I'm glad to hear you say I have a future here, but my stream of income is important to me. While I'm flattered, your praise doesn't help me pay my daughter's college tuition.*

Not a partner: *I understand what you're saying. You're asking me to participate in the success or failure of the company, but I'm not an owner [or] a partner.*

You and the company linked: That's where you're wrong. To the extent the company succeeds financially, you will as well. To the extent the company must sacrifice financially, you will have to also. And unfortunately, to the extent the company must sacrifice financially, you will have to also.

No commitment: *Are you saying you can't give me any kind of commitment about a raise in the near future?*

Personal commitment: I personally will give you a commitment that when things improve, I will come to you with an increase, based on the argument you made today. You won't have to come back to me again.

ADAPTATIONS

This script can be modified to:

- Deny requests for nonmonetary benefits that could create morale problems.

- Deny requests from children for more spending money or an increase in their allowance.

KEY POINTS

- Let the subordinate make his pitch without interruption or argument.

- If correct, accept his assertions and numbers openly.

- Respond to every request, regardless of which pitch is used, with the same answer: the money isn't there right now.

- Accept a certain amount of anger, sullenness, or annoyance—it's understandable.

- Make a personal commitment to come back with an increase as soon as it's possible.

Asking a Subordinate to Do Something Not in Her Job Description

35

STRATEGY

It's a fact of life today. Almost every manager will one day need to ask a subordinate to do something not in his job description. The secret to making this a smooth discussion is to frame it as good news. Don't feel manipulative. Since the alternative is termination, it is good news. Astute subordinates will realize that and go along with your spin—at least superficially. Feel free to point out that the added work will increase her value—and marketability. Subordinates who aren't as swift or who take a piecework attitude toward their jobs will need to have it made clear that there's no alternative. If she's not willing to accept that, she is free to look elsewhere.

TACTICS

- **Attitude:** Realize that this really is good news. You could be telling this person she's terminated. Instead, you're telling her that she still has a job.
- **Preparation:** Give some thought to the subordinate's attitude toward her job. That will make her response less of a surprise.
- **Timing:** As soon as you're made aware of the new arrangements, tell the subordinate. You don't want her to hear it through the grapevine. If it comes from you first, you'll be able to put things in perspective.
- **Behavior:** Don't be gleeful about the situation, but on the other hand, there's no need to be glum either. This is a fact of life in today's workplace, so treat it as such.

35. Asking a Subordinate to Do Something Not in Her Job Description

Icebreaker and pitch: I have some good news so I came right over to tell you. Your job is safe for now. I was able to convince the people upstairs that our department could cut costs by becoming more efficient rather than by downsizing. They've decided to cut a position in international sales instead and pass some work on to us.

Workload objection: *Does that mean we're going to have to start staying later?* [or] *I'm already overloaded; I simply can't take on any additional work right now.*

Financial objection: *I hope I'll be getting a pay raise to go along with the increase in my responsibilities and the change in my job description.*

Little price to pay: Yes, I suppose so. *[or]* I'm afraid you're going to have to have to. That's the price for holding on to our jobs in this kind of economy.

Look long-term: No, I'm afraid not. But look at the long-term benefits. It's an opportunity to prove ourselves, increase our skills, and improve our job profiles. All of that will help in the future—either here or someplace else.

Piecework attitude: *Still, I expect to be paid for the work I do. If I do more, I expect to be paid more.*

Grudging acceptance: *I suppose you're right . . . but I'm used to getting paid for the work I do.*

The company needs us: I understand. It's perfectly reasonable to want fair compensation for your work. But right now we're going to have to put that aside and help the company pull through this crisis period.

Evaluate your job: I understand. If you feel that strongly, perhaps you need to evaluate how important this job is to you . . . if in fact it is.

ADAPTATIONS

This script can be modified to:

- Give more tasks to a day worker without increasing his hours.
- Get a contractor to increase the scope of his work without increasing his bid.

KEY POINTS

- Present this as good news.
- If the subordinate objects to the increased workload, point out that she could have no job.
- If the subordinate objects on financial grounds, explain that in the long run, the added responsibilities will increase her value—here or elsewhere.
- If the subordinate still balks, and is a valuable member of your team, say this is something she will simply have to accept for the good of the company.
- If the subordinate still balks and isn't a key person, say she can leave if she doesn't like it.

Announcing a
Salary Reduction

36

STRATEGY

Here's one of the more difficult workplace dialogues in this book. Reducing salary is tough. The subordinate is bound to be very angry, so don't be glib or try to put too positive a spin on the situation. The great danger here is that he will take it as a sign that he isn't appreciated and will look elsewhere for a job. That's why it's essential you do everything you can to impress on him that you'd like to keep him. But at the same time you can't pull any punches. Don't imply it's only temporary if you know it's intended to be permanent, and don't promise to make it up to him in other areas if you can't. One secret is to go to the subordinate's workspace, rather than having him come to yours. That reduces some of the fear and also puts you more in the role of supplicant. Normally that's not appropriate, but in this case you *are* a supplicant. You're asking him to stick around even though you're cutting his pay.

TACTICS

- **Attitude:** Accept that you're asking the subordinate to give up a great deal, so a bit of fear and anger on his part is justifiable.
- **Preparation:** Make sure you understand the organization's rationale for the pay cut and can explain it succinctly. It's essential you use the same explanation with every person you speak with—mixed messages will imply a hidden agenda, and that will destroy the already battered morale.
- **Timing:** Present the news as soon as you know it's official, regardless of the time of day, day of week, or status of any other activities. This may require dramatic action on the part of employees, and they deserve as much lead time as you can give them.
- **Behavior:** Do all you can to reassure the subordinate that his job is safe and his future with the company secure. Absorb

36. Announcing a Salary Reduction

Icebreaker and pitch: I wanted to speak with you for a few minutes about how the company is changing to respond to increased competition. First, I want you to rest assured that your job is safe. The company is very concerned with your long-term happiness. In fact, that's why I'm here. The last thing we want to do is cut staff, especially productive team players like you. But our recent round of management audits pointed out that we need to reduce our payroll. That's why starting next month there will be an across-the-board salary reduction of 5 percent.

Fearful: *Please be honest with me. Are you really telling me I should look for another job?*

Offer reassurance: On the contrary, we look at you as a partner in this. We want to keep you on board. It's our goal to keep all of our valued employees—and you are someone we value very highly.

Is it temporary?: *I assume this is a temporary reduction. When will we all be brought back up to our normal salaries?*

Stress permanence: This isn't a temporary reaction to a problem; it's a permanent restructuring. In effect, we're creating a brand-new company in order to meet the challenges of the coming years.

Self-centered: *But I've helped increase revenues by more than 10 percent in the past year. You yourself told me how well I'd done at my last review. Is this how the company rewards achievement?*

Not criticism: This has nothing to do with your performance. The cuts are being made in order to keep the company alive and healthy. And whatever is in the long-term good of the company helps you as well.

Quid pro quo: *What is the company offering in exchange for all that I'm losing with this reduction?*

Can't afford it: *I can't afford a salary reduction. In fact, based on my positive review, I was planning on asking you for an increase soon.*

Issues threat: *I hope you understand that this means I'm going to have to start looking for another job.*

Be frank: Frankly, we're offering you employment with a healthy company that is positioned well for the coming years and that has an extra-ordinary future in front of it.

Show concern: The company wants you to stay. I want you to stay. I care about you and your family. You have a very promising future here if you choose to remain a part of the team. I hope you will.

Offer sympathy: I'm not surprised to hear that. I know this may cause some short-term problems for you and your budget. We're all going to have to tighten our belts. But all I can offer you is a wonderful long-term future in exchange for the short-term discomfort.

anger—it's a legitimate response to these circumstances. Be as compassionate as you can, but refrain from making promises you can't keep or sugar-coating the news.

ADAPTATIONS

This script can be modified to:

- Reduce staff, benefits, or perquisites.
- Increase subordinates' contribution toward a medical or pension plan.
- Transfer a subordinate.

KEY POINTS

- Be clear and direct, presenting this as an unavoidable and final decision that doesn't reflect on a subordinate's performance or standing in the organization.
- If the subordinate cites his own success in response, reiterate that the cut isn't linked to performance, it's across the board based on the company's needs.
- If the subordinate asks if it's temporary or asks what he'll be receiving in exchange, be honest.
- If the subordinate expresses fears about his position, reassure him that this isn't a question of performance.
- If the subordinate expresses fears about his finances, commiserate but stress that there's no alternative.
- If the subordinate asks if you're taking a reduction, be truthful.
- If the subordinate threatens to look for another job, stress the company's desire to retain him but accept that there's nothing you can do to stop him.

Warning a Subordinate to Stop Drinking

37

STRATEGY

In large organizations there are official policies for dealing with subordinate drug and alcohol problems and perhaps even individuals on staff trained in bringing such issues up with subordinates. But most small companies have no formal procedures or resources for these troubling matters. Instead, it often falls to a manager. If you're eager to retain the individual, you're going to need to impress on her the need to rehabilitate, or at the very least to clean up her act during working hours. Expect anger, denial, and projection, but reiterate that this is a workplace problem that needs to be addressed. Regardless of how the dialogue ends, offer whatever information about treatment you can. Then, keep your fingers crossed that the shock therapy works.

TACTICS

- **Attitude:** Be determined—subordinates' personal problems cannot be allowed to interfere with the workings of the company. A subordinate with a drinking problem is a danger to both you and the company.
- **Preparation:** Find out all you can about the company's health insurance coverage for such problems and local programs or facilities.
- **Timing:** Do this as soon as possible after an incident where the subordinate's problem was obvious.
- **Behavior:** Hold this meeting in your office. Make sure it's entirely private and confidential. Be as businesslike as possible. It's not your role to explore the causes of the problem—leave that to a counselor. Your job is to make it clear that her behavior is affecting her work and you cannot allow that to continue.

37. Warning a Subordinate to Stop Drinking

Icebreaker: I called you in here to tell you that your job performance is not as good as it should be, and I think the reason is your drinking during business hours. You're not here to maintain potential. You're here to realize it.

Complete denial: *I don't know what you mean. I don't drink during business hours.*

It's the job's fault: *This is an awfully stressful job. I need a drink or two at lunch to be able to handle the stress.*

I'm still tops: *Listen, even after I have a couple of drinks at lunch, I'm still the best person you've got. Nobody does this job better than me.*

Angry: *You have no right to say that to me. My personal life is none of your business.*

No debate: I don't want to have a debate with you. Something is affecting your performance and whatever it is has to stop. When I hired you I looked forward to a long relationship. I still want that . . . if possible.

Less pressure?: When I hired you I saw someone who could handle pressure. No amount of drinking is going to make this job easier. If you want me to take some of the pressure off you, that could be arranged.

Needs your best: You're right. You do your job very well. But you're even better when you don't have a couple of drinks in you. The company, and you, need you to be the best you can be.

You're right but: You're right. Your personal life is none of my business. But this is affecting your work and that *is* my business. It could end up affecting how you earn your money.

Apologizes: *I'm sorry. I'll handle it. It won't happen again.*

Accept apology: Thanks. I was hoping you'd respond that way. I know you care about this company and want to do the best job you can. If I can be of any help, let me know.

Confrontational: *Are you threatening to fire me?*

I don't want to: We're having this conversation because I don't want to have to fire you. I'll fire you only if I have no other choice. We have a problem here. I need you to address it. I'll help if I can, but it has to be addressed.

Provide information: Meanwhile, I've checked and the company's health insurance plan will cover outpatient treatment and/or counseling. Here's a list of services and practitioners in the area.

ADAPTATIONS

This script can be modified to:

- Stop a subordinate from proselytizing in the office.
- Stop a subordinate from gossiping.
- Curtail disruptive behavioral problems, such as loud radios.

KEY POINTS

- Be businesslike, determined, clear, and direct. Remember this is a business discussion even though it revolves around a personal problem.
- If the subordinate denies she has a problem, refuse to get into a debate. Instead, stress there's a problem that must be corrected.
- If the subordinate blames job-related stress for her drinking, offer to help relieve some stress.
- If the subordinate claims her performance is still good, despite her drinking, say that it could be better yet.
- If the subordinate says his personal life is none of your business, agree, but note that when personal problems affect the workplace they become business problems.
- If the subordinate remains confrontational, say her job is in jeopardy.

Turning Down a Promotion Request

38

STRATEGY

Despite the changes in the workplace, most employees believe that positions should be filled from within by moving individuals up the chain of command. But today, such strict adherence to the hierarchy isn't the norm. Openings are usually filled on a case-by-case basis or not at all. Sometimes people are moved laterally. Sometimes a replacement is brought in from outside. And sometimes people are indeed moved up the ladder. When a subordinate requests a promotion you cannot grant, the secret to breaking the bad news is to offer him praise and explain that his future lies elsewhere, to say he isn't quite ready for the job, or to suggest that the particular job description will be changed, making his experience—his major selling point—irrelevant. All three must be done gently, particularly if the person has a promising future in the company. Keep this discussion short and sweet. You're breaking the news of the decision, not engaging in another job interview. If the subordinate doesn't accept your primary rationale, be friendly but firm and note that he isn't the one who makes these decisions.

TACTICS

- **Attitude:** Think of yourself as a coach, inspiring a player to try again after falling short.
- **Preparation:** Decide prior to the meeting how important he will be to the company's future. If he does figure strongly in your plans, discuss these, vaguely, reassuring him of his value. If he's not likely to play an important role in the company's future, you can lean more toward his not being ready for the job.
- **Timing:** Do this as soon as you know he won't be getting the job. The last thing you want is for him to hear it through the grapevine before you've had a chance to add your spin to the message.
- **Behavior:** Be concise and businesslike. You're not passing a death sentence. Offer your best explanation and then move on, refusing to engage in another job interview.

38. Turning Down a Promotion Request

Icebreaker: Greg, I've called you in here to let you know that you won't be taking Jack's place as manager of the department. I have other plans for you. I want to thank you for making yourself available for the job. Once again you've demonstrated how much you care for the company's success and we're excited about your future here.

Why not?: *I don't understand why I'm not getting Jack's job. I replaced him when he was on vacation. I'm the next in line. I've covered for him when he was sick. I know everything he does. Even he said I was the best man for the job.*

What plans?: *Naturally I'm disappointed. But I'm excited to hear you and the company have plans for me. If they're not for me to take Jack's place, what are they?*

Job changed: The job Jack did may no longer exist. We're reviewing the structure of the entire department and, in all likelihood, there will no longer be a manager's position. However, let me repeat that we admire your sense of urgency and your ambition, and there is a future for you here.

Not ready: You're not ready yet. Moving you into this kind of spot prematurely would do more harm than good to your long-term future. When you're more seasoned, you may well be moved into a more important position. Let me repeat, there's a future for you here—we don't want to see you self-destruct.

No specifics: Actually, we believe your progress in the company may not follow the traditional path. There's nothing specific just yet, but we're considering you in our long-term plans. You're part of a group that we'd like to play a major role in our future.

Hidden agenda?: *You make being turned down sound wonderful. But I've still been turned down. Is there some other agenda? Are you sending me a message about my career here?*

Close the issue: Listen, we're happy with you. We want you to stay with us. I've said we think you're valuable and you have a future here. But we're not about to have you tell us how to run the company. You may get to that position one day . . . but you're not there yet.

ADAPTATIONS

This script can be modified to:

- Turn down a transfer request.
- Turn down a request for an assistant.
- Turn down a request for a change of title.

KEY POINTS

- Be clear, direct, and concise, holding out the suggestion of a future with the company.
- Let him ask for a reason, since he may instead ask about your suggestion of an alternative future for him—that gets you into a more positive line of conversation.
- If he does ask for a reason, say he's either not ready or the job description will be changed.
- If he asks about his future, remain vague but hopeful.
- If he tries to engage in further dialogue, cut him short, wielding your authority firmly but with good humor.

Giving a Negative Performance Review

39

STRATEGY

Delivering criticism requires a delicate touch. You need to present the problem strongly enough so the subordinate gets the message and hopefully changes her behavior, but not so strongly that you undermine her confidence or create lingering resentment. The best way to accomplish this is to start with positive comments before delivering the criticism. If the information is received openly, reaffirm your confidence and set up a future meeting. If the subordinate disputes your perception or gets angry, give her a chance to get over reflexive defensiveness by offering specifics. If that doesn't calm her down, stop pulling your punches and make it clear her future depends on improved performance.

TACTICS

- **Attitude:** Think of yourself as a teacher or a mentor, not a judge and jury. Be willing to absorb a little anger without retaliating—it's not easy to take criticism submissively.

- **Preparation:** Make sure your list of criticisms is accurate and detailed—you don't want this to turn into a debate over facts. Have specific suggestions and advice ready to help the subordinate improve her performance.

- **Timing:** If this isn't a formal review, it should take place as soon after a problem as possible so it's fresh in everyone's mind. If you can, schedule it for early in the week so the subordinate has a chance to act on your advice right away and won't have to dwell on it over a weekend.

- **Behavior:** Lead off with positive comments so the meeting doesn't seem like a one-sided attack. If the subordinate won't get past her initial anger or denial, forget subtlety and make it clear her future is at stake unless she cleans up her act.

39. Giving a Negative Performance Review

Icebreaker: I'm generally very pleased with your work—especially the way you're handling the arrangements for the sales conference—but there is one thing you need to work on. Maybe I haven't made it clear that you're also responsible for supervising all the promotional materials, because lately I've found quite a few mistakes and some sloppy work.

Accepts criticism: *I'm really sorry. I didn't realize that I'd slipped up. I won't let it happen again.*

Denies problem: *Really? I've been very careful about reviewing those pieces. I don't think there were any mistakes when they left my desk.*

Gets angry: *I've been working overtime to get everything set for the sales conference. I can't believe you're complaining about this given all I've accomplished here.*

Chance to get past denial: Let me show you what I mean. Here are copies of the last three promotional pieces that you okayed. I've marked the problem areas.

Chance to defuse anger: I'm surprised by your reaction. I thought you'd be eager to improve your performance. Is something else troubling you?

Gets past denial: *I guess you're right. I didn't realize that all the time I was spending on the conference was affecting my other work. I'll be more careful from now on.*

Still denies problem: *I'm not the only one whose job it is to check the promos. I can't believe that some of those mistakes weren't inserted after I signed off.*

Remains angry: *I think you're being very unfair. On the whole, my work has been excellent; you're just nitpicking. You've been overly critical of me from day one.*

Gets over anger: *I'm sorry that I got so defensive and snapped at you. It's just that I work very hard and really want to do the best job that I can.*

Issue a warning: I have a real problem with your uncooperative attitude. If you want to make it in this company, you'll need to address this problem. Please come back to me in a day or so to discuss how you propose to handle it.

Schedule a meeting: I'm so glad to hear you say that and I want to help you in any way I can. Let's schedule a meeting for a month from now to talk about how things are progressing.

ADAPTATIONS

This script can be modified to:

- Review a student's poor performance.
- Discuss a partner's lack of effort.
- Speak with a volunteer about lethargic efforts.

KEY POINTS

- Soften initial criticism by suggesting that perhaps your instructions weren't clear or that the subordinate has been overworked.
- If your criticism is denied, offer specifics without getting defensive.
- If the subordinate responds with anger, show surprise and ask if there's something else troubling her.
- If the subordinate accepts the criticism immediately, or after having a chance to blow off some steam, reiterate your desire to help and schedule a subsequent meeting.
- If the subordinate refuses to get past her anger or denial, say you have a problem with her attitude, warn her it must change, and demand immediate action.

Turning Down a Subordinate's Request for Time Off

40

STRATEGY

As a manager, you're no doubt aware that the easiest way to earn a reputation as a bad guy is to say "no" to a subordinate without being able to give him a good, solid reason for your refusal. However, if you can legitimately back up your rejection, you've a chance of coming across as a human being while still maintaining managerial control of the office. When a valued, hardworking subordinate has already used up all his sick/personal time, you must be clear in your own mind as to what you and the company consider legitimate reasons for additional time off. For example, time off for a doctor's appointment or having to close on a home purchase might be acceptable: both events must be scheduled during business hours and are important. On the other hand, time off for sports events or taking a son to look at a college shouldn't be acceptable because these are activities that easily can be taken care of on the weekend and aren't essential. If your subordinate's request is legitimate, the only reason you can give for turning him down is that his timing is bad: things are simply too busy at work for you to let him have that day off . . . at least not without compensation time. If you feel his request is unacceptable, your tack will be to invoke precedent, as in, "If I let you have the day off to go to the Monster Truck Rally, before you know it I'll have everyone coming in here asking for days off." Just remember: whatever your personal feelings about the subordinate and his request, the language of your refusal must pertain to business, period.

TACTICS

- **Attitude:** While your first instinct might be annoyance, try to keep an open mind and be fair. Let him state his case and then decide accordingly.
- **Preparation:** Although each request for time off must be handled individually, you can expedite the process greatly by knowing what you and the company consider valid reasons for time off and reasons that are beyond the pale.

40. Turning Down a Subordinate's Request for Time Off

His opener: *Mark, may I speak with you a minute?*

Polite response: Sure, Steve. What's up?

Legit reason for time off: *I need to know if I can have Friday off to go to the doctor. I know I've used up my sick and personal days, but Friday is the only day I could get an appointment to see her, and I'm having some tests done that require me to fast for 24 hours beforehand.*

Bogus reason for time off: *It's my kid. He wants to go to Springfield U next year, and I thought maybe I could take Friday off, beat the traffic, and take him up there to have a look around.*

Thumbs up: We're not under any time pressures right now so . . . sure, no problem. Make sure you let me know how everything turns out, okay?

Time pressure: Normally, it wouldn't be a problem. But as you know, that report absolutely has to be on Harold's desk on Monday, and I need you to be here. Would it be possible for you to try to reschedule?

Thumbs down: Springfield U is a great school, but unfortunately company policy doesn't allow time off for parents who want to take their children to look at colleges. If I let you do it, everyone will want to do it. I'd suggest you just leave after work on Friday or early Saturday morning.

Being unfair: *You gave Jackson a day off to take his mother to look at nursing homes.*

Our secret: *No one else but you has to know why I'm not here on Friday.*

Can't reschedule: *The problem is, I really had to jump through hoops to get this appointment, and, even then, I'm lucky they're squeezing me in. I know the timing is bad, but I really need to see the doctor.*

Suggest comp time: If you can't reschedule, you could stay late on Thursday and come in on Saturday morning. I'd have no problem with you taking Friday off if you guarantee that report will be on Harold's desk first thing Monday morning.

Agrees: *I'll be here Thursday night and Saturday morning and the report will be on Harold's desk Monday morning. I promise. Thank you.*

Will try to reschedule: *I'll see what the doctor's office says about rescheduling and get back to you.*

Stick to your guns: I'll know why you're not here, and it's not my policy to lie for employees. How about this? If you can get your work done on time, you can leave an hour early. But there is no way I can give you the entire day or even half the day. There's simply too much to do.

Not comparable: I gave Jackson the day off because that was an emergency situation that could not be rescheduled. You may not have known this, but Jackson stayed late three nights in a row to be able to take that day off.

Should have lied: *Are you saying I should have lied to you, maybe told you I had to go to the doctor?*

Honesty is the rule: No, I'm saying there are valid reasons for taking time off and there are invalid reasons for taking time off, especially when you've run out of sick days and personal days. If you actually had a doctor's appointment, I've no doubt we could work something out. However, lying isn't the way to behave in the workplace.

- **Timing:** Unfortunately, this is one request you're likely to be blindsided by: one minute you're sitting in your office working, the next you've got a subordinate poking his head around the door asking if he can have a word with you. If you can handle it there and then, great. However, if you can't, ask him to stop by after work or set up an appointment for the following day when he might speak to you in your office. If he corners you in the hallway, do the same.

- **Behavior:** Be polite, attentive, and sympathetic. Stop what you're doing when he makes his case and maintain eye contact. Don't interrupt. You're his boss, not the Grand Inquisitor, so avoid playing twenty questions. Whatever your personal feelings about the request, don't roll your eyes, sigh heavily, or chuckle. No one likes to be belittled.

ADAPTATIONS

This script can be modified to:

- Deal with a spouse or child seeking release from an obligation.

KEY POINTS

- Before a conversation even takes place, have a clear sense of what you and the company consider legitimate as well as unacceptable reasons for time off.
- If the request is legitimate but the timing is poor, simply tell him he can't have the time because he's needed at work.
- If the request is unacceptable, tell him you can't give him the time for that kind of reason and say it would set an unwanted company precedent.
- Be fair and open-minded about suggestions for compensation time.

Reducing the Size of a Subordinate's Staff

41

STRATEGY

Downsizing. Streamlining. Doing more with less. Call it what you will, laying off staff is one of the most difficult tasks a manager must perform. Managers often must be the conduit to our subordinates for difficult decisions made by those "upstairs." The goal of this script is to show you how to effectively inform a subordinate she must reduce her staff. The necessity of maintaining the bottom line and the realization that, like it or not, this is one of her responsibilities are the twin pillars that will support your dialogue.

TACTICS

- **Attitude:** You must embody confidence and objectivity. Acknowledge the difficulty of the task at hand, but don't be drawn into dwelling on it. Be businesslike. Focus all efforts on accomplishing a difficult task. Your approach will serve as a model for your subordinate to emulate when she deals with her staff.

- **Preparation:** The most important preparation is making sure all your information is accurate. There can be no question about what must be done, who must do it, when it must be done, and why it must be done. Review the personnel in each of your subordinates' sections because the ultimate recommendation to superiors will be yours. If cuts are being made in specific sections, have the necessary backup to support their selection.

- **Timing:** Schedule the meeting as soon as possible. Meet first thing in the morning. Establish a "first thing tomorrow" deadline for her recommendation. Tell her you are available throughout the day for clarification and advice. The more rapid her response, the greater time for review and the less time for agonizing and procrastination.

- **Behavior:** Act professionally, but recognize the difficulty of the task and be ready to absorb initial objections.

165

41. Reducing the Size of a Subordinate's Staff

State problem: It's official: we have to downsize our operation. I need a $100,000 salary reduction from your section. Your choices can bring you over that figure, but you can't be under it. I want your recommendations at the start of work tomorrow. Names, salaries, and bulleted reasons for the choice. Prepare this personally and discuss it with no one. Staff reductions are a part of every business. But the more efficiently we do what we have to, the less hurt for everyone.

Seeks alternatives: *That's a lot. Can't we soften that and reduce other places? Supplies? Hardware? Equipment?*

Dispel alternatives: Those were considered. We're near bare bones in some of those areas now. Salaries are our highest expenditure.

States anxiety: *We're going to lose some good people. This is really going to be tough.*

Focus on responsibility: I know, but it's part of the job. Make the selections to meet the baseline figure and keep your section functioning effectively.

Questions timeline: *That's really sudden. Can't I have more time to think about this?*

Justify timeline: The longer we delay, the tougher the job becomes. You know your people. I have confidence that you'll do what is best.

Seeks clarification: *Is my section the only one that's being asked to make these reductions?*

Cuts targeted: Your section is one of two that are being cut. I reviewed the entire department and decided where we could take the hits and still function effectively. I went through the same process I'm asking you to do.

Questions decision: *That doesn't seem fair. Why not spread it out over the whole office? That would make it easier on all of us.*

Spread equally: No. I've been given a total figure that I'm spreading equally through the office. Everyone is being hit.

Expresses approval: *That's fair. That will make it a little easier for me to justify.*

Fairness isn't issue: We have to do what's effective, not fair or easy. I'll be available all day if you need help. Nothing will go upstairs that I haven't reviewed with you and approved.

ADAPTATIONS

This script can be modified to:

- Reduce the size of a subordinate's operating budget or reduce/reorganize job responsibilities.

KEY POINTS

- Be certain your facts and figures are accurate and review personnel for each subordinate's section.
- Inform your staff as soon as you know.
- Require rapid turnaround to you. This will limit procrastination and harmful leaks.
- Stress professional responsibilities and job requirements. Don't let personal misgivings interfere with the task.
- Provide support to your staff.
- Be clear that the final recommendations will be yours.

Changing a Subordinate's Workspace to a Less Private One

42

STRATEGY

Whether they have one desk among the multitudes in a "bullpen" or a corner office, individuals take ownership of their workspace. Just look at the photos, pictures, posters, and personal curios that decorate the average workspace. Making a workspace yours creates a sense of comfort. So what to do when someone must be shifted to a less private space? Present it as inevitable and not indicative of his perceived value. Expect unhappiness and disappointment. There will probably be some mild resistance and questioning ending in resigned acceptance. If you should face an aggressive and angry response, do not engage in any debate. Restate the facts and offer the chance to go over your head with any concerns.

TACTICS

- **Attitude:** There's no reason to be uncomfortable or to lack confidence. Your conversation will be based on a decision about effective use of space. There will most likely be objective recommendations from experts. Job performance, attitude, or any other individual work traits of the subordinate have nothing to do with the decision. It is, quite literally, a case of "nothing personal." Your manner should mirror this.

- **Preparation:** Keeping your staff informed of your plans is the key. As soon as a decision has been made to add staff, equipment, or machines, let all the affected subordinates know. Emphasize that the changes are improvements that will benefit everyone. Be open about the fact that some staff will lose some of their privacy to make room for this improvement. Assure staff that the physical structure of the workplace will be the basis for determining the area to be modified, nothing else. Tell them when a specific decision has been reached that the subordinate involved will be informed first. Openness builds trust and confidence and underlines that the subordinate losing the space is the object of circumstance, not managerial disapproval.

169

42. Changing a Subordinate's Workspace to a Less Private One

States action: George, you're going to have to move to a cubicle to make room for the new equipment.

Unhappy acknowledgment: *I knew it. I knew it was going to be me.*

Urges alternative: *Why can't we put the new equipment with our other machines? It would keep it all in one convenient area.*

Emphasizes rationale: Remember, George, it's not you that was selected. It was the area best suited to be modified.

Rebuts alternative: We definitely looked at that. The room is just not there. Our plan gives us the best option to support the effectiveness of the entire staff.

Seeks clarification: *So what exactly does this change mean for me?*

Provide specifics: We're going to move you to a six-by-six-foot cubicle opposite your current office.

Expresses anxiety: *Six by six! That seems like an awfully small space. It's going to be tight.*

States support: I know. But everything needed to continue as you are will be intact. It will just take some getting used to.

States self-doubt: *It's going to make everything more difficult. I really thought I was doing a good job.*

Reclarifies: Your work is not an issue in any way, George. If someone else was in that office, the same space would be taken. It's the space, not the person in that space.

Accepts situation: *I understand. You have to do what you have to do.*

- **Timing:** As soon as you know, meet with the subordinate. Delaying enables leaks and rumors (which undermine your efforts to be open and fair with all) to start. Remember, everyone is anxious about being the "lucky" choice. Delaying increases the anxiety. Reschedule other business to deal with this.

- **Behavior:** Sit with your subordinate in your office. Removing the official barrier of the desk enhances your image as an understanding supervisor. You sympathize with his unhappiness and understand it, just as you know he understands there is no other choice.

ADAPTATIONS

This script can be modified to:

- Deal with the reassignment of job responsibilities when adding additional staff.

KEY POINTS

- Keep your entire staff well informed every step of the way.
- Be specific about what will happen, why it will happen, and when it will happen.
- Emphasize the change as an improvement for all, acknowledging the hardship for one.
- Affirm that the actions are dictated by architectural necessity and not managerial choice.
- Let the individual affected know as soon as you do. Then let the entire staff know.
- Don't hesitate to encourage a disgruntled subordinate to speak to a superior.

43

Questioning a Subordinate's Expense Report

STRATEGY

When questioning a subordinate's expense report, remember to be calm and collected. The last thing you want is a conversation laced with accusations and denials. If you chastise the subordinate, nothing productive will arise from the meeting. Your goal is to make the subordinate aware of a mistake in judgment and be sure it doesn't happen again. Perhaps she took a client out to an expensive dinner or charged the company for a hotel in-room movie. The first example is about judgment and experience. Help the subordinate recognize the problem and discuss future solutions. In the second example, it's more a question of acceptable behavior. Don't blame her for ordering the movie, just calmly explain that it isn't appropriate to charge the company for personal entertainment. If you educate rather than punish, most subordinates will appreciate your advice and guidance. If the problem persists, you must deal with the subordinate in a harsher fashion. For a first offense, however, give her the benefit of the doubt and show her how to behave appropriately in the future.

TACTICS

- **Attitude:** Be calm and collected, even friendly. Don't embarrass or accuse the subordinate. This will only lead to resentment. An upbeat and positive approach will ensure that the subordinate learns from her mistake.
- **Timing:** Have this meeting in private. Never question a subordinate in front of other subordinates. Try to schedule the meeting after lunch when the subordinate will be most relaxed.
- **Preparation:** Anticipate your subordinate's protests and excuses. Have two copies of the expense report in question. That way you can look over it together.

43. Questioning a Subordinate's Expense Report

Icebreaker: I've been reading over your most recent expense report. There are a couple of items I'd like to discuss with you.

Expensive dinner: I'm glad you took the clients from Acme out to dinner. The bill for dinner, however, was over four hundred dollars. I think that's a little too much for a dinner tab.

In-room movie: I noticed you included the cost of an in-room movie on your expense report. You may not be aware the company does not pay for movies and other entertainment not directly related to work. I'm sure you'll understand if we don't reimburse you.

Blameless: *What was I supposed to do? Ask them to split the check? I had to pay. They're clients, I can't suggest McDonald's for dinner. They wanted an expensive dinner, and I got stuck with the bill. It happens.*

Spin doctor: *We need to keep the client happy. I know the dinner was expensive, but in the long run it's a small price to pay for their business.*

Protests: *C'mon, I'm on a long business trip with nothing to do. I already had a great meeting with Acme, Inc., and I ordered a hotel movie. What's the big deal?*

Apologizes: *I'm sorry. I completely forgot about the movie. I didn't mean to add it to the cost of the room. Sorry about the oversight.*

Explain: Don't get me wrong, I'm glad you took the clients to dinner. Next time, however, be prepared. Do a little research and try to find an affordable restaurant that you can all enjoy. Take control of the situation. That way the client is happy, and we don't lose money.

Make your point: Naturally, the client comes first. Next time, however, take the initiative. Suggest an affordable restaurant where the clients will be comfortable. If you take control of the encounter, we can keep the client happy and save money.

Reason: It's not the cost of the movie that's at issue. It's simply a matter of judgment. Entertainment not pertaining to business shouldn't be charged to the company. I'm sure you understand.

Soothe employee's concern: Don't worry about it. It happens all the time. That's why we have accountants.

Humble: *I understand what you're saying. I'll try to control our future business dinners. I let the situation get out of my control.*

Gives in: *I see your point. I hadn't thought of it that way. It won't happen again.*

Close positively: The only way to learn is from experience.

- **Behavior:** Even if the subordinate becomes upset at the suggestion of poor judgment or disallowed charges, don't lose your temper. Remind her you're trying to help. Don't threaten her with disciplinary action unless the problem has repeated itself several times.

ADAPTATIONS

The script can be modified to:

- Confront a student about an unintentional cheating incident.
- Coach a worker about appropriate behavior with clients.

KEY POINTS

- Don't lose your temper. It only makes the situation worse.
- Illustrate the error in judgment, thoroughly explain the subordinate's mistake, and offer possible solutions.
- Remember the goal of the meeting is to educate, not scold. Show your subordinate the mistake and try to be sure it isn't repeated.
- Don't undermine your subordinate's confidence. Show you still have faith in her.

Offering Constructive Feedback to a Subordinate

44

STRATEGY

The best time to offer constructive criticism is right after there is a mistake or a problem. However, sensitive employees may still be a bit frazzled by a problematic situation. That could result in excessive denial, fear, anger, or defensiveness. The best way to overcome these reactions is to get the subordinate past them as quickly as possible and move right into teaching mode. It's essential that the feedback be presented as help for dealing with similar problems in the future, not a recrimination for past behavior.

TACTICS

- **Attitude:** This is an excellent chance to teach as long as you can get past the staffer's insecurities. It's worth the effort.
- **Preparation:** Have a short, simple explanation prepared in advance so you can be as clear and concise as possible in offering your suggestions.
- **Timing:** While the best time to learn is right after a mistake, it's possible that waiting overnight could help frayed nerves heal and ease the acceptance of the suggestions.
- **Behavior:** Be calm, friendly, supportive, and compassionate. Assume the role of teacher and mentor, not critic.

44. Offering Constructive Feedback to a Subordinate

Icebreaker and pitch: Ken, I wanted to speak with you about the way you handled Ms. Robertson earlier today.

Defensive: *I know that didn't go very smoothly, but she's very difficult to deal with.*

Denial: *Why, was something wrong? I thought I handled her pretty well.*

Frightened: *Am I in trouble? My job is important to me. I thought I was doing well.*

Angry: *Are you going to criticize me for one isolated situation, particularly one we've had problems with before?*

Relax: You're right. It didn't go well. That's why I wanted to speak with you about it.

Inform: Actually, it didn't go well. She was angry and your response may have placated her, but it cost the company more than was necessary.

Reassure: You're not in trouble. Overall, I'm very happy with your work. I just want to give you a tip so you can handle this type of situation better in the future.

Assert authority: It's my job not to criticize you but to help you become better at what you do. And it's the problem customers that give us all the most opportunities to learn.

Not an inquisition: First, I just want to make it clear that this isn't an inquisition or a pop review of some kind. I want to offer you some help on dealing with situations like this in the future. And the best time to go over these things is right after they occur. When a difficult customer puts you in a situation like that, the best thing to do is to humor her as much as you can and then plead ignorance or powerlessness. Say you don't know something or you need to get approval, ask the customer to wait, and then go get whichever manager is on duty. He or she will know how much of an adjustment can be made without the company absorbing too much of a financial hit. Do you have any questions?

Still fearful: *This isn't going to cost me my job, is it?*

Reassure: I told you this wasn't an inquisition. I'm not reviewing you now, and when I do, it will be based on how you apply these kinds of lessons, not on whether or not you're perfect. Any more questions?

Resists suggestions: *Well, there was no manager around when she launched into her tirade.*

Reiterate or expand: Then all you need to do is say you can't find a manager and say she's free to either wait until one becomes available or come back later at her convenience to speak with one. Any more questions?

Accepts suggestions: *No, I understand.*

ADAPTATIONS

This script can be modified to:

- Offer constructive criticism to a friend or family member.

KEY POINTS

- Be specific in both citing the problem and providing advice on future solutions.
- Reassure, calm, and inform when dealing with frightened or anxious staffers.
- Gently reassert your authority if necessary, but be aware that the anger is probably just an expression of fear.
- Reiterate that this is a learning opportunity, not grist for a negative review.

Asking a Subordinate to Be More Aware of Ethical Issues

45

STRATEGY

Ethics in business can be a slippery slope. If minor or occasional ethical lapses by employees are tolerated, either openly or by looking the other way, there's no telling where the situation will end up. That makes it essential to deal with such problems immediately. However, smacking down a subordinate for a minor transgression can be counterproductive. By all means confront the employee as soon as possible. In order to soften the blow but to make sure it's effective, offer understanding without letting that be an excuse. Allow the subordinate to offer his own explanation or to blow off steam. But make it clear that the ethical lapse is unacceptable and not to be repeated.

TACTICS

- **Attitude:** This is an important matter, but it needn't be a confrontation unless you need to respond to an attack.
- **Preparation:** You need to have the utmost confidence in your facts. Making a mistaken approach of this kind could damage your future relationship.
- **Timing:** Have this conversation as soon as possible after learning of the ethical lapse.
- **Behavior:** Hold this dialogue in your workspace, in private. Your manner should be serious yet understanding. Think of yourself as a forgiving parent, rather than a supportive pal or a zealous prosecutor.

45. Asking a Subordinate to Be More Aware of Ethical Issues

Icebreaker: Stan, it's obvious that you're a great salesman. I'm very pleased by the numbers you've put up in your first few months. You're a great advocate for the company. But I think you're sometimes letting your enthusiasm and excitement get the better of you. Some of the delivery dates you've been giving customers are impossible to meet. I know that in the short term, stretching the truth that way could gain us some sales, but we need to keep our eye on developing long-term trust, too. You need to stop overpromising.

Everyone does it: *Sure I'm sometimes a bit optimistic in the dates I give customers. But everyone does it. All our competitors give delivery dates that they know are impossible to meet. If I don't do the same, I won't be able to compete effectively. Besides, no one has complained yet, have they?*

Attacks: *Okay. I stretched the truth a bit. But it's only because I'm under such incredible pressure to produce. Our sales goals are so high that the only way any of us are going to meet our quotas is by exaggerating a bit.*

One time: *I'm really sorry about this. I only stretched the truth one time, with Acme, Inc. You know how tough they can be, and we really needed to close the sale and keep them from jumping to our competitor. I promise it won't happen again.*

Long term: I don't doubt that some of our competitors have some ethical shortcomings. But that's no reason for us to stoop to their level. Our long-term reputation is more important than a single sale or short-term success. Don't do it again.

Still wrong: Once is once too often. That one fib could be enough for us to lose our reputation. I know how good you are at your job and that Acme can be a real pain to deal with. But that doesn't make what you did acceptable. I hope I've made myself clear.

Counterattack: That's no excuse. One thing has nothing to do with another. I have no problem discussing the sales quotas with you, but right now we're talking about ethics, not numbers. Your behavior was unacceptable. Don't do it again.

ADAPTATIONS

This script can be modified to:

- Confront a family member about a minor ethical lapse.

KEY POINTS

- This is serious, however minor it may seem to the subordinate.
- Make it clear that you understand and forgive, but you don't excuse.
- If you're told everyone does it, explain this is a way to set the company apart.
- If it's a one-time event, stress that's no excuse, but make it clear you don't think poorly of the subordinate.
- If you're met with an attack, assert your authority and press the issue.

Tactfully Suggesting Better Hygiene to a Subordinate

46

STRATEGY

Having to tell someone her breath or body odor is offensive may be one of the most awkward situations you'll ever face in the workplace. Yet sometimes it's essential that you take action, not only for the comfort of you and other coworkers but for the company and the person's future as well. Such problems are almost certain to undermine the image of the company if the offending subordinate comes in contact with clients. Hygiene problems will erode her standing in the company and will block any future progress in the organization. Begin with the assumption that she isn't conscious of the problem. Start off by subtly suggesting the same tool(s) you use to avoid similar problems. If she takes the hint, let the matter drop. If your subtext isn't understood, you'll have to press further.

TACTICS

- **Attitude:** Try not to be embarrassed. The other party will be embarrassed enough for both of you. Remember, you're doing this for the person's own good.
- **Preparation:** Buy some breath mints or look around for a nearby drugstore.
- **Timing:** Do this immediately after lunch and privately. That way you minimize embarrassment and have an excuse for your actions.
- **Behavior:** Start off being subtle, but if necessary, shift to sincere concern. There's no need to be apologetic because you're doing the person a favor.

46. Tactfully Suggesting Better Hygiene to a Subordinate

Bad breath: *[Show mints, pop one in your mouth.]* Would you like one? I don't know about you, but sometimes I really need these after lunch.

Body odor: You won't believe the sale I stumbled on. The drugstore up the street was offering 50 percent off on antiperspirants and deodorants. You should check it out. If you want, I'll go over there with you after work.

Takes the hint: *Um . . . sure. I'll take one.* [or] *Oh, I never . . . uh . . . Thanks, I appreciate it.*

Doesn't take hint: *No, thanks. I never use those kinds of things.*

Gets angry: *Excuse me. Are you suggesting there's something wrong with me?*

Be direct: There are some things even your best friend is too embarrassed to tell you, but you should know. You have a discernible body *[or]* breath odor, and you need to address it. I'm bringing this up primarily for your own good because it could cause you problems.

Gets defensive: *I don't have a problem—you do. No one else has said anything to me. This is just a way to humiliate me, isn't it? Well, it's not going to work.*

Reasonable excuse: *I'm sorry. I've been having extensive dental work* [or] *I've been taking a prescription medicine and was told this might be a side effect. I'm not sure what I can do about it, however.*

You are the company: This isn't an attempt to humiliate or intimidate you. As an employee, you're a representative of the company. The impression you make reflects on it. I'm simply asking you to take care of a problem. That's all.

Embarrassed acceptance: *Oh, I'm so embarrassed. It's just that . . . . I'm sorry. I'll take care of it.*

Suggest professional help: I thought it might be something like that. Why don't you give your dentist *[or]* pharmacist a call and ask for advice. Until then, why don't you try these *[indicating breath mints or deodorant].*

ADAPTATIONS

This script can be modified to:

- Discuss hygiene problems with a teen.
- Discuss hygiene problems or erratic behavior with a parent or older relative.

KEY POINTS

- Start off subtly, but if necessary, be direct.
- If she takes the hint, drop the issue.
- If she doesn't take the hint, be direct.
- If she gets angry, say it's a business problem, too.
- If she says it's none of your business, explain why it is something you need to be concerned with.

Demanding Better Work Habits from a Subordinate

47

STRATEGY

Time really is money. The time-shaving employee—late in, early out—is stealing from you and the company. You are paying a full-time salary for less than full-time service. The longer the problem is ignored, the more comfortable the offender feels in continuing and adding to this behavior. By dealing effectively with this one individual, you'll also help ensure that others don't emulate his behavior. Even though you'll be confronting the subordinate's actual behavior, expect a torrent of excuses as to why the behavior took place. Stress that what has happened is the issue, not *why* it has happened. Focus on what has taken place and the effect it is having on both cost and job effectiveness. Stick to this tack, and the individual will ultimately acknowledge his destructive behavior. After he does, be clear about the outcome if the abuse continues. Only then should you consider ending the meeting on a practical, humanistic note by offering advice to help the subordinate deal with the "whys" of his problem.

TACTICS

- **Attitude:** Be totally confident and at ease. You hold all the cards going in. You'll be citing a problem easily observed and documented. A vacant work station is a red flag. And, if there's a time clock, you have ironclad evidence. The actual time shaving and the cost in money and job effectiveness are undeniable. Be confident and indignant that such obvious and blatant behavior is taking place.

- **Preparation:** At the point you realize there's a pattern of neglect, start writing down dates and times the subordinate is away from the job. Documenting these specifics is the most critical part of your preparation. Create a "memorandum for the record" indicating what you're doing and why. This becomes part of the documentation. Clearly, if the subordinate's actions hadn't prompted it, there would be no such memo. Time sheets or cards

189

47. Demanding Better Work Habits from a Subordinate

Establish control: [Holding up papers.] Friday, September 12, 9:20. Tuesday, September 16, 4:48. Wednesday, September 17, 9:13. Friday, September 19, 4:50. Frank, do you know what all these numbers mean?

Anxious curiosity: No, I'm afraid I don't.

State problem: Those are all the times you were supposed to be at your workstation but weren't. You were either not here yet or on your way home early. If you add them all up, it amounts to hours of wasted work time.

Personal excuses: I'm sorry, I've had a lot on my mind. There are things going on at home that I didn't want to burden anyone with. My head just hasn't been in the job.

Continued focus: I can understand that, but if you're going to keep working here, you must show up and leave on time. Right now you're costing us money and effectiveness. It has got to stop.

Rationalization: I'm not the only one. Everyone is late once in a while or cuts out early.

Reaffirm problem: I'm aware of that. In your case, however, it's more than once in a while—otherwise I wouldn't have started keeping a record. You need to understand that your job is on the line.

Begins excuses: I know I'm late once in a while and leave early now and then, but I didn't think it amounted to that much time.

Confirm accusation: [Wave your papers.] You wouldn't be here if it didn't. You're costing us money and affecting your coworkers. You're also placing your job in jeopardy.

Acknowledges responsibility: *My job! I can't lose my job. I'm sorry, it won't happen anymore. I swear.*

Clarify monitoring: I hope not. To be sure, I'm going to continue to monitor you for the next two months. If there's no further problem, I go away. If the problem continues, you go away. Am I being clear enough?

Acceptance: *I hear what you're saying. I'll take care of it.*

Reestablish rapport: I'm glad to hear that. As far as any personal problems go, why don't you speak with our personnel manager. There may be something that he can help with or at least recommend some other avenue for assistance.

are obvious support to be gathered. Comments from other managers who have experienced similar behavior aren't necessary but could augment your evidence.

- **Timing:** After you've observed an abusive pattern—a week, several weeks, a month—move quickly as soon as the behavior occurs again. Publicly ask the subordinate to come into your office just as he eases back to his workstation. You'll have seized control of the dialogue as well as the attention of the other workers who know perfectly well what is going on.

- **Behavior:** Be conspicuous in the work area at a time when the latecomer should be there. As soon as he returns to his desk and sits down, announce you want to meet—right now. Don't wait for a response, just move directly to your office. When he enters, silently gesture him to a seat while you remain engrossed in an open folder of documents clearly visible on your desk. When you're ready to speak, hold the documents up.

ADAPTATIONS

This script can be modified to:

- Deal with the subordinate who wastes time on the job or who is chronically absent, absent on particular days, or late for meetings and deadlines.

KEY POINTS

- When you believe a pattern of behavior is in place, document dates and times.
- Call for your meeting in front of other workers.
- Use physical evidence as a means of reinforcing your position.
- Stay focused on what the behavior has been and its effect on the workplace.
- Do not get sidetracked into debating why the behavior has occurred.
- Be clear about future actions and outcomes.

Asking a
Subordinate to Improve
Her Appearance

STRATEGY

There's no second chance to make a first impression. Even when a business may have a good track record, prospective clients are still greatly influenced by the "what you see is what you get" attitude. A staff that projects a professional appearance can only help build client confidence. A subordinate who doesn't reinforce a "dressed for success" image can only hurt your chances of securing and maintaining clients.

The goal of this script is to help you bring any sartorially challenged members of your staff to the high standard of appearance required as a norm in the world of business. Errant subordinates will try to make this an issue of personal taste because it's really the only argument they can muster. If you're dealing with staff members of the opposite sex, they may even try to lead you into the minefield of gender harassment. That's why you should consider having a fellow supervisor of the same gender as the offender present in your office when you deal with an opposite gender subordinate. This reinforces the professional tone of your position, safeguards potential future misreporting of events or comments, and serves as a role model for proper dress.

Though not absolutely necessary, refer to any print materials distributed previously to employees regarding dress. Don't waver from your responsibility for maintaining the highest professional standards in the workplace. All possible arguments to justify personal dress shatter against this brick-wall position.

TACTICS

- **Attitude:** This problem is visually obvious to any and all, so be confident in confronting it. Given this, project an air of disbelief and disappointment: how could anyone not know how to dress for work! Project this attitude in a clear, matter-of-fact presentation of the problem and the solution. This will underline that your concern is professional, not personal.
- **Preparation:** See if your firm has anything in print regarding appearance: an employee handbook, new employee handouts, or

48. Asking a Subordinate to Improve Her Appearance

Establish authority: Adrienne, I need to talk to you about something that may make you uncomfortable. *[Pause]* You may not be aware that an important part of my job is ensuring our staff looks and acts in a professional manner.

Curious concern: *I never really thought about it. What's it got to do with me?*

State problem: It has to do with my doing that job. Adrienne, your professional dress today is not acceptable for this office.

Clarify problem: I'm a little bit shocked by your dress. A tube-top and miniskirt? In the office?

Angry rebuttal: *Nobody else complained. You're the only one who seems to have a problem. Maybe you shouldn't look.*

Clarify problem: You look as if you are going to the mall. A sweatshirt and jeans! What were you thinking?

Offers resistance: *How I dress is my own affair. It's personal. Just like your not liking it is.*

Clarify problem: You look as if you've slept in that outfit—for several days. And the stains. You look disheveled.

Sympathy excuse: *I usually dress well. You know that. I was in a hurry this morning and I threw these on.*

Offer alternative: I'd rather see you come in a little late with an explanation than look unprofessional.

Embarrassed apology: *I'm really sorry. I understand. I didn't mean any harm.*

Accept apology: I'm sure you didn't. That's why I had to talk to you right away. This must not happen again.

Refutes argument: No, it's professional. I'd love to dress differently, but I can't any more than you can. Our jobs demand we look a certain way. Listen, did you dress like this for your interview?

Point taken: *Well, uh, no, I didn't.*

Press understanding: Of course you didn't! You wouldn't be here if you did. You dressed to impress us as a professional. I expect that each day.

Counter argument: Should I notify our clients and potential clients that they shouldn't look, too? That's absurd.

Stubborn deflection: *I don't believe this. I could lose my job because you've got a problem? I have a right to dress any way I want.*

Assert authority: I'm sure you do. You also have a right to seek work elsewhere if you can't dress as a professional here.

Make outcome clear: If I consider your appearance unacceptable in the future, I'll send you home to change immediately—on your time!

recent memos. Check with interviewers to see if they discuss appearance when hiring. Also see if you can get information on how your transgressor dressed for interviews. When you assumed supervisory responsibility of the individual, did you say anything about attire? Make note of all the information concerning the obligation for professional dress in the workplace. This supports your point that appearance is not a matter of any one individual's personal taste but a professional requirement. The proper appearance of fellow workers reinforces this view.

- **Timing:** The instant you see inappropriate dress, move on it. The first time should be the last time. Moving rapidly highlights the importance of the problem.

- **Behavior:** The moment you observe inappropriate dress, ask to see the individual. Be straightforward in stating the problem. Emphasize that the professional appearance of the staff influences client attitudes and actions. Your concern is, therefore, not a personal one but a professional one that could touch any staff member who does not realize this. You must stick to this and wave your banner throughout: professional not personal!

ADAPTATIONS

This script can be modified to:

- Deal with the subordinate who displays poor hygiene, a subordinate whose work area may be slovenly or inappropriately decorated, or a subordinate whose makeup or jewelry is out of place.

KEY POINTS

- Be familiar with any information given to staff regarding appropriate attire.
- State clearly that the concern involves professional decorum and not personal taste. Maintain this throughout.
- When dealing with a subordinate of the opposite gender, consider having a fellow supervisor of that gender present in your office when you confront the problem.
- Use the individual's interview dress as the key example of what you are after.
- Be specific as to what action you will take if you observe the problem again.

Handling a Subordinate's Personal Telephone Calls and Internet Use

49

STRATEGY

Some employees consider office telephones and Internet connections required for their work as available for their personal use. If paper-clip pilfering adds up, imagine the hidden costs for the worker who thinks "job ownership" means personal use of the firm's copiers, computers, postal machines, telephones, and anything else that plugs into an outlet. When the employee is a highly valued and productive subordinate, some managers look the other way, but this only encourages more of the same. Eventually, personal use of equipment may become so rampant that orders will come down from above to crack down hard. That's why it's essential to stop such problems before they attract attention from upstairs.

TACTICS

- **Attitude:** You'll be dealing with behavior you've observed so you can be confident. Be understanding in your approach because the issue is one workers easily rationalize as a job perk, not a problem.
- **Preparation:** The essential element of preparation is validating that abusive behavior is taking place. Your firsthand observations are often enough. But the more effectively you can corroborate those observations with tangible evidence, the more confident you can be of controlling the dialogue and ending the problem.
- **Timing:** Gathering tangible evidence will mean a stronger case but also more time. When ready, meet at the end of the day. This provides a night of thoughtful reflection and eliminates the potential for day-long gripe sessions with other employees.
- **Behavior:** Project confidence and authority from behind your desk. Have any backup materials clearly visible and peruse them before speaking. Be authoritative and direct but not necessarily

49. Handling a Subordinate's Personal Telephone Calls and Internet Use

Capture attention: Glen, I'm concerned about a problem I've observed over the last few weeks. You feel perfectly at ease going online for your own personal needs. *[Pointing to papers on desk.]* If it were just occasional I would say so, but these logs and records show use far beyond what is required for the job. Plus, I've seen it with my own eyes. It's costing us money and must stop.

Singled out: *Why are you singling me out? Everyone does this.*

No big deal: *I make the company a lot of money. I don't think a few e-mails is a big deal.*

Own fault: It's the facts that singled you out *[hold up papers]*. According to these records, you're the biggest offender. I'll speak with others separately, but right now I'm speaking with you. If you don't stop, this behavior will be noticed upstairs. It must stop now.

Bottom line counts: You know it's the bottom line that counts. This isn't a charity. Your actions are costing the company money and encouraging others to do the same. Eventually, they'll come to the attention of the people upstairs. This has to stop now.

Emphasize confidence: I'm glad to hear that. You're much too savvy a worker to get into more hot water over something like this.

Acceptance: *Fair enough. I'm sorry. It won't happen again.*

angry. You don't want to alienate a productive subordinate, but you can't ignore his behavior either.

ADAPTATIONS

This script can be modified to:

- Deal with the employee who borrows personal and professional materials from fellow employees.

KEY POINTS

- Be prepared to cite specific incidents based on observation and documentation.
- Do not link the problem to the employee's job performance unless it applies.
- Stay focused on the behavior as a cost factor.
- Be exact in regard to how the problem will be monitored.
- Be clear what the result will be if the problem persists.

Stopping Backstabbing among Subordinates

50

STRATEGY

If the coffee break is the number-one entitlement workers hold sacred, complaining is a close second. Employees consider gripe sessions as no more than a healthy "venting" of petty frustrations. But when someone repeatedly and maliciously directs complaints at colleagues behind their backs, it's not only the employee that's being attacked but also the efficiency of the workplace. The goal of this script is to bring such backstabbing to an immediate halt. The secret is investigation and verification. If you haven't witnessed the backstabbing first hand, you must verify it. That's because it's not uncommon for an employee to try to manipulate management into punishing an office enemy by alleging backstabbing. Verifying a complaint means interviewing all the affected workers, including the alleged perpetrator. Quite often the investigation is enough to bring the problem to a halt: word spreads you're aware of the problem, consider it serious, and are ready to deal with it accordingly.

TACTICS

- **Attitude:** Everything you do or say must demonstrate that management considers backstabbing a serious offense. Remember, as a manager you must overcome the time-worn "venting" viewpoint as well as the silent discomfort inherent in investigating employee-versus-employee issues. To do that your attitude must be serious and straightforward every step of the way.

- **Preparation:** The unease workers feel bringing backstabbing to the attention of management is part of the shield protecting the abusive subordinate. You must be prepared to penetrate this wall of silence. Subordinates should be told they're not being singled out but are among many being interviewed. Emphasize that all responses are strictly confidential. Solicit feedback about the problem in general without attaching a name to initial queries.

50. Stopping Backstabbing among Subordinates

Establish control: Jan, we have a serious problem. One of our staff is constantly criticizing and demeaning the work of others behind their backs. It's at the point where morale and productivity are going downhill. Such backstabbing is very upsetting. After personal observation *[or]* a thorough investigation, I've no doubt you're the person responsible for the turmoil.

Deflects accusation: *I don't believe this! Everyone complains. I do my job every day, no problem. Why are you singling me out?*

Validates accusation: You've singled yourself out. You know I carefully investigated this problem. You were one of the many people I interviewed. A number of your co-workers—a number, not just one—made it clear you are the source of the problem.

Confirms role: *I complain like everyone else. I never meant any harm.*

Establish conditions: Your comments went far beyond complaining. It stops right here, right now. Any further incidents and your job is in jeopardy.

Makes excuses: *This is unfair. I don't care what any of them said. They don't like me because I don't socialize with them. I don't believe you'd let them do this to me.*

Reasserts authority: It's too late for excuses. I wouldn't accuse you or anyone else of anything if I hadn't taken the time to make sure I was right. If you think this is unfair, you can go over my head. We can both put our cases on the table. Just give me the word.

Accepts conditions: *I understand. As I said, I didn't mean to hurt anyone. I was just joking around. I'm sorry. It won't happen again.*

Present expectation: Your actions were far from funny. You've placed your job in jeopardy and severely strained your relationship with your coworkers. Your "joking" will stop immediately. Any such incidents in the future will cost you your job.

Rationalized acceptance: *That won't be necessary. I was just blowing off steam. Maybe I got carried away. I didn't mean to hurt anyone; I was just joking around.*

Wants to appeal: *Fine. Please set it up as quickly as possible.*

However, once initiated, the interview should call upon specific incidents, and you must press for the identification of a specific individual. Collective anonymity can provide a cover that encourages honest responses. It will also add considerable weight to the meeting with the actual backstabber.

- **Timing:** Move quickly in confronting the problem. This shows the seriousness of the issue and the depth of your resolve in dealing with it. When you have finished gathering verification, notify the guilty subordinate in writing of the date and time of a meeting to discuss "a matter of serious mutual concern."

- **Behavior:** Establish that you consider the problem serious and that you're unquestionably in charge of solving it. Stay behind your desk, seated. Be straightforward and specific. Deal with the problem as an existing one, not a suspected one. Review what the problem is, how you verified it, and what you'll do about it. Don't engage in debate. Say you have the verification and want the problem to stop. Conclude the meeting by citing what specific action you will take if there are further occurrences of the problem.

ADAPTATIONS

This script can be modified to:

- Respond to other types of nonsexual harassment in the workplace.

KEY POINTS

- Take all observed or reported incidents of backstabbing very seriously.
- Verify that the behavior took place. Never act on hearsay or inconclusive evidence.
- Confront the individual involved from a position of absolute certainty—no debating.
- Be straightforward and humorless in presenting information and eliciting responses.
- Be unrelenting in underscoring the seriousness of backstabbing behavior.
- Be absolutely clear about what will happen if the behavior occurs again.

Putting an End to a Subordinate's Gossiping

STRATEGY

Gossip in the workplace is like an open jar of honey: everyone enjoys a small taste, a big gulp can make you sick, and getting the lid back on is sticky business. Unrelenting, focused attacks on a single worker create fear, resentment, and apprehension in all workers. The gossip monger is rarely called to task by colleagues, protected by the silent shield of everyone's penchant to gossip. The result is the undermining of the equilibrium and effectiveness of the workforce. This script's goal is to put an end to the pronouncements of your office gossip. Your willingness to acknowledge the problem, consider it seriously, and confront the source are the secrets to success.

TACTICS

- **Attitude:** Be firm and confident in your approach. No one will debate that gossip is a good thing. Stress that your intolerance and anger is for the activity, not the person.
- **Preparation:** Try to get actual examples of the gossip's bad-mouthing. The strength of your documentation will determine if you can, in fact, confront a gossip as the problem or must confront gossip *itself* as the problem. If subordinates come to you to complain, keep notes. Check with other supervisors, too. Your own experiences of negative behavior are key. Because subordinates may clam up when a supervisor is around, and probably won't snitch on a coworker for an activity they also have engaged in, getting solid documentation may be tough. Still, every workplace has a body of common knowledge—everyone just knows—so don't hesitate going with your feelings and instincts.
- **Timing:** As soon as *you* feel satisfied that you've determined who is the primary problem, confront the person. The longer you allow the behavior to continue, the more you send the message

51. Putting an End to a Subordinate's Gossiping

Establish control: Peter, we have a serious problem with gossip in the office. It's apparently becoming personal and hurtful.

No evidence: I've gotten reports from a number of people that someone is spreading malicious rumors about the personal life of one of the secretaries. Have you heard anything about this?

Some evidence: I couldn't help overhearing you holding court by the coffee machine this morning. I know everyone gossips, and I'm not saying you're responsible for the hurtful personal attacks I've learned of, but I wasn't pleased by what I heard earlier.

Stonewalls: *Gossip isn't anything new or uncommon. But still, I haven't heard about any particularly malicious personal attacks.*

Denies responsibility: *I'm sorry about that. I didn't mean anything by it. Even though I might have spoken out of turn this morning, I'm not the gossip you're looking for.*

Enlist support: I'm glad to hear that. Because you're very well connected with the rest of the staff, I'd really appreciate your help in solving this problem. Could you spread the word that I'm concerned about this and that I consider personal attacks and gossip to be completely unacceptable? Let everyone know that, whatever the intent, this kind of innuendo is hurtful and unprofessional and will not be tolerated. Can I count on your help in dealing with this situation?

Agrees to help: *Absolutely. I'll spread the word. You can count on me.*

Stress seriousness: Great. Together, I hope we can put an end to this problem. Otherwise, I'm going to have to start digging deeper into it and make some serious changes around here. Let me know how it goes.

that the problem is unimportant. If you delay, you'll have an office gossiping about your lack of concern for an effective, harmonious workplace.

- **Behavior:** Strongly state how professionally destructive and personally repulsive you find the activity. If you have firsthand examples and documentation, confront the person directly and tolerate no excuses. Anger, annoyance at the least, is appropriate. Without documentation, confront the behavior and not the person. Be concerned and solicitous, seeking help from the individual to solve a problem. You'll ultimately win acceptance that the problem is a serious one that can't be tolerated in the workplace. With documentation, you might even get a grudging acknowledgment of guilt. In either case, be clear what future outcomes will be.

ADAPTATIONS

This script can be modified to:

- Put an end to the antics of the office practical joker and the office know-it-all.

KEY POINTS

- Documentation may not be possible. Move on the problem based on your general knowledge and gut instincts.
- Move quickly as soon as you are aware of it. Do not let it linger.
- Focus on gossip as a harmful and destructive force in the workplace.
- If you've no evidence, ask if the suspect has any and then ask for his help in solving the problem.
- If you've some evidence, reveal it to the suspect and then ask for his help in solving the problem.
- Be clear there will be serious repercussions if the problem doesn't stop.

Turning Down a Subordinate's Request to Hire Her Offspring

STRATEGY

It's difficult to reject a subordinate's family member for employment without the worker taking it personally. To avoid this, you should reinforce her value to the company and make it clear the rejection is clearly a business decision, not a reflection on her. Let her know you share in her disappointment, while at the same time explaining your decision is non-negotiable. Your goal is to help her understand and accept the reasons behind your decision.

TACTICS

- **Attitude:** Be firm, but show understanding and appreciation for a subordinate who wants to help out her family member.
- **Preparation:** If the subordinate is asking that you hire a son or a daughter for summer work, know what the company's policy and history are on this practice. Also know what your budgetary constraints are. If you're being asked to hire someone full time, know what the applicant's qualifications are, what (if any) positions are open in the company, and what salary range the applicant is looking for.
- **Timing:** Especially in the case of the subordinate seeking a summer job for a son or a daughter, inform her as quickly as possible; they'll need time to look elsewhere. Also, keep in mind that this is a conversation best held at the end of the workday so she can get home and break the news to her child.
- **Behavior:** Show sympathy for what the subordinate is trying to do; don't sit behind your desk when the two of you talk, nod empathetically when she speaks, and keep eye contact to show your genuine concern. You want her to understand that her request is being rejected, not her.

52. Turning Down a Subordinate's Request to Hire Her Offspring

Icebreaker: Thanks for coming in, Mary. I received your request that I hire your son, Barry, for the summer. I've met him and I think he's a great kid, but I'm afraid we have no position for him right now.

Appeals: *I think he'd be terrific out on the loading dock. He'd give you more than your money's worth of work, and you wouldn't even have to pay him benefits.*

Personalizes: *Can't you just do this as a favor to me? After all, I've been a faithful employee now for over twenty years.*

Plea for sympathy: *But Barry simply has to find a job this summer.*

Veiled suspicion: *Haven't you hired employees' kids in the past? Didn't Bill Wilkin's boy work here last summer?*

No choice: Mary, if your son's work habits are anything like yours, I have no doubt he'd be a tremendous help to us. Unfortunately, I've been given absolutely no money in my budget this year to hire any additional personnel, even on a temporary basis. It's something our company simply can't afford right now.

Special circumstances: You're absolutely right. You have a very good memory. But Bill's boy was hired only because we received some last-minute orders in April and had both the authority and the money to bring someone on for a few months. That was an extraordinary situation. If that were to arise again, I'd hire your son in a minute. Unfortunately, that's not the case this summer.

Desperation: *Well, I just don't know what we're going to do. We really need to find him a job.*

Anger: *I was counting on you to help us out here. How can you let us down like this?*

Absorb anger: I can understand your anger. You assumed I'd be able to give Barry a job and, now that you know I can't, you're worried he's not going to find any summertime work. But maybe I can be of some assistance.

Support: As I said earlier, Mary, I value you as an employee, and I think your son is a fine boy. I've prepared a general letter of reference on his behalf, if you think it would be any help *[hand it to her]*. I've also checked the want ads in the newspaper. If I were in your position, I think I'd encourage Barry to look at the many seasonal employers in our area—the parks department, golf courses, recreation centers, county pools, landscapers, lawn-care companies, that sort of thing. They're always looking for strong, ambitious young men like Barry *[stand up]*.

Skeptical: *Well, I suppose.*

Resigned: *I appreciate the letter, and if you hear of any sort of opening, would you keep Barry in mind?*

I'll call: If I hear of an opening he might be suited for, I'll call you immediately. Good luck.

ADAPTATIONS

This script can be modified to:

- Turn down a friend or relative's request to hire her child.
- Turn down a subordinate's request to circumvent any company procedure.

KEY POINTS

- Be clear at the outset that it is impossible for you to hire the subordinate's son or daughter but that it's no reflection on either the child or the subordinate.
- Reinforce the subordinate's value to the company.
- Demonstrate your concern by suggesting alternative places of employment.
- Avoid taking responsibility for your subordinate's anger; make it clear that this is her problem the two of you are addressing, not yours.
- If necessary, stand up to indicate that the meeting is over.
- If the subordinate is asking you to do a favor by showing her child some form of preferential treatment, make it clear that you simply won't do this, while at the same time reinforcing the subordinate's value to the company.
- Offer a letter of reference to demonstrate to your subordinate that you have confidence in her child's abilities.
- Don't make promises you can't keep.

Suggesting a Subordinate Improve His Communication Skills

53

STRATEGY

Every business is in the communication business. Regardless of how technologically advanced the modern office becomes, the human voice remains the instrument for immediate personal contact. Communication style and manners can instantly affect the emotions, attitudes, and perceptions of people. The voices on the company's telephone lines, for example, belong to individuals, but what they say speaks for the business. That's why it's important that you correct any person whose communication style or manner is too informal, too rude, or too vulgar. If you accept it as serious and move rapidly to correct the errant subordinate, the problem can easily be solved.

TACTICS

- **Attitude:** If the staff member is too informal, be businesslike and straightforward but relaxed. Where rudeness or use of inappropriate language is the problem, be annoyed, even angry. He should know better.

- **Preparation:** Have a specific example of the improper behavior. This can be through firsthand experience, or complaints reported to you. You don't need to show the problem is long term and ongoing. Once is once too often and more than enough reason to move on the situation.

- **Timing:** Meet as soon as you have heard an inappropriate exchange. This emphasizes to all how seriously you regard the behavior. Do the same where a complaint has been made. This is critical when dealing with rudeness or inappropriate language and desirable in the case of informality. If meeting means cutting into a break or quitting time, so be it. This requires an instant remedy.

53. Suggesting a Subordinate Improve His Communication Skills

Icebreaker: Kevin, you do a solid job for us. There is, however, a problem I need to discuss with you, one that can be easily fixed. I couldn't help hearing you speak this morning.

Rude: You were being rude and short-tempered, seemingly annoyed. That's unacceptable.

Obscene: I heard you using obscene language. You just can't talk here as if you were in a locker room.

Informal: I felt your tone was much too informal.

Makes excuse: *I'm sorry. I just lost my temper with some intern who was being a real jerk. Believe me, it's never happened before.*

Apologizes: *I really am sorry. I intended no disrespect to anyone. You can be sure this won't happen again.*

Rationalizes: *Too informal? I thought that was good. I was trying to make the other person as comfortable as possible.*

Strong admonition: You represent this office when you communicate with others. Anything less than professional behavior shows disrespect to me, this office, and the person with whom you're talking. The people we work with find great comfort in being treated as professionals. Understand?

Accepts: *Yes, sir, I do. I'm really sorry. It won't happen again.*

Future outcome: Make sure it doesn't.

- **Behavior:** Be direct and to the point. Where appropriate, convey your annoyance. Stress that rude or vulgar manners are unacceptable in any business. Where informality is the issue, explain why it's a problem, and offer suggestions.

ADAPTATIONS

This script can be modified to:

- Suggest improvements to a subordinate's written communications.

KEY POINTS

- Act immediately to confront the problem, especially if rude or inappropriate language is involved.
- Don't be afraid to let your anger show if necessary.
- Be supportive of a too informal subordinate.
- Accept no excuse for inappropriate behavior or language.
- Emphasize that the individual always represents the company.
- Imply future action if the matter isn't resolved.

Handling a Flirtatious Subordinate

54

STRATEGY

The overfriendly worker's "hands-on" approach to work coupled with the occasional double entendre, body brushing, and personal compliments creates one of the most difficult and uncomfortable manager-subordinate problems you'll face. Your success at ending this behavior will depend on your objective, dispassionate approach, citing examples of the behavior. Your focus should be on linking the perceived behavior to the manner in which you and coworkers are adversely affected. Expect responses ranging from anger to embarrassed enlightenment. Don't be surprised at arguments accusing you of sexual harassment and/or male chauvinism. Don't get rattled. Be objective, cite your documentation, and focus on your professional concern for maintaining an effective workplace. Ultimately, it's not important to get agreement: recognition of your position and the reason for it should be enough to end the problem.

TACTICS

- **Attitude:** You need to be calm and controlled. You're a diplomat who must avoid personal entanglements while dealing with an issue that's clearly personal. Feeling flattered is a natural reaction. But you must maintain the objectivity of a manager who's simply dealing with another workplace problem.

- **Preparation:** Establish that a pattern of behavior is taking place. Keep a record of incidents to confirm not only the problem but your objective approach to the problem. Include dates to give your notes even more credence. Use fellow managers as sounding boards. If they confirm your observations, so much the better. If they haven't really noticed, ask them to be more aware and give feedback on what they see. Their support is helpful but not absolutely necessary. Your perceptions are enough to initiate action.

54. Handling a Flirtatious Subordinate

Icebreaker: Karen, an office works best when everyone feels comfortable with the people and the work—like one big happy family. But I haven't felt very comfortable as the head of that family lately. I'm afraid my discomfort has to do with you.

Seeks clarification: *With me? What on earth have I done to make you feel uncomfortable?*

State problem: I feel your behavior toward me in the workplace, often in the presence of others, can only be described as flirting.

Surprised questioning: *Flirting! Me! Whatever are you talking about?*

Shifts responsibility: *Colin, I don't believe what I just heard. I think you're seeing what you want to see.*

Detail problem: I'm talking about conversations where your hand is always on my arm or shoulder, going out of your way to brush against me, your constant compliments, and your frequent off-color insinuations. I've been keeping a record of the kind of behavior I described just to make sure I'm being totally professional and objective.

Authenticates feelings: It's not just me. Others have commented about your behavior to me. And I've been keeping a record of the kind of behavior I described just to make sure I'm being totally professional and objective.

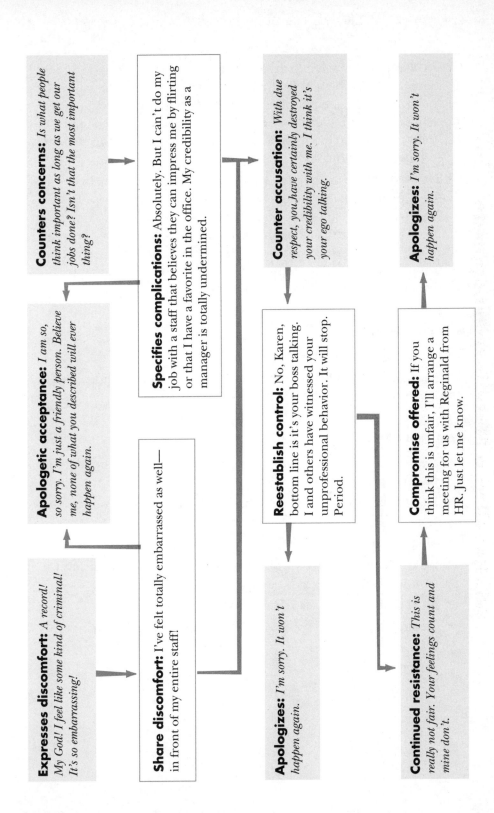

Expresses discomfort: *A record! My God! I feel like some kind of criminal! It's so embarrassing!*

Counters concerns: *Is what people think important as long as we get our jobs done? Isn't that the most important thing?*

Apologetic acceptance: *I am so, so sorry. I'm just a friendly person. Believe me, none of what you described will ever happen again.*

Specifies complications: Absolutely. But I can't do my job with a staff that believes they can impress me by flirting or that I have a favorite in the office. My credibility as a manager is totally undermined.

Counter accusation: *With due respect, you have certainly destroyed your credibility with me. I think it's your ego talking.*

Apologizes: *I'm sorry. It won't happen again.*

Share discomfort: I've felt totally embarrassed as well—in front of my entire staff!

Reestablish control: No, Karen, bottom line is it's your boss talking. I and others have witnessed your unprofessional behavior. It will stop. Period.

Apologizes: *I'm sorry. It won't happen again.*

Compromise offered: If you think this is unfair, I'll arrange a meeting for us with Reginald from HR. Just let me know.

Continued resistance: *This is really not fair. Your feelings count and mine don't.*

- **Timing:** Don't rush into this. The more time you have to document your view, the better. This also gives you a chance to see if the behavior is directed at others as well. Initiate the dialogue at the end of the day, on Friday if possible. This will avoid any co-opting of fellow worker sympathy or anger. It will also offer time for cooling off and reflection.

- **Behavior:** Be the objective manager throughout. Remain at your desk to underline the superior-subordinate relationship. Present your case in a straightforward, matter-of-fact manner. Stay away from comments that could move the conversation onto a personal track. You're dealing with your perceptions, and those perceptions cannot be argued with. You even have documentation of the behavior that shaped the perceptions.

ADAPTATIONS

This script can be modified to:

- Deal with the office flatterer or the favor seeker who provides freebies and all types of small gifts.

KEY POINTS

- Determine that the behavior perceived is part of an ongoing pattern.
- Document examples of the behavior to authenticate your perceptions.
- Maintain a tone of professional concern and control at all times.
- Be consciously aware of not responding on a personal level to counterarguments.
- Meet at the end of the day, on Friday if possible.
- Be clear about what you'll do if the behavior doesn't change.

Dealing with a Brownnosing Subordinate

55

STRATEGY

If the faint praise of a subordinate makes you uneasy, then intense praise will make you sick. The workplace brownnose who trumpets your praises no matter what you do is actually undermining your credibility and authority. The public nature of extravagant flattery, often in your presence, adds embarrassment to the mix. The longer the praise goes on, the more you risk having other subordinates believe this is how to impress you and is what you value in the workplace. Expect an initial response of shock and surprise to your efforts. Next will be pleas of innocence, not for his actions but for his intent. He may even try to brownnose you in this meeting! That's why you must be unrelenting in emphasizing that it is the perception of his actions and comments that is destructive, regardless of his intent.

TACTICS

- **Attitude:** You should be offended and annoyed by brownnosing behavior. Such a subordinate is calculating and shallow and implies to others by his actions that you may be the same. A subordinate who thinks you'll be impressed by transparent praise and unsought personal attention is insulting your integrity and should make you angry.

- **Preparation:** Be ready to refer to the instances the subordinate's behavior made you feel uncomfortable, why you felt uncomfortable, and the effect on others. Don't worry about exact times and dates, just make a list from your own memory. Highlight any daily or weekly pattern of brownnosing rituals. If other managers have commented to you about your unwanted office buddy, include their observations and comments.

- **Timing:** When your gut tells you you're a target, act. An ideal time to do so is immediately following a public display by the "suck up."

55. Dealing with a Brownnosing Subordinate

Establish control: *[Outside of office]* Howard! Right now! My office!

Assert authority: If I seem angry and annoyed, it's because I am. I've had enough of your fawning and flattery. There's a word for that, Howard—brownnosing!

Surprise or denial: *I haven't done anything.* [or] *You can't be serious. How can you even think that?*

Attempts deflection: *I don't understand. You're upset because I happen to be kind and considerate? And what's wrong with giving credit where it's due?*

Rationalizes behavior: *I'd think you would be pleased that I respect what you say and feel free to say so. I certainly don't feel embarrassed.*

Give examples: You personally deliver my mail, you bring me doughnuts, you praise me in meetings. It's embarrassing.

Maintain focus: What's wrong is that it comes off as calculated and transparent. It's embarrassing.

Clarify further: Obviously not. But I want it to stop. If others think that all I value is being flattered, no one will take me seriously.

State outcome: Let this be the last time we have this conversation. Let's move on. If you can't, I guarantee I'll call you on any further brownnosing on the spot. I won't care who's present. Now show me by your actions that neither of us needs to be made uncomfortable again. That's all.

- **Behavior:** Turnabout is fair play in the embarrassment department. By initiating your dialogue publicly, you'll also demonstrate your annoyance to other subordinates.

ADAPTATIONS

This script can be modified to:

- Deal with the giver of unsolicited gifts and office freebies.

KEY POINTS

- Initiate dialogue immediately after an incident takes place.
- Make a list of examples of incidents from memory, highlighting patterns.
- Be direct and forceful.
- Stress the debilitating effect such behavior has on others.
- Focus on job performance as the way in which a subordinate can impress you and gain respect.

Asking If a Subordinate Is a Victim of Domestic Abuse

56

STRATEGY

This is obviously a highly sensitive issue that you must broach with extreme caution, especially if you and the subordinate are of different genders. Be prepared for a tremendous amount of resistance and decide just how far it is useful to push. You may have to settle for half a loaf. Keep in mind that, just by airing the subject, you may be putting the worker on the road to actually addressing it herself later on.

TACTICS

- **Attitude:** You want to show compassion and at the same time maintain a certain distance from the subordinate. Remember that she will be feeling particularly vulnerable and exposed, so it will be up to you to keep some boundaries in place.

- **Preparation:** Read up a little on telltale signs of spousal abuse, such as bruises around the cheeks and eyes, swelling of the lips, and so forth. Also, gather information about local referral services in your community, such as women's shelters, hospitals, police liaisons, clergy, and therapists.

- **Timing:** Schedule a meeting on a Monday, as abuse is often prevalent on weekends. Also, arrange to meet early in the day. If your subordinate agrees to seek help, you want to ensure that there's enough time during that day to get her set up with the proper support system.

- **Behavior:** Meet in your office behind closed doors. Sit at some distance from your subordinate but not behind a desk. Maintain eye contact, adopt an avuncular demeanor, and display comfort while at the same time pressing the seriousness of the issue.

56. Asking If a Subordinate Is a Victim of Domestic Abuse

Icebreaker: Lois, I appreciate your coming in. Please sit down and make yourself comfortable. *[Brief pause]* This is extremely difficult for me to ask, but please hear me out. Lois, is there any possibility your husband is physically harming you?

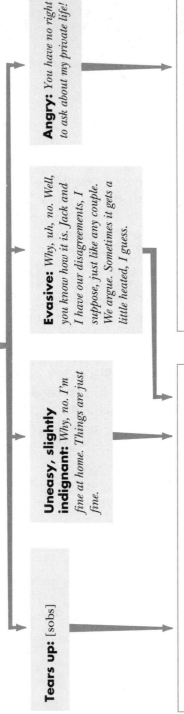

Tears up: [sobs]

Uneasy, slightly indignant: *Why, no. I'm fine at home. Things are just fine.*

Evasive: *Why, uh, no. Well, you know how it is. Jack and I have our disagreements, I suppose, just like any couple. We argue. Sometimes it gets a little heated, I guess.*

Angry: *You have no right to ask about my private life!*

Put it in context: I know this is a very private matter. I certainly don't mean to pry, and I don't raise this subject lightly. I mention it only because I care about you as a member of this company's family. I've noticed bruises on your face and arms, and you've seemed quiet and withdrawn lately. That's not like the old outgoing Lois, and that's why I'm concerned.

Absorb anger: I understand your feelings, Lois, and I don't bring this up lightly. I only raise it because I care about you, not because I mean to invade your private life. I've noticed your bruises, and you've been very quiet and withdrawn. Frankly, I feel I'd be remiss if I didn't say something.

Reluctant: Things have been a little tough lately. Bills have piled up, Douglas's dad's been sick, and we've both been really swamped at work. We really do still love each other, but, well, it feels like Douglas's changed somehow. I don't know; maybe things will get better.

Self-critical: Oh! I was such an idiot for marrying him! My mother was right! I'm so embarrassed. I'm such a jerk.

Self-blame: It's all my fault. I don't get dinner on the table on time. I don't keep the house clean. I know that other wives treat their husbands better, if you know what I mean.

Denial: I don't know what you're getting at. Honestly. I fell down the stairs last week, that's all. [Nervous laughter] I've always been a little clumsy.

Anger: How dare you accuse my husband of beating me! My marriage is just fine, thank you very much! And I'd appreciate it if you'd just mind your own business!

Persuasion and referral: My only concern is your health and well-being. I've noticed your bruises, and, as I mentioned a moment ago, your mood is very different lately. In the past, the company has referred employees who seemed troubled to a local counselor named Judy Brown. I just want to offer you her card. If you don't need it, who knows, some day maybe you'll know someone who does.

Dismissive: Fine, I'll take her card.

Reluctant: Well, it can't hurt to just talk to her. Okay.

ADAPTATIONS

This script can be modified to:

- Fit the needs of a child who is being abused by a parent (even if the child is an adult).

- Apply to a subordinate who is being psychologically—but not physically—abused by a mate.

KEY POINTS

- You want to make the route from the subordinate's needs to professional help a path of least resistance, so have resources available and be willing and able to help secure those resources.

- You don't want the subordinate to come to see you as her rescuer; instead, your efforts should be directed toward putting her in touch with professionals.

- Respect the fact that it is often difficult for abuse victims to admit even to themselves that abuse is occurring. Their resistance to admitting it to someone outside their own immediate circle of friends and family will only be stiffer. Your goal should be to at least send the subordinate out of your office with the business card of a resource person. The subordinate may indeed want to take steps to resolve the problem but not in front of you.

Apologizing to a Subordinate for Your Own Behavior

STRATEGY

In apologizing to a subordinate, you are in essence turning the tables on the power dynamic that exists between the two of you. A dicey proposition but one you can use to your advantage by demonstrating that you're not too big to admit when you've made a mistake. You also want to be clear about what you're apologizing for. For instance, you may have had every right to be angry with a subordinate for something she did or failed to do, but now regret the severity of your tirade.

TACTICS

- **Attitude:** Show honest contrition and a willingness to admit your mistake. But don't blur the distinction between superior and subordinate. Don't grovel.

- **Preparation:** Before meeting with the subordinate, make sure you've calmed down sufficiently and composed yourself adequately. Go over this script in your head; know what you want to say. Go to her office and tell her you want a moment of her time.

- **Timing:** Ideally, you want to have this conversation on the same day the behavior occurred. You also want enough time to elapse so that you've had an opportunity to cool down and the subordinate has recovered from the blow. But you don't want to wait too long; feelings will just fester. Getting on top of this quickly will be appreciated by the aggrieved.

- **Behavior:** Be firm, confident, and relaxed. Be prepared for some anger and resistance and don't surrender to any desire you might have to react impulsively. More important than making sure your apology is accepted, you want to make sure it's heard. Also, if necessary, at the end of the dialogue, reassert your status as this person's superior, perhaps by requesting some work from her.

57. Apologizing to a Subordinate for Your Own Behavior

Icebreaker: Hi, Michelle. I just need a minute of your time. I want to apologize for blowing up at you the way I did this morning. I'm terribly sorry.

Gracious: *Well, I appreciate that. Apology accepted.*

Angry: *You should apologize to me! I didn't deserve to be spoken to in that way, and I didn't appreciate it!*

Retaliatory: *Actually, I've asked for an appointment with Mr. Quimby [your supervisor]. I think he should know how you treated me.*

Icy: *I'd rather not discuss it right now. I have a lot of work to do.*

Appreciation: I appreciate your accepting my apology. It wasn't at all like me to explode the way I did, and if you don't mind, I'd like to explain why it happened.

Absorb anger: You have every right to be angry. My explosion was out of proportion. I was unhappy with the way you handled the McKenna account and I overreacted.

Persist: I certainly understand how you feel right now, but I need to take a minute to explain myself, and I think you need to hear me out. You and I have enjoyed a very healthy relationship, and it's important that we air this out.

Amenable: *Well, okay, but there's really nothing you need to say.*

Icy: *All right.*

Reluctant: *Okay, but don't think this is going to change my mind.*

Resistant: *I said I don't want to discuss it.*

Explanation: I think you know that our department has been under enormous pressure lately. I've been quick tempered with a few people today and, when I discovered you'd lost McKenna, I just blew up. I got angrier than I should have, I'm sorry, and I can assure you it won't happen again.

Patient: That's fine. But if nothing else, then I want you to please listen to what I have to say.

Still angry: *Look, you still shouldn't fly off at me like that!*

Absorb anger, bring closure: I think we're in agreement on that. I thought it would be helpful for both of us if you had my explanation *[stand to leave]*. Now I think it's time we both get back on the ball and see if there's any chance we can get McKenna back in the fold *[smile, offer a handshake]*. I'd appreciate getting your thoughts on that tomorrow.

Stonewalling: *Yeah, you certainly did blow up.*

Going upstairs: *Well, I may need to talk with Mr. Quimby.* [your superior]

Supportive: I understand. In fact, I went to see him myself this morning. I had to tell him about McKenna, and I also wanted him to know how I overreacted. He supported my suggestion that I come talk with you about what happened.

Agreeable, understanding: *I understand. And I'm sorry about McKenna.*

Closure: I'm glad you understand. This has been helpful.

ADAPTATIONS

This script can be modified to:

- Apologize for wrongly accusing a subordinate of some form of malfeasance.
- Apologize for chastising a subordinate in front of her colleagues.

KEY POINTS

- Be very clear about what you're apologizing for. You didn't harass your subordinate. You didn't unfairly single her out. You overreacted.
- Don't be hesitant about gently reminding the subordinate that she was being reprimanded for a mistake she made.
- Behave like a manager even when you're apologizing. Keep control over the discussion by making sure your subordinate listens to what you have to say.
- Make certain you have the last word.

Telling a Subordinate to Be Respectful of Diversity Efforts

58

STRATEGY

A company cannot expect its diversity efforts to be effective if resistance, whether overt or covert, isn't challenged. It's a manager's responsibility to respond whenever he or she hears or learns about comments that potentially challenge the company's diversity policy. That doesn't mean holding a public lynching or launching into a tirade. Investigate the matter and try to determine who the individual involved is. Then call that person into your office, explain what you've heard, and ask if it's true. This gives the subordinate a chance to deny the accusation. Whether or not a denial rings true doesn't matter. It is just an opportunity for you to get your point across without reprimanding the subordinate. If, on the other hand, the accusation is admitted, in whatever form, a reprimand is in order. Make it clear such behavior will not be tolerated in the future.

TACTICS

- **Attitude:** This is an extremely serious matter that could potentially cause legal problems for the company. It's also an important company value. It needs to be addressed firmly.
- **Preparation:** Try your best to determine who is the offender. However, don't feel the need to single out one person if that's not possible.
- **Timing:** Do this as soon as possible after the comments are made. The longer you wait, the more employees are apt to think the comments are acceptable. The sooner you respond, the stronger the impact you'll make.
- **Behavior:** Call the employee into your office. Remain seated and don't invite him to sit down. Dismiss him as soon as you're done without any further small talk.

58. Telling a Subordinate to Be Respectful of Diversity Efforts

Icebreaker: John, I've been told that you've been making comments around the office about Cheryl not being able to cut it as an installer and that it's no job for a woman. Are these stories true?

Denial: *Absolutely not! I would never say such a thing. Who did you hear this from?*

Make point: *My source isn't important. What is important is that the story isn't true. I'm glad to hear that.*

Just a joke: *It's no big deal. I was just joking around. You know how it is when everyone is taking a break and shooting the breeze.*

Not funny: You may have intended it as a joke, but it wasn't funny. This isn't something we should be joking about.

Sexist: *I'm not going to deny it. I just don't think this is a job for a woman.*

Reprimand #1: I don't care what your personal feelings are about this issue, but I do care what you do and say as an employee of this company. As an employee, your comments and behavior are both unacceptable and will not be tolerated in this company.

Performance problem: *I just don't think she can cut it. It hurts all of us to have someone out there in the field who can't do the job.*

Reprimand #2: If you have a problem with someone's performance, whether it's a man or a woman, you come to me to talk about it. You don't talk the person down to the rest of the staff.

State policy: We take our diversity efforts very seriously. But at the same time we value performance just as much. No one gets promoted here without merit, and we expect everyone to be able to do his or her job well. We also expect everyone in the company to be supportive of those diversity efforts. Have I made myself clear?

ADAPTATIONS

This script can be modified to:

- Tell a subordinate to keep his political, racial, or religious opinions to himself.

KEY POINTS

- Explain that you've heard about a possible problem.
- If it's denied, present the policy statement anyway.
- If it's claimed it was a joke, say it's not a joking matter and present the policy statement.
- If a prejudiced attitude is displayed, say it's not acceptable to express this or act this way in the workplace or anywhere else.
- If claims of poor performance are made, separate the two issues and then present the policy statement.

59

Terminating a Subordinate

STRATEGY

Companies have been using layoffs as a cost-cutting strategy for years. However, even though firing employees is an all-too-common part of their duties, few managers handle the process well. That's because, whatever the facts of the dismissal, most managers feel bad about letting someone go. Ironically, expressing those feelings of remorse can be cruel because they give the employee false hope. Instead, the best way to deal with a termination is to make it a quick, unambiguous act. Spell out exactly why you are letting the employee go, state clearly that the decision is final, and explain the details of the company's severance policy. Then ask the employee to sign a letter of acknowledgment and agreement which will make it more difficult for her to reopen the discussion or sue. Resist all attempts to turn the discussion into an argument or debate. The decision has been made and it's final.

TACTICS

- **Attitude:** Whatever your feelings, be dispassionate and businesslike—it's actually in the subordinate's best interests.
- **Preparation:** Have documentation of poor performance if any on hand. Also have details of the severance package written into a termination letter that can be signed at this meeting. Have severance checks written out and signed prior to the meeting.
- **Timing:** Do this as early in the week and as early in the day as possible so that the individual can apply for unemployment benefits and start looking for a job immediately.
- **Behavior:** Hold this meeting in your office. If possible, have a third party on hand to deter anger. Offer immediate severance payment in exchange for immediate signing of the termination memo. Absorb anger, deflect guilt, and acknowledge the subordinate's right to legal representation. Resist efforts to negotiate more severance or a second chance.

59. Terminating a Subordinate

Opener: I have bad news for you. I'm afraid your employment here is being terminated. The company has already cut a check for one month's severance pay and prepared a reference letter for you. I can give you both now.

Fired for poor performance: I must stress this decision is final. It was based on your inability to rebound from two unsatisfactory performance reviews. However, because we know you've tried, if asked, the company will say you were laid off for economic reasons. If you sign this letter that says you understand our discussion, we can put this behind us.

Laid off for economic reasons: I'm sorry, but this decision is final. It was based on the company's bottom-line profitability and has nothing to do with your performance. If asked, the company will say it was your decision to leave and I'll be happy to add my personal recommendation. If you sign this letter that outlines what I've just said, we can get this unhappy business over with.

Defends professional record: *I have to take exception to your decision to single me out. I think I've performed as well as anyone else in the department. I've never had anyone call my skills and abilities into question before.*

Gets teary or personal: *How could you do this to me? We've been friends. I've had you over to my home for dinner. Isn't there something you can do?*

Gets angry: *I expected something like this to happen. You've had it in for me from day one. You're just using me as a scapegoat for your own mistakes.*

Deflect defense: As I mentioned before, this is purely an economic decision having nothing to do with your abilities. You were simply the last hired. *[or]* We're not questioning your skills and abilities. We've simply decided that you're not as productive as we need you to be. That's something we warned you about in two prior reviews.

Asks for another chance: *Isn't there something I can do? I need this job. I promise my work will improve. All I need is another chance.*

Stress finality: I'm terribly sorry, but the decision really is final. Please sign this so I can give you your check and reference letter.

Deflect guilt: I feel terrible about this, but it's strictly a business decision. I can't let my personal feelings get in the way of the company's bottom line. I hope you understand. As your friend, I'll be happy to do everything I can to help you land another job. For now, though, I need you to take a look at this letter and then sign it.

Threatens legal action: *I'm not going to sign anything until I speak with my attorney. I think there are some issues I need to get a legal opinion on.*

State rights: You have every right to speak with your attorney if you'd like. I'll hold on to the check and paperwork until I hear from you. *[Stand up.]* Good day.

Absorb anger: I'm sorry you feel that way. Everyone here, especially me, wanted to see your relationship with the company work out. Unfortunately, it simply hasn't. Why don't you look at this letter and then sign it.

Demands more severance: *I'm not going to sign anything until we've had a chance to talk about this severance package. I've worked here for two years, and with the job market the way it is, this simply isn't enough.*

Not negotiable: I'm afraid my hands are tied when it comes to the severance offer. You can speak with the chairman if you'd like, but I must tell you that she is aware of, and approved, the offer. Please sign this so I can give you your check and reference letter.

ADAPTATIONS

This script can be modified to:

- Terminate a professional.
- Terminate an independent contractor.

KEY POINTS

- Be dispassionate, efficient, and businesslike.
- If she gets angry, absorb the outburst and push for closure.
- If she gets defensive, deflect the effort and push for closure.
- If she gets personal, deflect the guilt, stress this is business, and push for closure.
- If she gets teary, retain a businesslike demeanor, give her a chance to do the same, and then push for closure.
- Deny requests for more severance or a second chance.
- If she threatens legal action, acknowledge her right to representation.

Sending a Voluntary Termination Hint to a Subordinate

STRATEGY

"You can't fire me," legions of sitcom stars have shouted, "I quit!" How often managers wish this cliché could be reality. There are those times when regardless of what efforts everyone has made, an employee just doesn't fit. Attitude, performance, attendance, and all else combine to make it clear that a subordinate just isn't going to make it. The goal of this script is to help you to bring about the voluntary termination of such a subordinate by hinting at its desirability. By presenting evidence of work incompatibility in an understanding, nonthreatening manner, soliciting the subordinate's reflection upon that evidence, and indicating the advantages of voluntary termination, hints may become a reality.

TACTICS

- **Attitude:** Expect to feel a bit awkward. As difficult as terminating a subordinate is, it's still straightforward and businesslike. Hinting to a subordinate that he leave is often uncomfortable because it's so indirect and usually involves a "nice person, poor worker" scenario. Knowing your actions are driven by doing what's best for all should help.

- **Preparation:** Have specific actions and activities that indicate the poor working relationship. Be personally clear on what the advantages of resigning are so you can present them. Finally, carefully prepare and practice the script.

- **Timing:** Meet at least four days before the day you'd actually terminate the subordinate. Schedule the meeting at the end of the workday to allow the employee to think it over overnight and to avoid all-day coworker commiseration that will disrupt the workplace. If your hinting has been successfully "read," or your relationship with the subordinate has allowed you to be direct, meet immediately the next morning to implement the plan.

60. Sending a Voluntary Termination Hint to a Subordinate

Establish context: Mitch, I'm concerned. You seem very unhappy working here, and I worry about your future relationship with the company.

Questions: *Future relationship? Unhappy? I'm really not sure what you mean.*

Attitude problem: I see no interaction with fellow workers. You always look so tired and unenthusiastic.

Performance problem: The last six weeks you've been out at least one day a week, and we've had to talk before about your work being redone.

Excuse: *I just like working alone and keeping my feelings to myself, too.*

Excuse: *I can't help being sick. And I know I make mistakes sometimes, but everyone does.*

Plant seed: Mitch, can you really say you're happy here? Sometimes you look so harried and under pressure.

Explains behavior: *Well, there is pressure; it's work. Sometimes there is just so much to do. It gets to everyone.*

Encourage reflection: Certainly it does. But some handle it better than others. Why continue to be unhappy and under such pressure?

Direct statement: Mitch, the door is closed. This is entirely off the record at this point. But, yes, I'm afraid you are going to be let go. We both know it just isn't working out. Friday is to be your last day. I'd really like to see you resign before then.

Hurt response: *You mean you want me to do the dirty work for you?*

Clarify motives: I want you to get what's best for you in a difficult situation. It looks better to a future employer that you chose to leave, not that you had to be told to leave.

Future concern: *What if I do what you want and a new company checks up on me? What will you tell them?*

Questions directly: *It sounds like you don't want me to work here anymore. Am I going to be fired? Is that it?*

Deflect question: Mitch, at this point I want you to realize you are in control of the situation. You can take actions that are best for you.

Understands situation: *I see what's going on. I'm going to be out, but you would like me to quit so you don't have to fire me.*

Questions motives: *Are you saying you want me to leave? Is that what you want?*

Redirect challenge: I'm saying people should do what's best for them. They should find a work situation where they feel comfortable and committed.

Set timeline: Think about what we've discussed today and let me know first thing in the morning what you have decided.

Describe support: That you decided to leave to find something more challenging. Your leaving on your own also means we can give you a recommendation that could help. You decide how you want this to be done. I'll meet with you first thing in the morning to get your decision.

- **Behavior:** Be controlled and low-key. Because hinting at a course of action is involved, expect questions and confusion, real or feigned, about your position. Even if the message is received, expect being pressed to deliver it more directly. If your rapport with the subordinate allows it, move to being absolutely direct and to the point.

ADAPTATIONS

This script can be modified to:

- Hint that a subordinate voluntarily relinquish a supervisory role or give up job responsibilities.

KEY POINTS

- Be prepared to give examples of the subordinate's attitude and actions that support your decision.
- Provide enough time before any termination is planned for the subordinate to make a decision.
- Carefully prepare and rehearse what you are going to say.
- Remain low-key but in control and businesslike.
- If the relationship supports it, abandon any hints and be absolutely direct.
- Be clear on your expected timeline for action.

Telling a Subordinate to Have a More Positive Attitude

61

STRATEGY

While it's good to have at least one skeptic on your staff to keep everyone else honest, a constantly gloomy employee can cast a shadow over an entire department. This is definitely a problem but one that needs to be handled without too much fuss. After all, the more drama surrounding the dialogue, the more opportunities for the employee to spin out his negativity. Keep the conversation short and sweet. Humor can help lighten the tone. However, make sure you get your message across.

TACTICS

- **Attitude:** This is important, but it shouldn't be a major drama.
- **Preparation:** Don't worry about compiling a list of examples that will only lead to a debate over the merits of the negativity. Instead, present it as an overall perception.
- **Timing:** Do this as soon as possible after a negative comment.
- **Behavior:** Call the subordinate into your office. Sit down with him, out from behind your desk if possible, to create a warmer atmosphere. Smile and try to make him feel comfortable.

61. Telling a Subordinate to Have a More Positive Attitude

Icebreaker: Tom, I need to ask you a question and I want you to answer it honestly. Are you planning to leave the company?

Denial: *Absolutely not! Why do you ask?*

Make point: You've been displaying a very negative attitude to almost everything. It's really having an effect on morale in the department. I had assumed that because you seemed so unhappy you were about to leave.

Apologizes: *I'm sorry. It's just my personality. I didn't realize I was causing a problem. I'll try to be more upbeat.*

Voices complaint: *It's just that we work so hard and we get so little credit from the people upstairs. We're really not getting paid what we deserve, unlike those salespeople who are making far more than they should. And to top it off, the building is drafty.*

Exactly: This is exactly what I'm talking about when I said you have a negative attitude. If you really feel this way maybe you should look for another job. This isn't the greatest company in the world, but it's certainly not as bad as you're portraying it. I don't think you know how good you've got it. If you want to stay here you really need to be less negative.

Accept and reiterate: I'm glad to hear that. I don't expect you to be a Pollyanna, but you don't need to find the cloud behind every silver lining. Let's try to have some fun out there, okay?

ADAPTATIONS

This script can be modified to:

- Tell a friend or family member to be more positive.

KEY POINTS

- Make the dialogue short and sweet.
- Be as warm and friendly as possible.
- If he accepts the criticism, offer encouragement.
- If he continues to demonstrate the behavior, put him on notice.

III

Lifescripts

for Dealing with Office Politics

Confronting a Sexual Harasser

62

STRATEGY

Despite the trepidation and fear involved, if you're being sexually harassed you must deal with it immediately. If you don't put an end to the harassment, it will only escalate. The key to stopping harassment is to present a powerful, unequivocal objection, whatever the type of harassment and regardless of the harasser's motivations. An off-color joke should be treated with the same urgency as a pinch. Otherwise, your complaint won't be taken seriously. In many of these cases, power is as much an issue as sex. That's why you need to seize the power in this confrontation. You can do that by launching a direct assault.

TACTICS

- **Attitude:** All types of harassment are equal and require the same response—a powerful direct assault.
- **Preparation:** If you anticipate trouble, speak with a higher-up or the HR department prior to the meeting.
- **Timing:** Deal with it as soon as possible. Delay will only empower the harasser and make you feel powerless.
- **Behavior:** Go to his office or workspace, position yourself between him and the door so he cannot leave, remain standing, maintain eye contact throughout, and walk out as soon as you're done, ensuring that you have the final word.

62. Confronting a Sexual Harasser

Icebreaker: I want you to stop working and listen very carefully to what I'm about to say.

Implied threat: Your behavior toward me is totally unacceptable and must stop right now.

You're overreacting: *Relax, you're overreacting. It was just a joke. Don't take everything so seriously! Why don't you cool off a bit and we'll forget all about it, okay?*

Your word against mine: *Ooh, I love it when you get mad. But seriously, babe, it's just your word against mine. And no one is going to believe you. So why don't you forget all about this and let's go out to lunch.*

Refuse to play games: This is my profession. Ours is a business relationship . . . period. I come here to work, not to play games.

I'm sorry: *I'm sorry. I didn't mean anything by it. I was just joking. I didn't realize it would offend you. Can't we just forget all about it?*

Beat him to the punch: I thought you might respond this way, so I made sure to speak with personnel before I came here. They told me to speak to you prior to filing a formal complaint.

You're too sensitive: *Hold your horses. I said I didn't mean anything by it. You're exaggerating the importance of this. I really think you're being too sensitive.*

Put him on notice: I hear your apology, but there's no excuse for that kind of behavior. I've prepared a memo outlining what's happened, but I'll hold on to it for now. Maybe you'll be able to work things out.

You can't hurt me: *You don't scare me. I can make your life here miserable and destroy your future in this business. Go ahead. File your complaint. Nothing will happen to me.*

Imply legal action: That's not what my lawyer says.

ADAPTATIONS

This script can be modified to:

- Counter any type of on-the-job extortion.
- Counter an announced threat to your position by a coworker.

KEY POINTS

- Be as forceful as possible in your opening statement.
- Stress that there will be repercussions to continued harassment.
- If he says you're overreacting, state that this is a place of business, not a social club.
- If he says it's your word against his, explain that you've already gone to higher-ups.
- If he apologizes, say there's no excuse for his actions but you'll hold off taking further action for now.
- If he says that you're too sensitive or that there's nothing you can do, say your lawyer disagrees.

Confronting a
Backstabbing Peer

63

STRATEGY

The secret to confronting a backstabbing colleague is to show that the attacker, far from being constructive, is being unfair and personal. If the actions have been covert, deliver your message indirectly—that way the attacker can't simply deny involvement and end the conversation. If the attack was overt, or if the indirect approach doesn't work, deal directly. Ideally, you should conduct the discussion privately, which increases the chance of an honest exchange. But if that doesn't work, or if the attack is so damaging you must respond immediately, do it publicly. If all else fails, stress your willingness to take your dispute to a higher authority.

TACTICS

- **Attitude:** Don't feel defensive or uneasy. You are an aggrieved party looking for justice. You're coming from a position of honesty so you've a right to feel confident.
- **Preparation:** Jot down some notes about past attacks. For this script they'll simply serve as reminders. If need be, they'll help you prepare a memo if this dialogue doesn't work.
- **Timing:** If the incident demands an immediate public response, do so. If not, approach the attacker privately as soon as possible after the latest attack.
- **Behavior:** Hold this meeting in the attacker's office. Don't schedule it—simply arrive. If this is an indirect approach, you can sit down. If this is a direct approach, shut the door behind you and remain standing, keeping yourself between her and the door. In effect, this puts you in the dominant position, keeps her a captive in her office, and forces her to listen to you. As soon as you finish your script, turn your back on her and leave.

63. Confronting a Backstabbing Peer

Indirect private approach

Icebreaker: I've heard that someone has been complaining that I'm not pulling my weight. What do you think I should do?

Denial: *I can't believe someone would spread rumors maliciously. Maybe you misunderstood a comment that was meant to be helpful?*

Appeal for privacy: If that's the case, I would hope she or he would make any other comments to me directly—and in private. Then I would do the same.

Confrontation: *What do you expect? We all want to be promoted, but there's only one opening. It's every person for him- or herself.*

Threat of action: That's not the way to go. If these attacks continue, I'm going to suggest to the boss that we have a staff meeting to air our feelings openly.

Rationalization: *The same thing happened to me last year. This place has become so political, don't you think?*

Appeal for unity: I agree—and it's really too bad. We'd all get a lot further if we worked together. And if we can't do that, at least we should stop cutting each other's throats.

Direct public response/private approach

Direct public response: I can't understand why you'd want to slander me this way in public. I suggest you stop this public display and discuss any personal problems we may have in private. But right now, I suggest we get back to business.

Later that day

Icebreaker: What have I ever done to you to elicit this kind of behavior? I can't imagine why you're attacking me.

Rationalization: *Last year someone told the boss my staff was demoralized. I know it was you. I'm just responding in kind.*

Appeal for unity: I've never attacked you—that's not my style. I like working with you, not against you. But if we can't work together, I'd at least appreciate your cutting out the attacks.

Confrontation: *Listen, we all want this promotion. If you can't take the competition, maybe you ought to remove yourself.*

Threat of action: Listen, I'm for a fair fight. I know what you're doing. If you keep it up, I'll suggest we sit down with the boss and discuss our problems.

Denial: *I didn't attack you. I just pointed out a couple of mistakes you've made lately in the hope they won't happen again.*

Appeal for privacy: If you're really interested in helping me, come to me privately, don't bring things up at staff meetings. I'll do the same for you.

ADAPTATIONS

This script can be modified to:

- Confront a gossiping acquaintance or friend.
- Dispel a rumor.
- Handle an off-color joke.

KEY POINTS

- Respond in kind: indirectly to covert attacks, directly to overt attacks.
- If need be, respond publicly and immediately. Otherwise, have the discussion in private.
- If the attacker denies either being the perpetrator or that the attack was harmful, appeal for privacy.
- If the attacker rationalizes her action, appeal for unity.
- If the attacker is confrontational, threaten to bring the matter up with higher authorities or go public with it.

Ratting on a Colleague

64

STRATEGY

Deciding whether to complain about a peer's performance is a tough call. Even if your gripes are entirely justified and your superior supports you, you can end up being viewed as a backstabber. So pick your fights carefully. If someone simply rubs you the wrong way, that's your problem. The only time it's worth entering these dangerous waters is when someone's sloppy work or procrastination is jeopardizing your ability to get your job done, and you've already tried, unsuccessfully, to set things right. Your goal in this script is to enlist your superior's direct intervention without incurring criticism yourself. You want to minimize any damage to your reputation and avoid being labeled the boss's spy. You can accomplish all this as long as you stress the connection to your own productivity and the company's goals. Make it clear that this is an unusual situation, not your common practice.

TACTICS

- **Attitude:** Your first loyalty must be to the company. It's by following this credo that you'll achieve your own success. You aren't putting someone down to boost yourself—you're helping the company achieve its goals.
- **Preparation:** Make sure you've established what you feel is the problem—quality or delay, for instance—and that you've tried on your own to resolve the situation.
- **Timing:** The timing here is tricky. You want to wait long enough so that action is vital but not so long that it's a crisis beyond repair.
- **Behavior:** Show remorse at having to take this step, but offer no apologies. You have the company's goals at heart and there's no shame in that.

64. Ratting on a Colleague

Icebreaker: Excuse me, Susan, but I need to speak with you. I'm afraid there's a problem with meeting our deadline for the Oxford proposal [or] I'm afraid the Oxford proposal just isn't going to meet our usual standards. I've asked several times, but Diane has yet to turn in her final sketches for the project. [or] The sketches I've gotten from Diane just aren't up to par.

Wants to hear: *You know how important that project is. I'm not going to let anything keep us from delivering the kind of work we promised, and delivering it on time. What exactly is the problem?*

Upset at idea: *Listen, that project is crucial. I made you the lead person on it, and I don't want to hear any excuses or buck-passing. Your job—and hers—is to get it done right, and on time.*

Not doing work: I know Diane is under a lot of pressure—we all are. But I'm not sure she's even begun the sketches I need from her. I've asked for them repeatedly, but she hasn't delivered. And we're running out of time.

Work not up to par: I know Diane is under a lot of pressure—we all are. But the sketches she's given me just aren't the quality we need. We've spoken about it repeatedly, but there's been no improvement. And we're running out of time.

Offer reassurance: I appreciate your concern, and I'm sure we'll meet the deadline if we solve this problem now. But I really need your help. Without it, I don't think I'll be able to get what we need out of Diane.

Wants more dirt: *Have you had problems with Diane in the past? What do you think of the job she and the rest of her people are doing overall?*

Against ratting: *I'll make sure she delivers. But please remember, teamwork is important. I'm not happy about your coming here and complaining about a colleague.*

Insists on your involvement: *Okay, you go back to Diane and tell her that you spoke with me and I said she'd better shape up. Let me know how it goes.*

Deflect probe for info: *I really can't give you a general evaluation. This is the first time anything Diane has done has involved me directly, and I thought you should know.*

Deflect criticism: *Teamwork is important to me, too. But so is making sure we get the job done. If I could make headway with her, I wouldn't bring it up.*

Argue for reconsideration: *All right, I'll give it one last try. But if it doesn't produce the results we want, can I count on your help at that point?*

Accepts responsibility: *Okay. I'll speak with her, find out what the problem is, and make sure you get the sketches on time.*

Agrees to act later: *Deal. If you really can't get her in line by the end of next week, come back, give me an update, and I'll get involved directly.*

ADAPTATIONS

This script can be modified to:

- Speak to a customer or a supplier about the behavior of one of its employees.
- Speak to a partner at a professional firm you associate with about the behavior of another partner.
- Speak to a store manager about a clerk's behavior.
- Speak to a principal about your child's teacher.

KEY POINTS

- Be clear about the problem and present it entirely in business terms.
- If your superior initially objects to getting involved, insist that you need her in order to get the job done.
- If your superior probes for more information on your colleague, stress that you have none to offer and that your concern is this project.
- If she insists on staying aloof, ask for a commitment that she'll get involved if you're once again unsuccessful.
- If she criticizes your coming to her with complaints about a peer, stress that you've only done it because the project was in jeopardy.

Suggesting No Further Drinking to a Peer

STRATEGY

It's always awkward to discuss drinking habits with a colleague but never more so than at a sales conference or in some other out-of-the-office business/personal situation. Most large companies have established routines for identifying, warning, and assisting employees who show signs of chronic alcohol or drug abuse, but when a fellow sales rep blows a deal by getting drunk at a client dinner, there's no employee-assistance program around to intervene. There's probably little you can do at the time, short of making a scene—and he has probably already taken care of that; so your goal is to make sure it doesn't happen again. That means changing his behavior—at least in his business meetings with you.

TACTICS

- **Attitude:** Be direct, clear, and determined. You are doing this for his good, your good, and the company's good, so there's no reason for you to question your actions.

- **Preparation:** Expect efforts either to deny there's a problem or to shift the focus of the discussion from the issue of drinking. Consider "compromise solutions" short of abstinence.

- **Timing:** Do this as soon as possible after an incident where the problem was obvious. Breakfast the morning after a botched client dinner is fine—as long as he isn't too hung over.

- **Behavior:** Be compassionate, but keep the focus on business. Your goal is to keep from being embarrassed in the future, and make sure his problem doesn't hurt your career.

65. Suggesting No Further Drinking to a Peer

Icebreaker: I need to speak with you about something that's affecting the way we work together. I think you need to stop drinking when we're working together. It's hurting our chances to close deals. Drinking gives clients an excuse to drink more and lets them avoid making decisions. And to be honest, sometimes you're not careful about what you're saying.

None of your business: *My drinking is my business. It's not like I'm getting drunk on the job. What I do outside the office is none of your business.*

It is my business: It is. Your drinking in business situations affects the company and my livelihood.

You're exaggerating: *I don't drink that much. I think you're exaggerating. Maybe I got a little buzzed when we were out with the people from Acme, but so did they.*

I wish: I wish I were exaggerating, but I'm not the only person who has noticed it. You really should tone it down.

You're jealous: *Listen, just because you have a hard time letting your hair down and don't know how to have a good time with clients doesn't mean I've got a drinking problem.*

I'm on the job: I resent your implication. I'm not a robot, but when it comes to business I'm more concerned with closing the deal than having a good time. I think you should be, too.

It works for me: *I know it's not your style, but socializing with clients works for me. I think the people from Acme had a great time last night.*

But no sale: It may have looked that way, but here we are this morning without a signed contract. We didn't do any business last night.

You're not the boss: *Who died and made you boss? This isn't your company. I don't take orders from you.*

Did it for them: *Listen, I had no idea. I just thought they'd be insulted if I didn't drink with them. They did keep refilling their own glasses and asking us if we wanted more.*

Apologizes: *You're right. I'm sorry. I wasn't aware of it. We've always worked well together in the past. Let's put this behind us.*

Can't close every day: *You can't close at every meeting. You've got to warm some clients up before you close them. Last night was just warming them up.*

I've a stake: You're right. I'm not the boss. But I have a stake in the success of our working together. If your behavior continues to harm my ability to do my job, I will discuss it with the boss.

Next time, different setting: I know. I saw that too. That's why next time I think we should get together with them in a nondrinking situation—like over breakfast or for an in-office meeting.

Pay compliment: Listen, I don't know anyone who's better at getting along with clients that you are. But next time, let's try using some of our sales skills, too. I know we can do it.

Didn't even try: I understand, but we didn't even try to close them last night. We didn't talk any business. We're not going to make sales that way.

ADAPTATIONS

This script can be modified to:

- Address any form of antisocial behavior by a peer.
- Discuss the physical appearance of a peer.

KEY POINTS

- Be businesslike, determined, clear, and direct.
- If he says his drinking is none of your business, stress that when it happens in a work situation it is your business.
- If he says you're exaggerating, say other people have noticed, too.
- If he says you're too uptight, say you're simply interested in getting your job done.
- If he blames the clients, suggest having meetings at nondrinking times or places.
- If he accuses you of acting superior, just reiterate your stake in the situation.

Tactfully Suggesting Better Hygiene to a Peer

66

STRATEGY

Having to tell someone that her breath or body odor is offensive may be one of the most awkward situations you'll ever face in the workplace. Yet sometimes it's essential to take action, not only for the comfort of you and other coworkers but for the company and the person's future as well. Such problems are almost certain to undermine the image of the company if the offender comes into contact with clients. Hygiene problems will erode her standing in the company and will block any further progress in the organization. Begin with the assumption that she isn't conscious of the problem. Start off by subtly suggesting the same tools you use to avoid similar problems. If she takes the hint, let the matter drop. If your subtext isn't understood, you'll have to press further while still being somewhat diplomatic.

TACTICS

- **Attitude:** Try not to be embarrassed. The other party will be embarrassed enough for both of you. Remember, you're doing this for her own good.
- **Preparation:** Buy some breath mints or look around for a nearby drugstore.
- **Timing:** Do this immediately after lunch and privately. That way you minimize embarrassment and have an excuse for your actions.
- **Behavior:** Start off subtly, but if necessary, shift to sincere concern. There's no need to be apologetic because you're doing the person a favor.

66. Tactfully Suggesting Better Hygiene to a Peer

Bad breath: *[Show mints, pop one in your mouth.]* Would you like one? I don't know about you, but sometimes I really need these after lunch.

Body odor: You won't believe the sale I stumbled on. The drugstore up the street was offering 50 percent off on perfumes and colognes. You should check it out. If you want, I'll go over there with you after work.

Doesn't take hint: *No, thanks. I never use those kinds of things.*

Takes the hint: *Um . . . sure. I'll take one [or] Oh, I never . . . uh . . . Thanks, I'll take you up on that.*

Gets angry: *Excuse me. Are you suggesting there's something wrong with me?*

Strong hint: *Are you sure?* I always use them during the day when my breath gets stale *[or]* I find they make me feel fresher throughout the day.

You're not alone: No, not at all. We all have to watch ourselves. Working in such close quarters makes everyone a little sensitive.

None of your business: *I don't think my hygiene is any of your business. I think I take care of myself just fine, thank you.*

We're in this together: Under most circumstances I'd agree with you. But we work in very close quarters here. I'd expect you to do the same thing for me if the situation were reversed. We have to take care of each other.

ADAPTATIONS

This script can be modified to:

- Discuss hygiene problems with a spouse.
- Discuss hygiene problems or erratic behavior with a parent or older relative.

KEY POINTS

- Start off subtly, but if necessary, be direct.
- If she takes the hint, drop the issue.
- If she doesn't take the hint, make your case stronger.
- If she gets angry, say it's a problem everyone there shares.
- If she says it's none of your business, explain why it is something you need to be concerned with.

Asking a Peer to Pull Her Own Weight

67

STRATEGY

We've all been down *this* road: saddled with a heavy workload, you and everyone else in your department start working extra hard to compensate—everyone else except one lone soul, that is. She's at her desk at nine and out the door exactly at five, and you're all getting pretty ticked. If she just pulled her own weight, everyone's burden would be eased. The goal of this script is to get Ms. Nine-to-Five to work as hard as everyone else. Your first strategy will be to appeal to her sense of fairness. Point out the rewards of working harder, whether it's the bonus the department has been promised or simply getting the work done faster. Remind her she won't have to work this hard forever. If these tactics fail, point out that she's rapidly becoming an object of hatred among her peers. Unfortunately, some people don't care if coworkers dislike them. If even the threat of becoming a pariah fails, it's time to use your final weapon: let her know that if there's a problem with the project and the boss is looking for scapegoats, her name is likely to be number one on everyone's list.

TACTICS

- **Attitude:** Your attitude should be one of asking for help without resorting to begging, cajoling, or threatening. It's okay if she gets an inkling of how angry you and the rest of the department are, as long as your dissatisfaction with her isn't conveyed blatantly via yelling, cursing, or name-calling.

- **Preparation:** Talk with others in your department and let them know you plan on approaching her—alone—about her not pulling her own weight. Tell those who disagree that while they may feel differently about the situation, you'd appreciate it if they didn't tip your hand. Ask those who agree if they'd be willing to back you up if she demands proof that others feel as you do. If applicable, be able to provide concrete examples for her of how her refusal to work up to her capabilities has hurt the department.

67. Asking a Peer to Pull Her Own Weight

Appeal to sense of fairness: Hey, Paula, got a minute? You know that project the sales department dumped on us at the last minute? Well, the rest of us have been either coming in early or staying late trying to get it done on time, and we could really use your help. Would you mind putting in a little extra time?

Refuses: *No way. They're not paying us overtime! Besides, I already give enough of my life to this stinkin' company!*

Rationality and guilt: We're not being paid by the hour, Paula, we're being paid a salary. And while I might identify with not wanting to give the company a minute more than you must, the truth is, it's your coworkers you're screwing. And people are starting to get annoyed.

Scheduling problem: *I don't know if I can. I usually shoot right over to day-care after work to pick up Jamie, and if I come in early, it's going to mess up the whole family's schedule, since I'm the one who gets Ruthie off to school so Sam can get to his office early.*

Sympathy for scheduling, but . . . : Geez, Paula, I didn't realize you and Sam were juggling so many balls outside work. But, you know, so are a couple of other people, and they've been able to make temporary arrangements just until the project is completed. Maybe you could ask them what they did. We're not going to be swamped like this forever.

Doesn't want to know: *I hear you, but can I point something out? I don't see the sales department burning the midnight oil or showing up at the crack of dawn. We didn't create this problem; why should we have to pick up the slack?*

Grow up: Because picking up the slack is our job, Paula. Look, haven't there been times in the past when we've done the same thing to sales? It's just the nature of the beast. Besides, if we get this done on time we'll be up for a bonus, and we'll be able to kick back for awhile.

Agrees to juggle: *Well, let me see what I can do. I'll get back to you after I talk to Sam.*

Agrees to help: *Okay, I'll come in early tomorrow. I guess it's only fair, since everyone else in the department is doing it. But I'm not a happy camper.*

Refuses: *Look, I'm sorry, but I can't [or] won't do it.*

Explain to peers: Then you better be ready to explain to everyone why you won't put in the time when the rest of us are.

Won't budge: *I don't care.*

Express thanks: Thanks. We'd all appreciate it.

Veiled threat: Okay, but if we don't get the project done on time and the boss comes looking for a scapegoat, chances are it's going to be you.

You will: Well, we're all sorry you feel that way. *[Jokingly]* Gee, you better get used to eating lunch alone from now on, Paula. But seriously, think about updating your resumé, because if this project sinks because of you, you may need it.

- **Timing:** Talk to her while the project is still in progress, not after it's completed. Make sure the two of you are alone. After lunch is always a good time to talk to a peer, since satiated people tend to be in a decent mood. Avoid approaching her when she's on her way out the door at the end of the day; what you say will go in one ear and out the other.

- **Behavior:** Start out politely, appealing to her sense of fairness. If she refuses to even consider what you're saying, it's okay to throw a touch of annoyance into the mix. Don't be afraid of using a veiled threat, either. Whatever you do, don't beg or yell.

ADAPTATIONS

This script can be modified to:

- Request a friend, relative, or spouse to pull their weight on a joint project, whether it's planning a party or keeping a house clean.

KEY POINTS

- Get the backing of your coworkers before talking to her.
- Talk to her while the project is still under way.
- If applicable, be able to provide concrete examples of how her unwillingness to put in extra time has adversely affected the department.
- Appeal to her sense of fairness, pointing out she's the only person in the department who isn't coming in early or staying late.
- If that fails, make her feel guilty for not pulling her weight like everyone else.
- Point out the benefits of coming in early and/or staying late, such as the potential for a bonus, easing the work burden for everyone, and getting the project done that much faster.
- Point out the drawbacks of her behavior, such as alienating her coworkers.
- If you must, threaten her with telling the boss she's to blame should the project not be finished on time.
- Don't beg, cajole, or threaten.
- Let a touch of anger show if necessary, but don't yell or belittle.

Asking a Peer to Improve the Quality of His Work

STRATEGY

Most of us get along swimmingly with our coworkers, which is why it can be so disconcerting when the quality of a peer's work begins to slide. Where once the two of you functioned like a well-oiled machine, you now find that your job is harder to do either because (1) you're trying to compensate for his sloppiness, laziness, or inattentiveness or (2) the caliber of your work is slipping because it's contingent on the quality of his. The goal of this lifescript is getting a peer to improve the quality of his work without harming your professional relationship and/or coming across as holier-than-thou. Your first gambit will be to appeal to his sense of fairness, pointing out that it isn't right that you should suffer because he's turning out subpar work. That means you'll need to be able to prove his work "isn't what it used to be," as well as show how it's affecting you. If, after receiving concrete evidence of his lackluster performance, he still insists he's the best worker bee on the planet, resort to your most powerful gambit: making a superior aware that the inferior quality of his work is having a deleterious effect on yours.

TACTICS

- **Attitude:** Even if you're ready to blow a gasket, your attitude should be one of asking for help. Never resort to begging, yelling, or threats. If you can't kill him with kindness, you could turn the heat up a notch and show how ticked off you are—again, without blowing up. Just be aware that in showing any annoyance, you could alienate him. Cool, calm, and collected always work best.

- **Preparation:** Before you confront him and tell him in the nicest way possible that his work leaves a lot to be desired, you need evidence that demonstrates not only that this is true but also that the inferior quality of his work is making it hard for you to

68. Asking a Peer to Improve the Quality of His Work

Icebreaker: Walt, have you got a minute? I need to talk to you. You know I really enjoy working with you. But lately, the research you've been giving me has had some major holes in it, and it's really made it hard for me to turn in reports up to the boss's standards. I was wondering, could you possibly kick up the level of your work a bit?

Denial: *What are you talking about? My work is fine.*

Anger: *No offense, but who died and made you boss? My work is fine.*

Admission of guilt: *I'm sorry, Phil, but I've got a lot on my mind right now. I'm doing the best I can.*

Confront denial: I'm talking about the fact that the info you gave me for the Harrison report was two years out of date. If I didn't depend on you, it wouldn't matter to me. But I do depend on you, and it kind of bothers me that my work now looks bad because you're cutting corners. It's not fair.

Deflect anger: I'm not trying to be the boss, and God knows I never claimed to be perfect. All I'm asking is that you give 100 percent like you always did in the past, so I'm not stuck doing double time to make things right. Think how you'd feel if you were in my shoes.

Accept apology: I hear you. I know how hard it can be to keep your mind on work when there are a lot of outside distractions. But it would really mean a lot to me if you'd try. Besides, throwing yourself into work might even make you feel better.

Still defensive: *Are you threatening me?*

Admits guilt: *I know, I know, you're right. What do you need me to do?*

Agrees to try: *Hmmm, maybe you're right. I'll give it a try.*

Response to threat: No. But you should probably know that if you keep handing me research that's half-baked and makes extra work for me, I'm going to have to tell the boss.

Still in denial: *See if I care.*

Tell him your needs: I need you to get the absolute latest info on the Jefferson account. Can you handle that?

Your final word: I'm sorry you feel that way. I was hoping we could resolve this and get back to being a great team like we once were. I see now I'll have to look out for myself.

Express thanks: Thanks. I really appreciate it.

Accepts challenge: *I'll give it my best shot.*

maintain your own high standards. Any concrete examples you can point to will be useful, but written work showing when he hits his marks and when he doesn't is the most powerful.

- **Timing:** If you can, try talking to him before the two of you embark on another project together or while you're in the midst of one. Speak with him alone, preferably not first thing in the morning or when he's dashing out the door at the end of the day. Behind closed doors right after lunch is ideal.

- **Behavior:** You might be feeling virtuous because your work isn't inferior—at least, it wasn't until *he* started fouling you up—but whatever you do, don't come across that way. Act as if he's a valued colleague whose help you need. If push comes to shove, make it clear—politely, of course—that you're not going to let him drag you down with him.

ADAPTATIONS

This script can be modified to:

- Ask a child to improve the quality of his housework.
- Ask a spouse to improve the quality of his housework.
- Ask a partner to improve the quality of his work.

KEY POINTS

- Appeal to his sense of fairness, making it clear that his sloppy and/or subpar work is having a direct effect on your work.
- Be able to provide concrete evidence of above.
- If asking him to improve fails, threaten to tell a superior what's going on.
- Don't beg, yell, or belittle.
- Don't lose your temper.
- Approach him as a valued colleague to whom you're appealing for help.
- Speak with him alone, preferably after lunch.
- Be calm and polite no matter how abusive, upset, or defensive he might become.

Asking a Peer to Stop Gossiping

69

STRATEGY

When you're the subject of gossip, your natural instinct might be to lash out at the person you suspect is playing Gossip Columnist and give her a piece of your mind. Don't. The goal of this script is to help you convey your displeasure with her tongue wagging—and to get her to stop—without a direct accusation. This is important, since (1) you could be accusing her falsely; (2) confrontation could disrupt your work relationship; or (3) you could cause the other person, if spiteful, to spread even more falsehoods designed to damage your reputation, both personal and professional. For this lifescript to work, you can't let on you know you're talking to a gossip. Instead, approach the gossiper as if you're confiding in her about what has taken place.

TACTICS

- **Attitude:** Depending on what has been said, you might be furious, wounded, or worried. Don't let it show. Instead, act calm. Your attitude should be one of disbelief at the gossiper's unprofessional behavior, tempered with annoyance at being the subject of office chatter.
- **Preparation:** Gossip spreads geometrically; while it usually springs from one source, before long lots of folks are telling the same tale. For that reason, it's crucial you be as sure as you can you're dealing with the original perpetrator. Ask around. Eventually, you'll be able to deduce who the motormouth is.
- **Timing:** Enticing as it might be to imagine your talk taking place in full view of the whole company in the employee cafeteria, this discussion should take place in private. If you must, come in early to catch her alone or ask her to stay after work for a few minutes. If either of you have your own office, do it there, preferably after lunch, when people are usually in a good mood. An empty rest room can work too, although you risk interruption. If you must, talk to her quietly in the hall.

69. Asking a Peer to Stop Gossiping

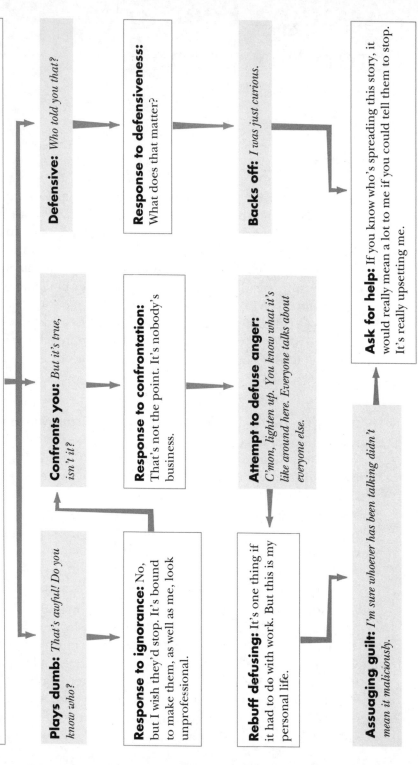

Icebreaker: Tina, can I talk to you? I'm so upset. Someone is going around telling everyone I'm dating Drew. Can you believe that?

Defensive: *Who told you that?*

Response to defensiveness: What does that matter?

Backs off: *I was just curious.*

Plays dumb: *That's awful! Do you know who?*

Confronts you: *But it's true, isn't it?*

Response to ignorance: No, but I wish they'd stop. It's bound to make them, as well as me, look unprofessional.

Response to confrontation: That's not the point. It's nobody's business.

Attempt to defuse anger: *C'mon, lighten up. You know what it's like around here. Everyone talks about everyone else.*

Rebuff defusing: It's one thing if it had to do with work. But this is my personal life.

Assuaging guilt: *I'm sure whoever has been talking didn't mean it maliciously.*

Ask for help: If you know who's spreading this story, it would really mean a lot to me if you could tell them to stop. It's really upsetting me.

- **Behavior:** Remaining calm throughout, approach her as if you're troubled and seeking her advice. Segue into disbelief followed by mild indignation. Finally, ask her to help you squash the gossip. Don't say or do anything that tips your hand and makes it obvious you know it's she, whether by smirking, glaring, or being sarcastic.

ADAPTATIONS

This script can be modified to:

- Nip gossiping by a friend or family member in the bud.
- Derail gossiping about a friend or coworker.

KEY POINTS

- Avoid direct confrontation.
- Make sure you've got the right person.
- Pretend you're confiding about how upset you are.
- Express your anger and disgust at the gossiper's unprofessional behavior.
- Finish by asking for her help in curbing the gossip, reiterating your distress.
- Keep calm, never letting on you're fully aware she is the guilty party.
- Don't smirk, glare, or use sarcasm.
- Have the discussion in private, if possible.

Correcting a
Peer's Mistakes

70

STRATEGY

In the workplace, handling the mistakes of a fellow worker requires a delicate touch. You need to deliver your message strongly enough so your help is heard and understood but subtly enough so it doesn't undermine operations or create resentment. The secret is to present yourself as a friend, someone who has been through the situation before and can help. Outline the nature of the mistake and why it causes others problems, but affirm your confidence in your peer's abilities. If your comments are received favorably, suggest ways to correct the mistakes, then offer to be available for questions and help. If your peer disagrees with your perception or gets angry, remain calm, but restate your prior comments and how the mistakes interfere with efficiency. He must be made to understand that either he corrects his mistakes or you'll go over his head.

TACTICS

- **Attitude:** Think of yourself as a friend, even a mentor, someone who has been where this person is and can help. Be prepared to accept a little anger or frustration—criticism is never an easy pill to swallow, especially when given by a peer.
- **Preparation:** Have examples in mind so you can stay on the topic and give detailed and accurate information. Also, have specific suggestions ready to offer.
- **Timing:** Meet as soon as possible after the offense occurs so it's fresh in both your minds. Do it when you're alone, but don't make it seem like an ambush.
- **Behavior:** Remember, you're both in the same boat, so you want to help, not hurt. Lead off empathetically. If that doesn't work, make it clear you need to maintain a good, positive working relationship, so correcting each other's mistakes is essential.

70. Correcting a Peer's Mistakes

Icebreaker: Jeez, isn't the filing system confusing? It has taken me ages to get it straight. It totally defies logic—you'd think accounts would be filed under clients' names, but they're kept under product. Maybe that's why some of your account files have been popping up in weird places. I lost half a day searching for one of them.

Accepts criticism: *You had trouble with it too? That's good to know. I'm trying really hard to get the hang of it. I didn't realize I was causing so much confusion. I'll have to think twice before I file!*

Denies the problem: *What are you talking about? No one else said anything to me. I'm pretty careful about where I put my files. Maybe you should check with everyone in the department— could be someone else is confused.*

Reiterate your point: Don't you handle the Joyce and O'Casey accounts? You wouldn't believe where I found them, and it's not the first time. You know what I do? I think about their product as I go for their file.

Gets angry: *My files? No way! Who are you to get on my back about filing problems? I know what I am doing. You do your work, and I'll do mine. Anyway, nobody's perfect.*

Defuse the anger: Hey, relax. I told you, I only figured out the system a short time ago myself. Someone mentioned it to me at the time, and I realized my mistakes were slowing the whole office down. I'm not trying to come down on you, just letting you know we all have to be really careful.

Gets past denial: *Yeah, they're mine. Did I put them in the wrong place again? I'm kind of glad you brought this up—I've been embarrassed I was having so much trouble with the system. I'll try to be more careful next time.*

Still denies the problem: *Sure, those are my account files, but I'm not the only one who ever pulls them. Someone else in the department might have moved them, not me.*

Remains angry: *I really can't believe you're pulling rank on me. You really think you run this department, don't you? Well, I already have one boss, and that's quite enough. Worry about your own performance, not mine.*

Gets past the anger: *I'm sorry I snapped. I'm on deadline for this proposal, and the pressure is really on. Thanks for the warning.*

Get tough: Okay. I just tried to help. You need to realize that when you misplace files, it throws everyone else off. I'd hate to do it, but if things don't get better, I'll have to speak to Vincent and see if he can help.

Offer to help: Don't sweat it. If you have any questions, feel free to ask me. Like I said, it can get pretty confusing, and we all have enough to do without worrying about filing, too.

ADAPTATIONS

This script can be modified to:

- Correct a friend, acquaintance, or fellow volunteer whose mistakes are affecting your efforts.

KEY POINTS

- Soften initial criticism by being empathetic, sharing your understanding of the problem.
- If your criticism isn't accepted, show your evidence without becoming defensive or angry yourself. Reaffirm your empathy and understanding, but remain firm.
- If your criticism meets with anger, remain calm, then reassure that you're only trying to help.
- If he accepts your criticism, reassert your desire to help anytime.
- If anger and/or denial continue, make it clear you were trying to help, but that resistance could call for further action, since mistakes affect productivity.
- Remember the goal is a successful, productive, stress-free work environment. You don't want to alienate or polarize, but you do want to be able to get your work done efficiently.

Refusing to Lie
for a Peer

71

STRATEGY

When a peer asks you to lie, chances are it's to avoid getting in hot water with a superior for something she did or didn't do. Since you don't want to get a reputation as a liar or appear to be a partner in crime—both of which could jeopardize *your* job—the goal of this script is to make clear to your peer that you won't lie without sounding as condescending or holier-than-thou. Basically, you're walking a tightrope between maintaining good relations with your coworker and your superior. If this is the first time the coworker has asked for your "help," you can lean a little to her side of the tightrope. If this is clearly a habitual problem, lean toward your superior's side. But if this incident falls somewhere between unique and habitual, you'll have to try to strike a balance.

TACTICS

- **Attitude:** Whether it's the first time or the fiftieth she's asking you to cover for her, stand firm. Don't lose your temper or belittle her for screwing up. If it's the first time she has come to you, tell her you'll exaggerate the reasons for her behavior when relating the story to the boss and leave it at that. If she appears to be falling into a pattern of bad behavior and subsequently asking you to lie, calmly point out she'd better make an effort to change her behavior. If she's clearly a habitual offender, despite your prior warnings to her, feel free to bluntly convey your annoyance, saying in no uncertain terms that lying is out of the question.

- **Preparation:** There's no way to prepare for this situation, other than realizing that if you're there when she loses it, chances are she's going to ask your help in covering her butt.

71. Refusing to Lie for a Peer

Asks you to lie: *Bonnie, I need your help. You know that obnoxious woman I just lost my temper with? Well, she said she's going to complain to the boss that I was rude to her. If she comes to you and asks what happened, will you tell her that woman's full of it?*

Response to habitual behavior: No way. You've been warned about this before, Beth. The boss isn't stupid. She'll know I'm lying for you and then we'll both be in trouble. Forget it.

Becoming a pattern: If she asks, I won't deny the customer was a nightmare. In the meantime, you better get a grip, Beth. This is happening way too much. We're not going to be able to keep covering for you.

Unique behavior: I'll definitely let her know the customer was giving you a hard time.

Upset: *But I would do it for you!*

Catches implication: *But what if she asks how I behaved?*

Doesn't catch implication: *Thanks.*

Not the issue: That's not the issue. The issue is the way you chewed her out, which was entirely unprofessional.

Will tell truth: Then I'll tell her the truth. The customer was obnoxious, but let's face it, you were pretty rude to her.

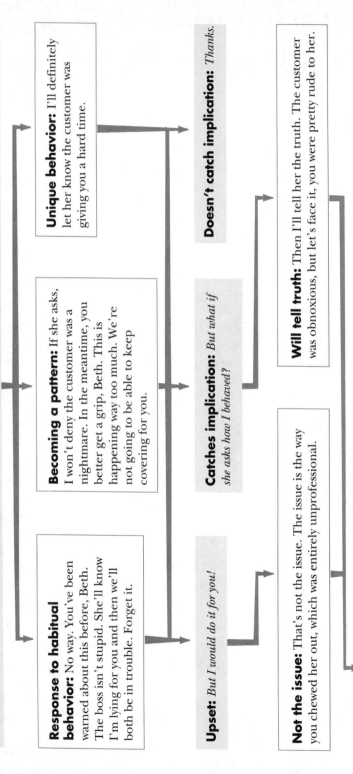

Defends herself: *But you saw what she was like!*

That's no excuse: You're right. But you know the rule: the customer is always right.

Final appeal: *So you're not going to help me?*

Final advice: I'll help you, but I'm not going to lie for you. My advice is that you better get your act together when it comes to dealing with the customers. If you don't, you might lose your job.

- **Timing:** You can't control the timing of her approach, but you can control the timing of your response. If she asks you to lie for her in front of customers, tell her you'll discuss it later. If she asks you in front of other coworkers, deal with it immediately. That will send a clear message to all present that you don't consider lying for peers part of your job description.
- **Behavior:** Even if your track record is spotless, avoid pointing this out, as you'll sound pompous and condescending. Instead, be firm but friendly, even if she becomes increasingly distressed by your unwillingness to "help."

ADAPTATIONS

This script can be modified to:

- Respond to a request to lie in any situation that may jeopardize a personal or business relationship.

KEY POINTS

- Be firm, but friendly, in your refusal to lie.
- Don't lose your temper or humiliate the other person.
- Avoid blowing your own horn.
- If it's the first time she asks, offer gentle corrections.
- If it has happened before, warn her this behavior could get her into trouble and advise her to change.
- If the behavior is habitual, tell her you refuse to compromise your credibility and risk your job for her.
- Respond to a request immediately if coworkers are present.
- Postpone the conversation if you're approached in front of clients or customers.

72

Asking a Peer to Clean Up Her Work Area

STRATEGY

You probably won't care if the gal in the next cubicle is the reincarnation of Oscar Madison until you have a hard time finding something you need in her workspace; her mess starts spreading into communal or your own workspace; or your superior starts referring to your whole department as "the pit." The goal of this script is to get your coworker to clean up her work area as soon as it affects either your reputation or your ability to do your job. Without calling her a slob—at least not to her face—you need to make it clear that if she doesn't tidy up and provide easy access to material others need, you'll be forced to blow the whistle. Avoid making comparisons or offering put-downs. If she acknowledges her desk is a mess, offer to help. If she gets defensive, point out how the six-foot-high piles of files and faxes reflect badly on the whole department. If she insists that only she needs to know where everything is, calmly bring to her attention the information she keeps that you require as well, and subtly threaten a trip to your superior if she doesn't get her act together. If she says she can't stand the thought of your nosing through her things, tell her all she needs to do is separate work items from personal items, and the problem is solved.

TACTICS

- **Attitude:** Most people aren't deliberately messy. A few are, however. They believe that making things difficult for others to find makes them indispensable. But even if you think this description fits your coworker, you can't call her on it without causing a major upset. Your attitude should always be one of offering friendly advice.
- **Preparation:** Your request needs to be backed up with a concrete example of how her sloppiness has negatively affected you, whether it was a disparaging comment made by management or

72. Asking a Peer to Clean Up Her Work Area

Icebreaker: Thelma, I need to speak with you. You know the report we've been working on? Well, Nicolas asked to see it on Friday when you were out. It took me twenty minutes just to find it under all that stuff you have piled on your desk. I really think you need to clean up your work area.

Agrees: *Geez, Rachel, I'm sorry. I know my office looks like a bomb hit it, but you know how busy it's been around here. I haven't had time to clean up.*

Offer to help: Things have been crazy around here, I agree. But if you need some help getting organized, I'm here. Between the two of us, it wouldn't take long.

Admits paranoia: *No offense, Rachel, but I hate the thought of anyone going through my things when I'm not here.*

Defensive: *Are you calling me a slob?*

Not an attack: Of course not. But Nicolas walked through here the other day, saw your desk, and called the department a "pigsty."

Oblivious: *I know where everything is.*

We work together: Yes, but I don't. And since we work together on so many things, I really need to be able to find things in your office quickly.

Maintains privacy: *If you need to know where things are, just ask. You can even call me at home.*

Stress need for access: Suppose you're on vacation or out of the office? What are we supposed to do then?

Offer solution: Well, if you organized your materials so work and personal items were separated, you wouldn't have to worry about that. Why don't you try it?

Comes around: *Okay. I'll try to be more organized.*

Still obstinate: *You're making a big deal out of nothing.*

Veiled threat: It *is* a big deal. Margaret asked me what took me so long. I didn't tell her I had trouble finding the report because your office is a nightmare. But I really think you need to get organized.

your being late to a meeting because you couldn't find the sales report that was supposed to be in her out-basket.

- **Timing:** You need to speak with her as soon as possible after something has happened.
- **Behavior:** Don't confront her in front of anyone else in the office. If you do, embarrassment might compel her to make things really difficult for you to find. Don't yell, beg, or belittle. Though you might be tempted to touch things in her workspace to drive your point home, don't—if she's very jealous of her privacy, that could send her over the edge.

ADAPTATIONS

This script can be modified to:

- Help you convince a spouse, roommate, partner, friend, or family member to keep her room, house, or car neater.

KEY POINTS

- Act as if you're giving friendly advice.
- Avoid coming across as superior. Don't put her down.
- Don't touch her things.
- Have a concrete example of how the sloppiness has affected you.
- Speak with her as soon as possible after something has occurred.
- Speak with her in private.
- If she admits her work area is a mess, offer to help her clean it.
- If she challenges you, point out how her messiness makes everyone look bad.
- If she claims only she needs to know where things are, have an example of why that isn't true.
- If she says she doesn't like anyone going through her things, suggest she separate work items from personal items.
- If nothing else works, issue a veiled threat.

Asking a Peer to Turn Down Annoying Music

73

STRATEGY

People have a need to personalize and humanize their work environment. Many employers, eager to get employees to spend as much time as possible at their desks, often bend over backward in allowing self-expression, as long as it doesn't interfere with work or create a poor public image. Most forms of self-expression, such as hanging up artwork or having plants, are benign. But one of these forms that can be problematic is playing music. Playing music in your office isn't a right, it's a privilege, particularly with the option of headphones being readily available. Even so, it makes sense to complain about a peer's music in as diplomatic a manner as possible. The best techniques are to blame a third party or outside force and present the issue as a group, not as an individual, problem. Transparent or not, such gambits can keep a feud from developing. However, if diplomacy doesn't work, you've no choice but to subtly threaten to bring the issue to your superiors.

TACTICS

- **Attitude:** Your ability to do your work effectively outweighs other employees' right to self-expression.
- **Preparation:** Make sure you're not the only person bothered by the music.
- **Timing:** It's best to do this when the music is being played.
- **Behavior:** Hold the conversation in the other party's workspace but as privately as possible.

73. Asking a Peer to Turn Down Annoying Music

Icebreaker: Gary, can you turn it down for a second? Thanks. Aren't the acoustics in here awful? We've been asking the office manager for some help in making it easier for us all to hear, but he keeps putting me off. Would you mind helping out by turning your music down until they get around to fixing the problem?

Open to idea: *Not a problem. I'll turn it right down. I didn't realize you all were having trouble hearing.*

Defends turf: *Listen, I don't know about any acoustic problems you're having. All I know is playing my music is the only thing that gets me through the day here.*

Veiled threat: I can sympathize with you. But this isn't just about me. Your music is making it tough for a lot of us to do our work. We'd rather not bring it up to the office manager. He'd probably see taking your radio away completely as the answer to our complaints about the acoustics.

ADAPTATIONS

This script can be modified to:

- Ask a peer to refrain from cooking or eating certain foods in the office.
- Ask a peer to hold loud personal conversations outside the office.

KEY POINTS

- Blame the problem on the environment, not the music.
- Frame it as a group problem, not your problem.
- Subtly threaten to bring the problem to management if it's not resolved.

Confronting a Chronic Interrupter

74

STRATEGY

Chronic interrupters threaten not only your presentations but your image in the office. After repeated occurrences, the situation will become either comical or embarrassing to the rest of the staff, and the content or import of what you say will be lost. Try to deal with this in private first, even accepting some of the responsibility. If that elicits an apology, leave well enough alone. Denials should be met with examples and a blunter request. Attacks, on the other hand, should be met with a sharp rebuke and even a veiled threat. If the problem crops up again, respond with all the ammo you can muster. Failing to be forceful at that point will guarantee that the problem becomes worse.

TACTICS

- **Attitude:** There's no excuse for rudeness. Still, realize that bending over backward is the best way to stop the behavior. But be prepared to get tough if your sensitivity doesn't work.
- **Preparation:** Have an example in mind in case you're met with denial.
- **Timing:** Bring this up as soon as possible after the incident.
- **Behavior:** Hold this conversation privately in the other party's work area. The more secure his surroundings, the more likely he'll apologize. If it happens again, however, respond immediately and publicly, regardless of where it takes place.

74. Confronting a Chronic Interrupter

Icebreaker: Bob, I have a problem and I need your help. I'm a very deliberate speaker. You, on the other hand, are very exuberant and enthusiastic when you speak. Sometimes when I'm speaking, your energy makes it tough for you to wait for me to finish my points. I appreciate your input, but I need you to give me the time to get my ideas across without interruption. I'll invite comments when I'm done.

Attacks: *Listen, I'm just making important points. Time is money and, to be honest, you take forever to make your points.*

No excuse: I didn't come here to get your input on my presentation style. I simply came here to ask you to stop being rude and interrupting me when I'm speaking. I don't want to have to resort to rudeness in return, but I will if necessary.

Apologizes: *I'm sorry. I know I tend to jump into conversations. I'll try to rein myself in.*

Accept: No damage done. I appreciate your response. I'll try to be more concise in the future as well.

Denial: *What do you mean? I don't interrupt you when you speak.*

Example: Yesterday when I was trying to give my department's quarterly sales figures at the staff meeting, you interrupted me to point out that they were down from last quarter. That was not on point, and to be blunt, it was rude.

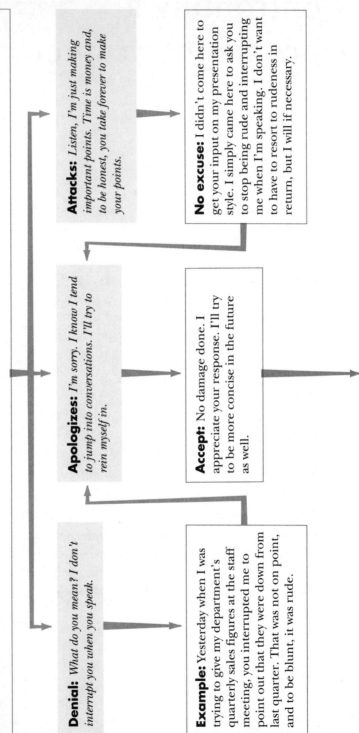

If it happens again

→

Interjection: Bob, please stop. You're interrupting me again. We talked about this earlier. I know this is reflexive with you, but you need to wait until I'm finished.

ADAPTATIONS

This script can be modified to:

- Put an end to any form of repeated public rudeness.

KEY POINTS

- Bring the matter up in private first.
- Cast it as a mutual problem.
- Criticize the timing, not the content.
- Accept apologies graciously.
- Respond bluntly to denials.
- Respond in kind to attacks or to future incidents.

75

Confronting a Peer's Dishonest Behavior

STRATEGY

Confronting a peer's dishonest behavior is more problematic than confronting the same behavior in a subordinate. When you're in a position of authority over someone, it's part of your job to monitor her behavior. With a peer, you're in the uncomfortable position of being a bystander, torn between getting involved and being accused of meddling or ignoring the transgression and being guilty of aiding and abetting. The best strategy is to outwardly assume that this is all a matter of misperception rather than actual malfeasance. You are warning your peer that her actions could be mistaken for dishonest actions by someone who didn't know her as well as you do. Transparent or not, this gambit should be effective enough to at least put the other person on notice and, it is hoped, prevent future problems.

TACTICS

- **Attitude:** Your goal is to stop the behavior without actually accusing your peer of dishonesty. That would only lead to anger or denial.
- **Preparation:** Do your due diligence so it's clear you're not over-reacting.
- **Timing:** Make the approach as soon as you perceive the dishonest behavior. The sooner it is spotted, the less damage will be done.
- **Behavior:** Have this conversation in private in the other person's work area. Be informal but serious. Sit down to talk, but lean forward and speak in a lowered tone of voice.

75. Confronting a Peer's Dishonest Behavior

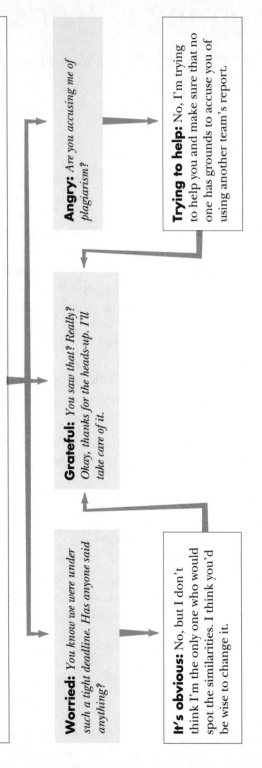

Icebreaker and pitch: Martha, I need to speak with you about the Anderson report you just prepared. I know you would never consciously do anything dishonest, but the way the report is written and presented is strikingly like a report done earlier this year by the Milwaukee team for the McMichael project. Maybe you should revise and rewrite it, and rethink the way you're presenting it, so no one could perceive that it was so similar to the earlier report.

Angry: *Are you accusing me of plagiarism?*

Trying to help: No, I'm trying to help you and make sure that no one has grounds to accuse you of using another team's report.

Grateful: *You saw that? Really? Okay, thanks for the heads-up. I'll take care of it.*

Worried: *You know we were under such a tight deadline. Has anyone said anything?*

It's obvious: No, but I don't think I'm the only one who would spot the similarities. I think you'd be wise to change it.

ADAPTATIONS

This script can be modified to:

- Warn a friend or family member off doing something dishonest.

KEY POINTS

- Stress that you don't question her honesty.
- Describe the problem as one of others' perceptions, not her actions.
- Say you're here to help, not to accuse.
- Note that you're not the only person who might "perceive" things this way.

Confronting a
Pilfering Peer

76

STRATEGY

Floppy discs, toilet paper, rubber bands, file folders, legal pads—when it comes to items people steal from the workplace, the list is endless. The goal of this lifescript is to stop a pilfering peer without coming across as smug, saintly, or a member of the FBI. Caught red-handed and confronted in a *gentle* way (yelling "Up against the wall, sucka" is a bad move), your coworker will either fall to his knees and beg you not to tell the suits; snarl that the very least the company owes him is a case of paper clips, since they pay coolie wages; or minimize his foray into larceny by claiming it's something everyone does. If he's got an iota of conscience and common sense, he'll see the error of his ways (after you point them out to him, of course) and put the goods back voluntarily. But if he doesn't, you need to make it clear that if you catch him stealing again, and you're later asked if you know who made off with the couch from the employees' lounge, you're not going to cover for him.

TACTICS

- **Attitude:** Whether you're shocked by your coworker's stealing from the office or secretly wish you had the guts to do it yourself, your attitude should be calm yet no-nonsense disapproval. Whatever you do, don't come across as morally superior, or you'll have an enemy for life.

- **Preparation:** Unfortunately, there's little you can do to prepare for this discussion, since it's likely to arise spontaneously the minute you come across your pilfering peer in action.

- **Timing:** Confront your peer the minute you catch him in the act—not after or before he strikes again.

76. Confronting a Pilfering Peer

Icebreaker: Tim? I can't help but notice that's a whole case of floppies you're putting in your briefcase. Taking one disc to bring home is one thing, but the big guys are definitely going to notice if a whole case is missing. You sure you want to do that?

Unashamed: *What's the big deal? Everyone does it.*

Rationalizing: *Why the heck should I pay for this when the company pays us slave wages? Besides, they consider this part of our "compensation." They owe me this.*

Frightened: *Oh my God, Dan, please don't tell the boss.*

Appeal to conscience: That's not true. I don't do it. And even if everyone did do it, that still doesn't make it the right or the smart thing to do.

Appeal to rationality: I hear you, and you're right: The pay around here leaves a lot to be desired. But if you're caught, your job could be in jeopardy. And if they find out I knew and covered for you, I could be in trouble, too. Besides, if stuff keeps disappearing, they'll keep using it as an excuse not to give us a raise. I think you should put it back.

Allay his fear: Mum's the word, if you put it back.

Sees the light: *You're right. I'll put it back.*

Now mad at you: *Hey, mind your own business, okay? Who do you think you are, anyway? Mother Teresa?*

Parting words: I'm not joking around. I'm not going to bust you this time. But if it happens again and the boss comes creeping around trying to find out who stole what, I'm not going to cover for you, either.

- **Behavior:** You're not Sherlock Holmes, so avoid behaving like him. Be supremely cool and calm, making your first volley on the light side, if possible. Don't try to wrest the pilfered item from his sticky fingers; similarly, avoid standing there smugly with your arms crossed like a disapproving schoolmarm. On the other hand, maintain eye contact at all times.

ADAPTATIONS

This script can be modified to:

- Confront a pilfering relative, friend, or guest.

KEY POINTS

- Keep your tone light.
- Confront him the minute you come upon him stealing.
- Avoid acting like a member of the FBI.
- Appeal to his conscience. If he doesn't have one, make it clear you won't cover for him if the suits come snooping around wanting to know who has sticky fingers.
- Maintain eye contact.

77

Asking a Peer to Cover for You

STRATEGY

The goal of this script is getting a coworker to cover for you when you have personal business to take care of outside the office but don't want to lose a personal/sick day. First a warning: if you're on probation or have been warned in any way about absenteeism, do not use this script—it's too dangerous. If you ask someone and get turned down, you won't be able to ask someone else without the risk of being discovered. Your only option will be to take time off without pay or use a sick day. The secret to achieving your goal is to encourage an immediate, albeit subtly subconscious, receptivity to your pitch on the part of the listener. You can do that by making her feel important—you're turning to her for help rather than to someone else. Opening with a heartfelt appeal helps, too—after all, no one likes to refuse a request for help. If you're sure she won't gossip, you can be as specific as you please in furnishing the details of your absence. If, on the other hand, you're afraid the word might spread, be as vague as possible, saying only that you have some personal business to attend to. If pressed for more information, say that you prefer not to talk about it. Be aware, however, that a refusal to provide the gory details could lead to a flat-out refusal to help. Consider subtly pointing out how assistance can benefit her, whether it's a promise of reciprocity or a more manageable workload.

TACTICS

- **Attitude:** Your attitude should be one of humility, whether you're asking a good friend or an acquaintance. Opening with a statement like, "I need your help" establishes that tone.

77. Asking a Peer to Cover for You

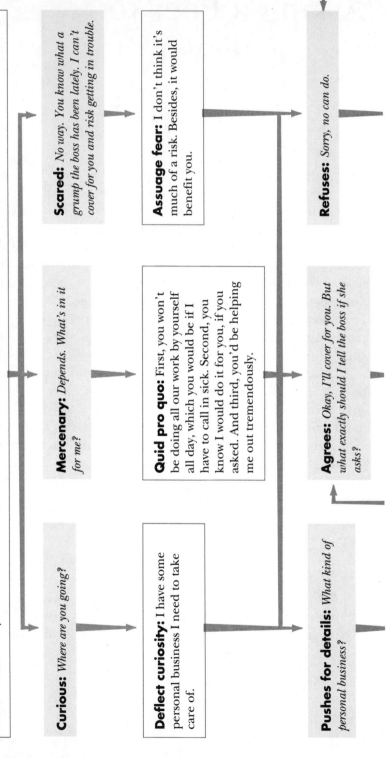

Icebreaker and pitch: Melanie, I need your help. I have to take a few hours off Thursday afternoon. Normally, I would just call in sick, but we're so swamped and I don't want us to fall too far behind because I'm out for a whole day. If the boss asks where I am, could you tell her that I'm *[mention a work-related errand]* and will be back at *[fill in the time]*?

Scared: *No way. You know what a grump the boss has been lately. I can't cover for you and risk getting in trouble.*

Assuage fear: I don't think it's much of a risk. Besides, it would benefit you.

Refuses: *Sorry, no can do.*

Mercenary: *Depends. What's in it for me?*

Quid pro quo: First, you won't be doing all our work by yourself all day, which you would be if I have to call in sick. Second, you know I would do it for you, if you asked. And third, you'd be helping me out tremendously.

Agrees: *Okay, I'll cover for you. But what exactly should I tell the boss if she asks?*

Curious: *Where are you going?*

Deflect curiosity: I have some personal business I need to take care of.

Pushes for details: *What kind of personal business?*

Remain vague: No offense, but I really don't feel comfortable talking about it, since it is a family matter.

Reiterate excuse: Tell her I'm *[work-related errand]* and I'll be back at *[fill in time]*.

Define relationship: Well, at least I now know where we stand.

- **Preparation:** Guesstimate how long you'll be out of the office before approaching your peer. In addition, try to discern her attitude toward using work time to attend to personal business. Some people go strictly by the book and look down on those who bend the rules, whereas others are always glad to help out with any activity that "cheats the suits." Have a backup plan in mind, just in case you find out your first choice isn't apt to go along with you.

- **Timing:** Ask for help at least a few days in advance. That way you'll have time to implement your backup plan, if necessary. After lunch is usually the best time for a private conversation like this.

- **Behavior:** Speak with her alone. Remember, you're asking for a favor, so be humble. Keep cool at all times, even if she's pushing for details. Do not, under any circumstances, break down, beg, threaten, or lose your temper. If, after presenting your case, she *still* turns you down, end with a cool and quiet, "Well, at least I now know where we stand with each other," and walk away.

ADAPTATIONS

This script can be modified to:

- Ask a friend to back up a social excuse.

KEY POINTS

- Open with the line, "I need your help." Be as humble and sincere as possible.
- Let her know how long you think you'll be out of the office.
- If she's a friend whom you trust not to gossip, you can tell her why you'll be out, if you choose.
- If you don't trust her not to gossip, tell her you have personal business you need to take care of and leave it at that.
- If she presses, tell her you don't want to talk about it.
- Demonstrate how she can benefit from helping you.
- If she won't help, end with a cold statement of your perception of the relationship.

78

Asking a Peer to Switch Vacations with You

STRATEGY

In many companies, vacations are spread out so as to minimize their effect on ongoing business. There may come a day when the only way to get the time you want is to switch with a peer who has already reserved that week or weeks. Approach him as soon as you realize you need to switch vacations and be prepared to be flexible. The more notice you give, the better the chance he'll agree, though you may have to alter your ideal plans slightly to make the switch work for both of you. Try to take into account his background and personality. Does the time you're asking for fall on a religious holiday, or is he just religious about spring skiing? If he has chosen to be out of the office when a supervisor or important client is also on vacation, asking him to switch may appear a strategy to outshine him. Having a compelling argument prepared for why you need the time will assuage any such fears. If he can switch but isn't inclined to, be clear that you consider the switch a favor that you'd be pleased to return at a later date. If he still can't or won't capitulate, and if it's truly essential, you can approach your superior with a modified version of this script—just realize that you could be creating an enemy.

TACTICS

- **Attitude:** Depending on the kind of plans he has, you could be asking for a big favor, or it could be no big deal. Be prepared to take no for an answer, but be persistent about wanting the time.
- **Preparation:** Have a compelling list of reasons why you need the time, and be ready to juggle days and times with him. Decide if switching with him is the sole or merely the most expeditious option. Have an alternative plan, in case he can't or won't accommodate you.
- **Timing:** The sooner the better. The more notice he has, the better the chance he'll be willing and able to switch.

78. Asking a Peer to Switch Vacations with You

Confirm your information: Jeff, are you still planning to take your vacation the last week of August?

Information confirmed: *Yes.*

Information faulty: *No. I changed that yesterday. My wife couldn't get free that week.*

Ask for switch: I'm scheduled for the third week. Would it be possible for you to switch with me?

Agrees to switch #1: *Sure. In fact the third week is better for me.*

On the fence #1: *Why do you ask?*

Make it official: Great. Let's call Joe and give him the new dates for each of us.

Make your case: I just found a beach cottage I can rent for a song, but it has to be that week.

Declines switch #1: *Sorry. Can't. We're driving my son to college that weekend.*

Offer to juggle days: I could be back the Friday before that weekend, if you could take the following week off instead.

Agrees to switch #2: *Sure, I could accommodate that.*

Declines switch #2: *Sorry. I've got things planned all week leading up to the weekend.*

On the fence #2: *Well, I don't know. I usually watch the U.S. Open on television all that week.*

Agrees to switch #3: *Well, I guess if it would mean that much to you, why not?*

Emphasize importance: You'd sure be doing me a favor if you could switch.

Declines switch #3: *Sorry. I just can't do it.*

Thanks anyway: Well, thanks anyway. If your plans change, please let me know.

- **Behavior:** Be positive and upbeat. Enthusiasm for your plans *and* his will help bolster esprit de corps and encourage him to make the switch.

ADAPTATIONS

This script can be modified to:

- Ask a peer to switch days off.
- Ask a peer to switch assignments with you.
- Ask a superior to change your vacation time.

KEY POINTS

- The more notice you give, the better the chance he'll agree.
- Be flexible and prepared to juggle days with him.
- Make your plans sound as compelling and necessary as possible.
- Be polite and positive. You're asking for a favor, but it isn't necessarily a big one.

79

Telling a Peer Her Job May Be in Danger

STRATEGY

If you've learned, from either a conversation with a superior or loose talk around the office, that one of your peers may be terminated, you may want to let her know while there's still a chance for her to save her job. Your goal should be to encourage her to make a candid self-assessment and once she has hit on areas management finds problematic, to suggest simple, effective changes to her work habits. Depending on your relationship and how bad things are, you might also encourage her to start looking for another job. Remember, while some people have a sixth sense for when their tenure at a company is shaky, others don't. If she isn't getting the hint or simply doesn't want your advice, you're better off leaving her be. Avoid being too explicit or naming your source so as not to endanger your own job.

TACTICS

- **Attitude:** Sure you're doing her a favor, but your primary concern has to be the welfare of the company. Tell her what you think she needs to know to remedy the situation and offer to help in any way you can. But remember, it's up to her to make the changes or move on.

- **Preparation:** Have a couple of her key performance issues in mind and a couple of simple solutions to offer. Realize that personality and corporate culture are sometimes hard to reconcile, so stick to improvements she can realistically accomplish.

- **Timing:** Downtime is the best time to approach your peer as a friend. Arrange to talk outside the office so your conversation will not be overheard, and at the end of the week so she'll have the weekend to cool down and decide how best to alter her performance or redraft her resume.

- **Behavior:** Be friendly and easygoing but earnest about the points for improvement you've outlined. You don't need to put the fear of God into her, but you do want her to take you seriously.

79. Telling a Peer Her Job May Be in Danger

Icebreaker: I asked for this chance to talk because I think your job may be in danger.

Receptive: *Yeah, I have been getting the cold shoulder a lot in meetings.*

Wants to blame someone: *Who told you that? I'll wring her neck!*

Defensive: *You're crazy. I do a great job and everybody likes me.*

Emphasize your respect: I think you're a valuable asset to this company, and I want to help you keep your job.

Decline to name source: It isn't something or someone in specific, it's just a sense I've gotten.

Don't back down: No, I'm not crazy. From what I've heard, you should consider making changes to your work habits or start looking elsewhere for a job.

Encourage self-evaluation: Can you think of anything you could do to improve your performance?

Offers wrong answer: *Well, sometimes I fall asleep at my desk after lunch.*

Offers correct answer: *Well, I have a hard time getting assignments done on time.*

Declines advice: *Whatever. You're paranoid. If they fire me, they fire me.*

Accepts advice: *Thanks for the good advice.*

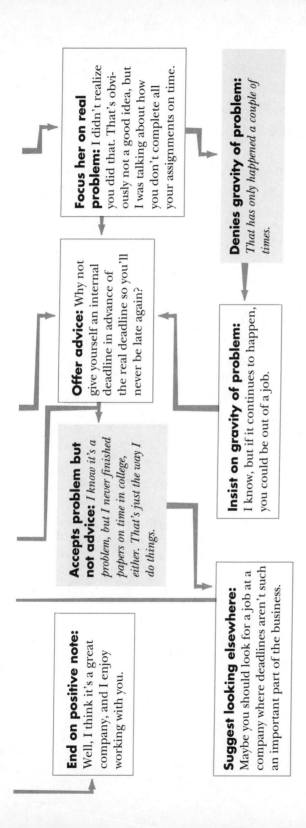

Focus her on real problem: I didn't realize you did that. That's obviously not a good idea, but I was talking about how you don't complete all your assignments on time.

Denies gravity of problem: *That has only happened a couple of times.*

Offer advice: Why not give yourself an internal deadline in advance of the real deadline so you'll never be late again?

Accepts problem but not advice: *I know it's a problem, but I never finished papers on time in college, either. That's just the way I do things.*

Insist on gravity of problem: I know, but if it continues to happen, you could be out of a job.

End on positive note: Well, I think it's a great company, and I enjoy working with you.

Suggest looking elsewhere: Maybe you should look for a job at a company where deadlines aren't such an important part of the business.

ADAPTATIONS

This script can be modified to:

- Tell a peer to shape up at the request of a superior.
- Break bad news so as to encourage action through strategic planning.
- Encourage teamwork to improve a project or department.

KEY POINTS

- Focus on ways she can improve, not what she has already done wrong.
- Decline to name your information source; remain focused on performance, not politics.
- Say what you have to quickly and don't be swayed to say it another time.
- Listen carefully to her self-assessment. If you decide to, you can advocate her side to management and assure them steps are being taken to improve the situation.

Helping a Peer Set More Realistic Goals

80

STRATEGY

Faulting an ambitious coworker isn't justified—unless, of course, in his quest to climb the corporate ladder in record time, he has taken on so much additional work he has let his basic responsibilities slide, leaving the rest of you to pick up the slack. The goal of this lifescript is getting a peer to keep up his basic responsibilities without damping his enthusiasm for more. Begin by telling him how much you and the rest of the staff admire his dedication and zeal. Then, gently point out how in taking on so many extraneous projects, he hasn't been paying attention to the work at hand, resulting in the rest of you having to cover for him. Ask that he rededicate himself to his basic responsibilities. He will admit he hasn't been paying much attention to his basic work; deny he has let things slide while playing the eager beaver; accuse you of being jealous; or accuse you of being lazy. Whatever his response, you'll need to provide proof you and the rest of the staff have been covering for him while he has been scheming to land a corner office by age twenty-five. If push comes to shove, let him know you're all "mad as hell, and you're not going to take it anymore."

TACTICS

- **Attitude:** Even if his incessant brownnosing and volunteering for extra work makes you gag, your attitude should be one of appeal. Whatever you do, don't put him down or overtly threaten or undermine him. Remain calm and in control at all times.
- **Preparation:** Talk to your peers and make sure they, too, are feeling resentful of carrying the ball for this guy as he attempts to score brownie points. Once that's confirmed, tell them you plan on having a friendly chat with the gentleman in question, and get their assurance they'll back you up if need be. Concrete examples are crucial.

80. Helping a Peer Set More Realistic Goals

Icebreaker: Felix, have you got a minute? I, along with the rest of the department, just wanted you to know that your dedication and enthusiasm lately have really been inspiring. Heck, we're having a hard time keeping up with you! But we've got a slight problem: you've piled so much extra work on your plate that you haven't been paying as much attention to your regular work. The rest of us have been forced to pick up the slack. Maybe you should think about refocusing on your core responsibilities a bit more before taking on anything new.

Thinks you're jealous: *Gimme a break. You're just jealous. You see me taking on all this extra work, and you're afraid it's going to make you look bad.*

No jealousy: I'm not in competition with you, Felix, and neither is anyone else in the department.

Thinks you're incompetent: *Hey, pal, I don't need to slow down. The rest of you need to speed up.*

No incompetence: The rest of the department may not be as ambitious as you, but I don't think you could ever accuse any of us of not being hardworking.

He's clueless: *What are you talking about? The boss hasn't said a thing to me about the quality of my work not being up to snuff.*

Open your eyes: That's because the rest of us have been carrying the ball for you. Remember that report Jerry asked you to write? You were so busy working on that extra project for Mike, you left out major portions of information that were vital. The rest of us had to scramble around piecing things together before we gave it to him.

Your pitch: Look, Felix, there's nothing wrong with dreaming big and wanting to get ahead. But that's never going to happen unless you set realistic goals and pay attention to your basic responsibilities. You need to have a solid foundation to rest your reputation on. Without that, you're just building castles in the air that are bound to come crashing down at some point.

Hears threat: *What's this "crashing down" garbage? Are you threatening me?*

Sees the light: *You're right, Alex. I've been so obsessed with getting ahead, I've let my regular work slide. Thanks for pointing it out to me. I'll definitely work on getting my priorities straight from here on in.*

Final response: Of course I'm not threatening you. But none of us appreciate, nor will we continue, picking up the slack caused by your overreaching ambition. *[Walk out.]*

- **Timing:** Talk to him alone, behind closed doors, preferably after lunch when he should be in a good mood or when he should be getting down to core tasks.
- **Behavior:** Initially, behave as if you admire the person for working so hard. From there, act as if you're appealing to the person's sense of fairness and rationality. If that fails, make it abundantly clear—without getting nasty—that you and the rest of your cohorts are in no way, shape, or form going to serve as his stepping-stones.

ADAPTATIONS

This script can be modified to:

- Ask a spouse, partner, child, or sibling to stop pursuing so many extracurricular activities.

KEY POINTS

- Flattery rarely fails. Open the conversation by saying how much you and your colleagues admire his dedication.
- Inform him in delicate terms that his enthusiasm to get ahead has resulted in the rest of you picking up his slack.
- Be able to provide evidence of doing this.
- Ask him to please be fair to the rest of you and refocus on his core responsibilities.
- If this fails, make it clear you and the rest of your peers won't cover for him anymore.
- Remain calm at all times.
- Speak with him alone, preferably after lunch or at a time when he should be focusing on his core responsibilities.

81

Asking the Information Technology Department to Be More Patient with Your Staff

STRATEGY

One of the great paradoxes of the information age is that those in an organization with the most knowledge of technology are often also those equipped with the least patience and skill at explaining the technology to others. In addition, IT departments are as overworked and understaffed as everyone else. Invariably their priority is getting the technology in place, not getting the users comfortable with the technology. Commiserating may be enough to get the added help you need. But if it isn't, you'll need to express your willingness to go over the IT department's head and hope that you won't have to criticize him too much in the process.

TACTICS

- **Attitude:** Try diplomacy but don't waste too much time on the effort. This is important and pressing.
- **Preparation:** Check to ensure that this is a department-wide problem, not just a single vocal individual who'd be better served by individualized education.
- **Timing:** If possible, do this before the initial training period has ended. It is easier to extend the effort than to relaunch one.
- **Behavior:** Stop by the other person's office to have the conversation. That shows your respect for his position. But sit down without waiting to be asked to subtly demonstrate your equality. When you ask who you need to speak with upstairs, stand up as if to leave.

81. Asking the Information Technology Department to Be More Patient with Your Staff

Icebreaker and pitch: I can't imagine how tough your job is, and I hate to add to your burden, but I have a problem and I need your help with it. I'd personally appreciate it if you or one of your staffers could do some more hand-holding with my staff over this transition to the new operating system. I know it may not seem like a big transition to people with technical expertise, but to a bunch of salespeople it's a huge transition.

Annoyed: *We've only been allocated one week to transition each department and we've already exhausted that with your group. I just don't have the time or the people to go through it all again. We've got deadlines too, you know.*

I'll go upstairs: I realize you have a limited amount of time and resources. Tell me who I need to speak with upstairs about getting some additional time from you for my department.

Readily agrees: *You're right, it's a tough job, but that's what we're paid to do. It won't be a problem. I'll have Carol come over tomorrow. She's very good at taking newbies by the hand through*

Offers up name: *Linda Jones is the VP who's been riding hard on the operating system transition.*

Issue threat: I'll speak with her as soon as possible, and either she or I will get back to you. Don't worry, I'll try not to put you in a bad light.

Backs off: *Before you go upstairs, let me see what I can do. Perhaps I can squeeze a few more days of training out of the schedule. Finance seems to be ahead of pace so maybe I can cut it from their allocation.*

ADAPTATIONS

This script can be modified to:

- Get extra care or help for a family member or friend from a teacher or health-care worker.

KEY POINTS

- Express sympathy with the IT department's mission and burden.
- Blame problems on your staff's technophobia rather than on IT's incompetence.
- Express willingness to go over the IT department's head if necessary.
- Subtly note that you'll "try" not to portray him poorly.

82

Asking a Peer to Remove You from Her Mailing List

STRATEGY

E-mail has quickly evolved from innovation to vital tool to nuisance. The ease with which newsletters can be drafted and the simplicity of adding recipients to the mailing list has led to e-mail overload. It's not unusual to receive daily summaries of how the T-ball team of the daughter of a business associate is doing. Explaining how inane or inappropriate such communication is will only cause animosity. The best way to get off the mailing list without getting on an enemies list is to blame the nature of e-mail itself. Explain how deluged you've become and note that you're no longer going to be viewing the messages yourself. If this isn't enough for your point to sink in, gently note that the e-mails will be filtered out in the future.

TACTICS

- **Attitude:** This is a big enough problem to do something about but not so big that you need to make yourself an enemy.
- **Preparation:** Change your e-mail procedures prior to the conversation so you can present it as a done deal.
- **Timing:** Do this soon after receiving the most recent missive.
- **Behavior:** Stop by the other person's office to let her know what is happening. Don't make it a big deal. This is one conversation best held while you're leaning in the doorway on the way to the restroom or water fountain.

82. Asking a Peer to Remove You from Her Mailing List

Icebreaker and pitch: Cindy, I've changed my office procedures and I need to explain them to you. I've been getting deluged by e-mail so I'm now having my assistant, Daniel, go through all my e-mail and reduce it to only the essentials before forwarding it on to me. You probably should remove my e-mail address from your personal mailing list. In the future if you have something personal or vital to speak with me about you should just contact me by telephone.

Gets message: *I'll take you off the list right away. I know how easy it is to get overwhelmed with e-mail. Let me know how it goes. Perhaps I'll implement the same procedure.*

Doesn't get message: *That's okay. I don't mind if Daniel sees my mailing.*

It will be trashed: Confidentiality wasn't my only concern. I was also trying to cut down on Daniel's work-load. I'll just have him filter out the messages from now on. As I mentioned, if you need to speak with me, just call.

ADAPTATIONS

This script can be modified to:

- Ask someone to stop sending you a holiday card or newsletter.

KEY POINTS

- Blame the nature of e-mail in general, not the specific content of the messages.
- Raise a red flag over lack of confidentiality.
- Offer alternative means of personal contact.
- If confidentiality isn't sufficient, blame workload.
- Directly state the messages will be filtered out in the future.

83

Asking a Peer to Treat Your Staff with More Respect

STRATEGY

Every office has a manager who thinks he can tease or boss around everyone in the company of a lower rank, regardless of to whom they actually report. Sometimes the staffer is able to handle the situation on his own. But there are times when an abrasive manager confronts a sensitive subordinate and trouble ensues. In order to maintain the chain of command, as well as the respect of your own staff, you need to address these problems. Whether you learn of the situation third-hand or are approached by the staff person, keep the junior employee out of the discussion. This is a meeting of equals. Start by rationalizing the problem by characterizing it as an attempt at humor and the employee as being sensitive. But if that doesn't work, assert your sovereignty.

TACTICS

- **Attitude:** This may not seem important to the other manager, but it actually is a challenge to your authority that threatens your relationship with your staff. That makes it an important issue.
- **Preparation:** Make sure this is an ongoing problem and not a one-time event that can be brushed off for the time being.
- **Timing:** Do this as soon as possible after a "confrontation" occurs.
- **Behavior:** Stop by the other person's office to have the conversation. Sit down without waiting to be asked to subtly demonstrate your equality to the other party. Deliver the initial request leaning back in a relaxed manner. Deliver the follow-up leaning forward.

83. Asking a Peer to Treat Your Staff with More Respect

Icebreaker and pitch: Paul, I know you like to joke around, but my assistant, David, is overly sensitive, and he's having a hard time handling your teasing. I'm sure he'd be embarrassed if he knew I asked you, but I'd really appreciate it if you go easy on him.

Gets message: *No problem. You know I don't mean anything by it. I'll cut it out.*

Annoyed: *Hey, it's not like I'm heckling the kid or anything. He needs to grow up a little bit and develop a thicker skin.*

You're right, but: That may be. He is a little wet behind the ears, but he's doing excellent work and is progressing nicely. He's my assistant, and I really think any toughening up or life lessons should come from me, not you.

Backs off: *Ouch. No one can say you're not tough enough. Just kidding. Okay, I'll cut it out. I didn't mean to step on your toes.*

ADAPTATIONS

This script can be modified to:

- Ask a friend or family member to stop teasing your child.

KEY POINTS

- Rationalize the disrespect by characterizing it as humor.
- Demonstrate an awareness of the assistant's sensitivity.
- Explain that you're making this approach unprompted.
- If a simple request isn't enough, assert your sovereignty.

84

Cold Calling for an Informational Interview

STRATEGY

Cold calling—contacting someone with no forewarning—is always difficult. It's even more of a problem when the call is about your career. The objective of this script is to make contact *inside* the organization. That way you'll only have to make one cold call.

TACTICS

- **Attitude:** Don't look on what you're doing as demeaning. Consider that you're actually offering the other party a wonderful opportunity—the other party just doesn't know yet how wonderful a chance it really is! If you're feeling desperate, you'll get nowhere. Feel confident and you'll get surprisingly far.

- **Preparation:** You definitely need a name to drop for the other party's security and comfort. Obviously, the more impressive and familiar the name, the better . . . but any name is better than none. Even a headhunter or secretary will do in a pinch. Before making the telephone call, it's important to discover everything you possibly can about the organization (especially its recent history). Your knowledge of the company may help compensate for your lack of a contact. It certainly won't hurt.

- **Timing:** Many individuals in supervisory positions come to the office early in an effort to get work done before regular business hours, then spend the first hour or so launching their staff. From 11:30 A.M. until 2:00 P.M. they're either thinking about, traveling to or from, or eating, lunch. From 3:00 P.M. on they're thinking about bringing the day to a close. That gives you two small but decent windows of opportunity to make your call: from 10:00 A.M. until 11:30 A.M. and from 2:00 P.M. until 3:00 P.M.

- **Behavior:** The more comfortable, friendly, and relaxed you sound, the more likely you'll be able to connect.

84. Cold Calling for an Informational Interview

Icebreaker #1: Fred Connor, please. It's *[your name]* calling.

Direct Connection: *This is Fred Connor.*

Gatekeeper: *Can you tell me what this is in reference to?*

Drop name: Of course. Dale Landry told me to call Mr. Connor.

Icebreaker #2: I'm so glad I was able to reach you. Dale Landry suggested I give you a call.

Pitch: I'm thinking about a career change, and Dale said you were a great source of knowledge on the licensing industry. I was hoping you'd be able to spare about fifteen minutes to speak with me, just to share some thoughts about the business.

Suspicious: *If what you're really looking for is a job, give Richard Davidson in personnel a call. I'm a busy man.*

Negative: *I don't know what Dale was thinking. I'm really not the person to talk to about this.* [or] *I'm just too busy. I'm afraid I can't help you.*

Positive: *Sure. Why don't you come in Thursday morning at about eight.*

Solicit name: I appreciate your honesty. Would you have a suggestion of someone else you think I could talk to?

Offers suggestion: *Why don't you give Eric Anderson over at Alliance a call? He knows more about the licensing business than anyone else I know.*

Ask to use name: Thanks so much for your help. I'll give Mr. Anderson a call right away. Would you mind if I used your name?

Solicit meeting: Actually, I'm not looking for a job right now. What I would really like is some information.

Positive: *Oh. In that case I can spare a few minutes. Why don't you come in Thursday morning at about eight.*

Ask to use name: Thank you very much. I'll give Mr. Davidson a call. Would you mind if I use your name?

Express thanks: I appreciate your help. I'm looking forward to seeing you Thursday at eight.

ADAPTATIONS

This script can be modified to:

- Obtain information about an industry.
- Solicit new business for your company.
- Raise money for an organization.

KEY POINTS

- Use words like "need" and "told" with gatekeepers; they imply you're on a definite mission rather than a fishing expedition.
- Flatter them shamelessly and ask for a very short amount of time . . . at their convenience.
- Stressing you're looking for knowledge, not a job, improves your chances for a face-to-face meeting enormously. However, if they offer a personnel contact, grab it.
- If they decline, solicit another name and ask to use them as a reference. Having turned you down once, they're unlikely to do so again.

85

Responding to a Salary Offer

Most job seekers are so happy to have been chosen for a job that they immediately jump at the first salary offer. In their understandable eagerness, they're failing to recognize that the number is just the first card being dealt and not necessarily the best. The goal of this script is to ensure that you get as much as you possibly can when you're first being offered a job. That is important because your starting salary will be the major factor in determining your short- and long-term compensation (since increases are generally based on percentages of your starting salary).

TACTICS

- **Attitude:** While your first sentiment may be relief that you've finally landed a job, don't fall into the trap of complacency. You will never be more powerful in this company than you are right now. They picked you because you're the best person to satisfy a need they have. In this period between selection and actually starting the job, your potential is limitless. Your attitude should be one of confidence.

- **Preparation:** The most important preparation you can do is finding out what the market range is for the position in question. Assume there's a range of 25 percent from the lowest salary paid to the highest ($75,000 to $100,000 or $30,000 to $40,000). You can also assume the other party wants to get away with paying you a salary in the bottom third of that range. Your goal, on the other hand, should be a salary in the top third of the range. That will let you jump into the next range when you shift positions in the future. In addition, come up with a list of nonfinancial compensations you are interested in, such as added vacation days, a company car, or a clothing allowance.

85. Responding to a Salary Offer

Makes job offer: *We'd like to offer you the job. What kind of salary are you looking for?*

Deflect approach: I'm delighted that you've offered me the job. I want you to know I'm 100 percent committed to the company. As for salary, I'm looking for the market. What do you think that is now?

Won't name figure: *Well, what do you think that is?*

Name figure: Stream of income is important to me, but I also want to be fair. My research has led me to believe a salary of *[figure in top third of range]* would be appropriate for this position and someone of my experience.

Too much: *I'm not quarreling with your value, but I'm afraid we can only afford to pay [a figure in the bottom third of the range].*

Too big a jump: *That would be quite a jump for you. In your last job you were making 15 percent less than that. I'm willing to offer you an increase of 10 percent.*

Names figure: *We're prepared to offer you . . . .*

Much too low: I really don't know how to respond. I expected an offer more in line with the marketplace, which I think is *[upper end of range]*. Perhaps our perceptions of the job profile are different.

A bit low: I believe that's in the low end of the range for this position. I was thinking that with my experience and this job profile a salary of *[15 percent higher]* would be appropriate.

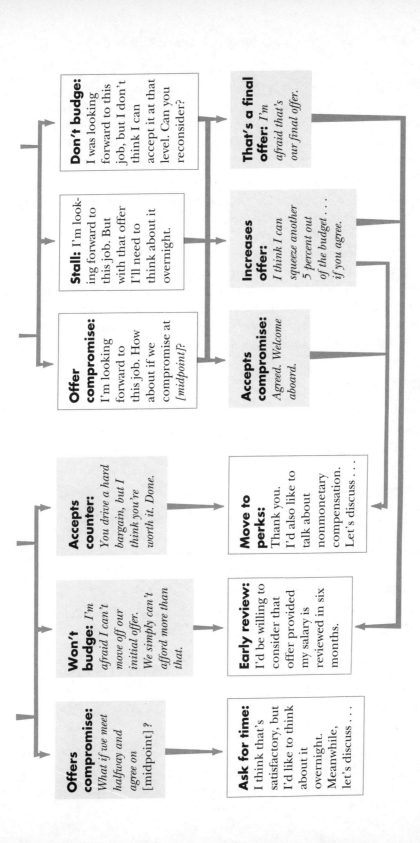

- **Timing:** You have only a little bit of time to work with here, but in order to maximize your return you need to push it as far as possible. That means, regardless of the offer that's on the table at the end of the conversation, ask to think about it overnight. This gives the other party one last chance to increase his offer in exchange for your immediate acceptance.

- **Behavior:** Your behavior should undergo a subtle transition when you move from job seeker to "anointed one"—you've shifted from seller to buyer. Obviously you should still remain polite and interested, but you no longer need to appear as eager and active. You can now sit back in your seat. You can break eye contact for longer periods of time. Most important of all, you no longer need to fill gaps in the conversation. While you don't want to play hard to get, a little resistance will encourage further offers. It's good to take notes during the dialogue.

ADAPTATIONS

This script can be modified to:

- Respond to a promotion, transfer, emergency assignment, or a significant increase in responsibility.

KEY POINTS

- Try, if at all possible, to force the other party into making the first offer. If that happens, the only direction it can go is up. If you are forced to name the first number, it can only go down. That's why, if you're cornered, you should come back with a figure close to the very top of the market range.

- If the first offer is below what you know to be the market range, say so, and suggest your perceptions of the job profile are dangerously different.

- If the first offer is within the range, counter it with a figure approximately 15 percent higher.

- If your prior salary is brought into play, say that it was one of the reasons you started looking for another job.

- If a compromise is offered, ask for time to consider it and move on to nonfinancial issues.

- If no compromise is offered, ask for a guaranteed early review and move on to nonfinancial issues.

Interviewing for a Career-Shift Job

86

STRATEGY

Most people are terribly afraid of interviews for jobs outside their own industry. They needn't be. The secret here is that if you've gotten an interview with a body outside of the HR department, someone in the company—very likely the person you'll be meeting—has realized your experiences are relevant and applicable. This interview is an opportunity, not an obstacle. They think you could work out but aren't sure. They're giving you a chance to convince them. In other words, you don't need to change minds during the interview, only reinforce beliefs they already hold. Still, you should be prepared for a series of probes.

TACTICS

- **Attitude:** Be confident. If the interviewer couldn't see how your past experience applied to this position, you wouldn't have gotten the interview.
- **Preparation:** You need to do a great deal of research and study on both the industry in general and the company in particular. Learn the buzz words, jargon, and politics of the industry by reading a year's worth of trade magazines. Research the company's role in the industry by searching for mentions of it in the past five years of trade magazines. Learn about the competition. You want to demonstrate that you have the ability to gain and comprehend industry-specific knowledge very quickly.
- **Timing:** You'll have little control over when this meeting takes place or over how long it lasts. That's why you need to make all your major points as early and as often as possible. If you get to the stage of the interview covered in this dialogue, you're a top candidate.

86. Interviewing for a Career-Shift Job

General probe: *What makes you think you're qualified to fill this position even though you have no experience in this industry?*

General response: While I've never been in your industry, I've solved the same kinds of problems, met the same kinds of deadlines, managed the same kinds of people, and done the same kinds of marketing. Even though I come from a different industry, I possess the same skills and abilities you require. For example, *[cite specific examples]*.

Jargon/players probe: *That may be. But you're not familiar with the jargon we use, the language and culture of our industry [or] the players in the business, the people who make things happen.*

Jargon/players response: As a matter of fact, I've made a concerted effort to learn the industry's language *[or]* to familiarize myself with the players in the industry. I want to make sure this job isn't an experiment for either of us. I'm determined to bring with me the skills, abilities, and knowledge I'll need to succeed.

Underlings probe: *I'm confident about your skills, but how will you deal with underlings who have more experience in the industry than you?*

Underlings response: I'll deal with them just as I've dealt with staffs in the past. I'll learn from them when I can and take their suggestions if valid. But I'll also demonstrate to them, as I have to you, that my experience and knowledge are transferable to this industry.

Peers probe: *I'm afraid the other department managers may perceive you as a threat or as a sign that massive changes are coming. After all, someone with your background being named to this position would be unprecedented for this company.*

Peers response: I think fear of change is natural to everyone. I saw the same kind of problems in other industries. I've discovered that once people show they can do the job, all those fears vanish.

Superiors probe: *You make a strong case for yourself. But you know, I may have a hard time selling you to the people upstairs. They're not as open-minded as I am.*

Superiors response: I understand. No matter how good an idea is, if it's new, it's tough to sell. Please let me know if there's anything I can do to help you with this. And also, please accept my gratitude for any efforts you can make on my behalf. No matter where I go in this industry I'll always be grateful.

- **Behavior:** Don't get upset by questions about the applicability of your prior experience, or about how you'll deal with others' reactions to your shift of industries. These are understandable concerns. The interviewer will have to answer these questions from others—as will you—and may need the ammunition you'll provide.

ADAPTATIONS

This script can be modified to:

- Shift the direction of a career within an industry; for example, an actor who has done only comedy could use a modification of this script to solicit a dramatic role.

KEY POINTS

- General probes should be met by general responses that reiterate how your skills and abilities, as demonstrated by your experience, are just as relevant to this industry as they were to the industry you came from. View this as a chance to make your case once again.
- Questions about your not knowing industry jargon, politics, or people should be answered with evidence that you've already started learning all three, showing you'll be up to speed in these areas very quickly.
- Questions about the reaction of underlings should be answered by explaining how this is simply a management issue like others you've dealt with in the past, and one that can be easily overcome.
- Questions about the reaction of peers should be answered by noting the universality of such reactions and stating that the best way to deal with them is simply to demonstrate the ability to get the job done.
- Questions about the difficulties of selling your hire to superiors are either veiled requests for help or subtle solicitations for gratitude that will extend into the future. In response, offer your help, gratitude, and future loyalty.

Responding to Tough Interview Questions

87

STRATEGY

In today's competitive job market, more and more personnel executives are using a technique called "the stress interview." Rather than trying to verify the claims on your résumé, which can be easily done with a few telephone calls, their goal is to see how you react when under pressure. Typically, the tough questions appear out of the blue and begin with a general probe about what you perceive to be your weaknesses. While the experience isn't pleasant, it can be turned to your advantage. Besides, getting a third degree like this means you're considered one of the top candidates.

TACTICS

- **Attitude:** The single most important thing you can do is not take these probes personally. In some organizations such stress interviews are now standard operating procedure. Look on these questions as a rite of passage rather than a torture session and you'll be fine.
- **Preparation:** The best way to prepare is to examine your résumé objectively and look for areas that could be probed. The three most common are: the frequency with which you've moved from job to job, your reasons for leaving your last job and why you may be without work at the moment, and the length of time you've spent either in one company or one position.
- **Timing:** In this situation you have little control over general timing. However, the best way to respond to these questions is to pause for one beat before launching into your defense. That shows you're not answering reflexively but that you're also quick on your feet.
- **Behavior:** The worst thing you can do is get angry. Instead, remain calm and try not to change either your body language or manner.

87. Responding to Tough Interview Questions

Probe for weakness: *Your résumé does a fine job of pointing out your professional strengths and skills, but I'd like to find out more about you as a person. For example, what would you say is your greatest weakness?*

Former weakness: When I started in sales, I tended to overbook my appointments. Then I realized I wasn't devoting enough time to each call, giving short shrift to some clients. Since then, I've learned not to schedule more calls than I can handle effectively.

Positive weakness: Sometimes I'm not as patient with the shortcomings of others as I should be. I'm trying to be more patient with coworkers who aren't as skilled or motivated as I'd like and to rely more on leading by example.

Stagnation probe: *You've been with XYZ, Inc., in the same position for five years now. Why haven't you been able to move up?*

Stagnation defense: The few positions that have opened up have gone to employees who have a lot more seniority than I do. That's why I'm looking for a company that offers a real opportunity to move up. What can you tell me about the possibilities for advancement here?

Job history probe: *Going over your résumé, I notice that you've changed jobs several times in the past few years. Why is that?*

Last job probe: *You've been out of work for a long time. Since you clearly didn't leave your last job for a new one, I assume you were let go. Why?*

Last job defense: Like so many places these days, my company was looking to cut payroll costs and wound up eliminating hundreds of jobs last year. I volunteered for the buyout program because I felt I'd reached the limit of what I could do there anyway.

Job history defense: As you can see, my job moves haven't been lateral; they've all led to positions of greater responsibility. Now that I've gained the experience, I'm looking to settle down with a company that will challenge me . . . like this one.

Stagnation follow-up: *Being in the same job at the same company for such a long time can make you stale. How will you cope with the challenge of a new job in a new organization?*

Closing stagnation defense: It's precisely because I don't want to get stale that I'm looking for new opportunities. From what I understand, your company offers just that. Can you tell me more about the kind of challenges I'd face in this job?

Last job follow-up: *You've been looking for a new position for several months now, apparently without any luck. What seems to be the problem?*

Closing last job defense: I'm not looking for just another paycheck. My severance was generous enough to allow me to take the time to find a company that's right for me, where I can make a real contribution. Can you tell me more about precisely what this job entails?

Job history follow-up: *With your history of job-hopping, I'm not sure that you'd be content to stay in one place for long. Would you say you're the kind of person who gets bored easily?*

Closing job history defense: Not at all. But I do enjoy being challenged. In fact, what's been most exciting in my previous positions has been finding new ways to keep a product fresh in our customers' eyes. Am I right in thinking that's a crucial part of the job here?

ADAPTATIONS

This script can be modified to:

- Deal with a co-op or condo board or club screening committee.
- Respond to probing informational interviews.

KEY POINTS

- If asked about a general weakness, offer one that's either a "positive"—such as being a workaholic—or one that you had in the past which you've since corrected—such as overbooking.
- If your job history is probed, point out that your moves have been vertical rather than horizontal and that they've been part of a search for a position . . . coincidentally, like the one you're interviewing for.
- If your departure from your last job is probed, blame layoffs on the economy and long job hunts on your willingness to wait for the right position . . . coincidentally, like the one you're interviewing for.
- If you're accused of stagnation, blame seniority and explain that's why you're looking for a job that rewards merit and offers challenges . . . coincidentally, like the one you're interviewing for.
- The best way to deflect such probes is to constantly bring the discussion back to the job itself. The more specifically you do this, and the more diligently, the quicker the interviewer will back off the stress questions.

IV

Lifescripts

for Dealing with Clients, Customers, and Vendors

88

Cold Calling a Potential Client

STRATEGY

There are few things more frustrating and daunting than making cold calls for new clients or customers. But in many businesses it's a necessity. First, don't try to sell anything in your initial conversation. You'll increase your success rate by simply pushing for a meeting rather than trying to close a sale. Second, have good retorts to the two most common responses—generally, those are a vague "not interested" or a cost objection. Third, don't waste your efforts and push more than twice. That will only lead to anger and be a waste of both parties' time. It's better to move on to another prospect. Assume you'll get appointments with, at best, 25 percent of those you call, and you'll only close deals with, at best, 20 percent of those you actually meet. This is a matter of volume so your dialogue is necessarily short.

TACTICS

- **Attitude:** Be enthusiastic, interested, and optimistic. You have to feel that you are truly offering her an opportunity—so never apologize for calling.
- **Preparation:** Have a written script prepared prior to making your calls.
- **Timing:** Since you'll be working on volume, you're apt to make these calls whenever you have free time. Consider saving your best prospects for the hours just before office hours begin or end.
- **Behavior:** Don't be antagonistic or condescending. Try to sound spontaneous, even though you're working from a script. Use the other person's name as often as possible. Ask questions as a way of trying to direct the conversation. Keep the dialogue short—save your sales pitch for in-person meetings.

88. Cold Calling a Potential Client

Icebreaker and pitch: Good afternoon, Ms. Carey. This is Sheila Sterling from Zenith Communications here in Topeka. Ms. Carey, the reason I'm calling you today is to introduce you to our new marketing consulting program which can dramatically increase the effectiveness of your marketing efforts. Ms. Carey, are you interested in boosting the effectiveness of your marketing?

Don't need it: *I'm really not interested, Sheila. We don't need any help with our marketing program right now.*

Financial objection: *I'm sorry, Sheila, we really can't afford to spend money on outside consulting services right now.*

Heard that before: Ms. Carey, I've heard that before from other people in your industry before I had a chance to explain our program. But after hearing about it they decided to enlist our help. I wonder if we could get together to talk about it. Is first thing Thursday morning good for you?

Cost not a problem: Ms. Carey, if it's a question of cost that's an issue, we usually have no problem overcoming it. As a matter of fact, Tekno, Inc., which I believe is up the street from you, had the same initial concern until we had a chance to sit down with them. How about 9 A.M. on Thursday?

Relents: *You know what, Sheila, that sounds interesting. But Thursdays are no good; we'll be tied up all day with deadlines.*

Still not interested: *I'm sorry, I'm really not interested in your service.*

Propose another time: I have an opening on Tuesday at 2:00 P.M. Would that be convenient?

Give up: I'm sorry to hear that, Ms. Carey. If you do need a service like ours in the future, please don't hesitate to call us. Thank you for your time, and have a good day.

ADAPTATIONS

This script can be modified to:

- Request charitable donations.
- Solicit political support.

KEY POINTS

- Be friendly, caring, enthusiastic, and, above all, concise.
- In response to general objections, say that others said the same thing until they heard about the product or service.
- In response to cost objections, say that's not an insurmountable problem—implying fees are negotiable—and cite another organization that was able to overcome price objections.
- If you're turned down twice, give up and move on to another prospect.

Breaking Bad News to a Client

89

STRATEGY

Being the bearer of bad news is never easy. It's even harder if you're being paid by the other party, and the bad news directly or indirectly reflects on your abilities. But potential disaster can be averted. The actual language you use depends on who is to blame for the problem. (If you truly are to blame, see script 93, "Apologizing to a Client for Your Own Mistake.") Remember, however, that in the final analysis you are responsible for your client's problems, whether or not you were culpable. That's why it's essential to express your regret and take responsibility, even if there was absolutely nothing you could do about the situation. From your first words, paint the situation as an obstacle that can be overcome rather than a disaster, and the sin as one of omission rather than commission. Then, offer your head, or a third party's head, on a platter to your client, along with your plan of action, in the hope that your mea culpa and solution will be enough. If it was the client's own fault, you should refrain from pointing that out directly, and just imply that that was the problem. Your goal is to explain the situation, offer a solution, and keep the client.

TACTICS

- **Attitude:** Be apologetic and contrite, but don't grovel or beg for forgiveness.
- **Preparation:** Make sure you know all the facts and can relay them concisely, and have a plan of action that requires only client approval to be set into motion.
- **Timing:** For your own sake the news must come from you so have the conversation as soon as possible.
- **Behavior:** Holding this dialogue over the telephone implies urgency and also protects you somewhat from anger. Put emotions in personal rather than business terms. Let the client vent—interrupting will only increase his anger.

89. Breaking Bad News to a Client

Icebreaker: I need to speak with you about an extraordinary situation that has come up. We've hit a roadblock, but together, I think we can overcome it.

Third party's fault: I'm afraid Acme Productions has let us down. I just got off the phone with them, and they told me they're not going to be able to deliver the spot on time. I've never had a problem with them before—in fact, they were my best vendor. That's why I chose them to work on your project. I feel just awful. I've found another production house, Zenith Studios, which can take on the job, and which will absolutely guarantee delivery by the end of next week. What I hold myself responsible. What upsets me most is that I've let a friend down. I'm terribly sorry.

Accepting: *It's not your fault. You can't control your vendors. Just make sure we get the project back on schedule.*

Angry: *Sorry won't cut it. You might not be to blame, but you're responsible. I'm out time and money, and your feeling bad won't make those losses go away.*

Client's own fault: I'm afraid the television spot we farmed out to Acme Productions isn't going to be completed on time, at least not without a big cost overrun. There's no point in assigning blame or fault. What's done is done. I was worried about all those special effects we asked for. I had a feeling they couldn't deliver them for the price they quoted. But what's important is to move on from here, learn from the mistake, and make sure we work together more closely in the future. I suggest we speak with Zenith Studios about taking over the project.

Accepting: *Don't be ridiculous. How could you plan for a hurricane? There's no reason to blame yourself.*

No one's fault: I'm afraid the television spot isn't going to come in on time. I just got off the phone with Acme Productions, and they told me their facility was destroyed by a hurricane over the weekend. They saved the preliminary tapes, but there's no way they can keep to schedule. I've spoken with Zenith Studios, and they're willing to take over the project, but I feel just terrible about this. You're the last person I'd want to let down this way. I keep asking myself, could I have done something, should I have planned for such a disaster?

Angry: *I don't know if you should have thought about the weather or not. All I know is my spot is going to be late, and I'm out big bucks.*

Reiterate: I appreciate your understanding. It will never happen again. If you agree, I'll call Zenith and give them their marching orders.

Deflect: You're right. I accept full responsibility. From now on I'll come to you for help in selecting outside vendors. Shall I call Zenith and give them the go ahead?

Reiterate: I appreciate your saying that. You know how important you are to me. If you agree, I'll speak to Zenith right away and get them started.

Deflect: I'm just as upset as you are. But I don't think there's anything to be gained by cursing the heavens. If you agree, I'll contact Zenith and get them started.

Accepting: *You're right. Blame and fault aren't important. What's important is getting the project back on track.*

Angry: *You're right. I don't care about who you think is to blame. All I care about is that I'm out time and money.*

Deflect: I understand. In the future if anyone is threatening to throw us off schedule, I'll fight them—even if it's you!

Reiterate: I agree. I'm looking forward to working even more closely with you in the future. For instance, do you agree we should ask Zenith to take on the project?

Asks for concession: *You do that. Just be aware that I don't want to pay for this fiasco. I expect you to pick up the extra costs.*

ADAPTATIONS

This script can be modified to:

- Revise the terms of an agreement due to unanticipated events out of your control.

KEY POINTS

- Use words like "obstacle" or "hurdle" rather than "problem" or "disaster."
- If it's clearly no one's fault, ask if it was your fault.
- If it's a third party's fault, say so, accept responsibility, and offer a plan.
- If it's the client's own fault, say you need to work more closely in the future, and offer a plan.
- If the client gets angry, deflect the anger by saying you understand the response, but urge moving on.
- If the client accepts the situation, reiterate your plan.

Refusing a Client's Request

90

STRATEGY

The business world has its share of unethical members. On occasion you may be unfortunate enough to have one of them as a client. Or perhaps you have a client who wants to use you to do something unethical in order to shield her. In either case, if you don't want or need to keep the client, you can simply refuse and tell her to find another professional. But if you need to retain the client, you face a dilemma. The solution is to offer an alternative, ethical course of action which, while it may not lead to the same results, will achieve some of the results without the potential side effects.

TACTICS

- **Attitude:** You are not a judge and jury, nor a board of ethics. You are simply trying to keep your client from harming herself—and you.

- **Preparation:** Understand, and be prepared to discuss, the ramifications of the proposed actions. At the same time, have the groundwork in place for an alternative course. Even if you complete the planning, don't say so. You want the client to have time to think over what you're saying in this dialogue and maybe become involved in the planning.

- **Timing:** Do this only after making sure that the request is indeed unethical or clearly improper. Once you've convinced yourself of that, have the dialogue as soon as possible.

- **Behavior:** This dialogue can be held either over the telephone or in person. But in either case refrain from being condescending and accusatory. Be specific, perhaps alluding to similar experiences you have had.

90. Refusing a Client's Request

Icebreaker: I've been thinking about your suggestion. The possible effects have been weighing on my mind. I've been thinking about how it should be handled, if at all. I need to know when you can spend as much time as possible to talk about it.

Receptive: *Right now is fine. I'm all ears. What's going on?*

Unreceptive: *Aren't you overreacting? I didn't think what I suggested was that significant.*

Not what you planned: I've been doing some research, and I've discovered that the ramifications of what you asked me to do could be significant and not at all what you want to achieve. *[Explain situation.]*

Still willing: *That may or may not be the case. But I'm willing to take the risk so I suggest you go ahead.*

Do your job: *Correct me if I'm wrong, but isn't it your job to protect me from any possible side effects?*

It's my job to protect: You hired me not only to do a competent professional job but to protect you and your family. I can't let you commit financial *[or]* professional *[or]* legal suicide.

That's what I'm doing: That's exactly what I'm doing by having this conversation with you. My job is to keep you and your family from getting into potentially dangerous situations.

I'm in charge: *Listen. You work for me. I've made my own judgment of the risk and I want you to move ahead.*

Now receptive: *All right. Show me how I can get what I want and still stay out of trouble.*

Refuse to assist suicide: I'm sorry. I won't help you to do something I know will be self-destructive.

Offer an alternative: I'm putting the final touches on a plan which, while it may not give you 100 percent of what you want, will keep you and your family from being exposed. I'll have it finished by this time tomorrow.

ADAPTATIONS

This script can be modified to:

- Dissuade a family member, friend, or coworker who wants your help in committing some questionable act.

KEY POINTS

- Be professional, not condescending or accusatory.
- Explain the potential ramifications of the proposed action.
- If the client is still willing to go ahead, say it's your job to stop her.
- If the client insists you just do your job, say that's exactly what you're doing.
- If the client demands compliance, say you can't and won't assist in her "suicide."
- Close by suggesting another course of action.
- If the client insists on the original course, say you'll have to withdraw from the project/case.

Resurrecting a Former Client

91

STRATEGY

Too many businesspeople stand on ceremony and foolish pride and never try to resurrect former clients. That's a mistake. It's far easier to get back together with a client you've lost or had no contact with than to get a new client—just take a look at script 88, "Cold Calling a Potential Client." Your goal in this script should be limited: to get a meeting with the former client at which you can pitch to become part of his life once again. The secret to achieving this is to play, as much as possible, on any personal relationship or event the two of you shared. Assuming there was a problem that caused your falling out, the former client may still be angry. Your response should be to absorb his anger and simply ask for the chance to tell your side of the story and make amends. To do either of those, you'll need a meeting.

TACTICS

- **Attitude:** Be cordial, humble, and, if necessary, persistent.
- **Preparation:** Before the call, gather as much personal data about the former client and his family as you can, if you don't remember names and ages. Be prepared to call back since your sudden reappearance may put him off balance initially.
- **Timing:** Try to call either early—before 9 A.M.—or late—after 5 P.M.—in the workday.
- **Behavior:** Don't call the former client at home or on the weekend. You'll get the most civil responses during normal working hours when he is at the office. Be prepared to absorb residual anger. If possible, imply that your request is a modest one.

91. Resurrecting a Former Client

Icebreaker: How are you? I ran into our mutual friend Edward Birch yesterday and it got me thinking about you. I'm just calling to patch things up and see how you and your family are doing. I hope I'm not calling at a time when you can't be bothered with a call like this.

It's a good time: *Uh . . . no, it's not a bother at all. We're all doing fine. How are you?*

It's a bad time: *Actually, it is a bad time. I'm very busy at the moment.*

Say you'll call back: Oh, I'm terribly sorry. I'll give you a call back later this week.

Miss relationship: I'm okay. But I think about you often. Even though we no longer have a business relationship, I've always wanted to call and chat and see how you're doing.

Over anger: *Listen. I'm over the problem we had. I know you did your best. It just wasn't good enough.*

Still angry: *I think about you, too . . . every time I look at that boarded-up storefront and the bills I still have to pay.*

Make amends: That's another reason for this call. I'd like to make amends and work for you again. What happened could never happen again. I think I could really be of help.

Absorb anger: I understand your anger. I hope one day you'll be able to sit down with me over a cup of coffee and hear my side of the story. I'm sorry for troubling you.

Not open to possibility: *I'm sorry, but you can't turn the clock back. I'm not interested.*

Open to possibility: *Hey, I don't harbor grudges. I'd be happy to speak with you.*

Meet for coffee: Why don't we just meet for a cup of coffee then. I miss our personal relationship and would really like to see you again—it meant a lot to me.

Ask for meeting: I'd like to come down and show you what I've been doing and how it might help your business. I'd really like to resume our friendship—it meant a lot to me.

ADAPTATIONS

This script can be modified to:

- Rekindle a dormant relationship for networking purposes.
- Tell a former client about a new product or service you're offering.

KEY POINTS

- Be contrite, humble, and personable—this is initially a personal call.
- Explain that you miss the relationship and would like to renew it.
- If the former client is still angry, absorb the anger and imply your request is too modest to justify such anger.
- If the former client is no longer angry but hasn't forgotten the matter, ask for a chance to make amends.
- If the former client isn't open to renewing the relationship, push for a personal meeting over coffee.
- If the former client appears willing to renew the relationship, ask for a more formal meeting.

Dealing with a Client Who Is Angry with Your Staff

92

STRATEGY

When a client calls to tell you that she is upset with one of your staff members, there's really very little you can do. Your goal is to keep the anger at the individual from being extended to you and your company. Whether or not you know about the situation, it's best to act as if this is the first you've heard of it. The best response is simply to allow the client to vent. Don't apologize for someone else—that will allow the anger to be shifted to you. And don't offer a defense. That will only turn the conversation into a debate. Instead, show personal concern, express your regrets over the whole situation, ask if you can bring the matter to the staff member's attention, and then offer to make amends. In most cases, all the client needed to do was to express her anger. By accepting her anger, without accepting blame or rising to your staffer's defense, you should be able to resolve the situation quickly and painlessly.

TACTICS

- **Attitude:** Be concerned and regretful—not reflexively defensive or apologetic.
- **Preparation:** You'll have little or no time to prepare for specific situations, so put a continuing policy in place for dealing with such issues.
- **Timing:** You'll have no control over the timing of this dialogue.
- **Behavior:** Moderation is the key. If you're too responsive, you'll open yourself up for blame. If you're unresponsive, you won't give the client a chance to vent. Listen, show you care, offer to do what you can, and leave it at that.

92. Dealing with a Client Who Is Angry with Your Staff

Makes complaint: *I'm very upset with your office. I just found out your assistant insulted my mother when she came to your office to pick up my order. You know, my mother isn't well and being upset doesn't help her health. I'm very concerned with the way your staff treated her.*

Show concern: First, and most important, how is your mother feeling? Is she okay?

Restates softened complaint: *She's as well as could be expected. Thank you for asking. I know she's hard of hearing and obstinate at times, but that's no excuse for how she was treated.*

Offer amends: Thank you for bringing this to my attention. I feel terrible that you had to make this call. May I mention this to my assistant to make sure it never happens again to your mother or to anyone else? Meanwhile, if there's any way I can make amends, please let me know.

Final venting: *By all means talk to her. There's no way to make up for it, just make sure it doesn't happen again.*

ADAPTATIONS

This script can be modified to:

- Derail criticism from someone important to you about someone important to you.

KEY POINTS

- Show concern.
- Don't apologize or rise to a defense.
- Offer to make amends.

Apologizing to a Client for Your Own Mistake

STRATEGY

When you've made a mistake that affects a client, financially or otherwise, you're obligated to apologize. If you want to keep the client, you'll need to come clean and offer a plan for addressing the situation. That said, you'll have to make an individual judgment on how far you're willing to go to keep the client. Remember: words cost you nothing other than pride, so I'd suggest you go pretty far verbally. On the other hand, lowering your fee probably isn't a good idea since it will cut into any future work you do for the client. A compromise solution is to pick up some, but not all, of the costs of cleaning up the problem you created. How much of the cost you absorb is a matter for negotiation.

TACTICS

- **Attitude:** Be contrite, honest, and apologetic. But move on to the solution as quickly as possible.
- **Preparation:** Do a thorough postmortem so you can completely yet concisely explain what went wrong and why. Have a solution in hand, one that requires only the client's approval to get launched.
- **Timing:** Do this as soon as possible after the mistake. You want to make sure the client hears about this from you, not someone else.
- **Behavior:** Having this conversation over the telephone could show a sense of urgency, and can also insulate you somewhat. Be prepared to absorb some anger. However, don't let unjustified threats go by—they're uncalled for unless your mistake was malicious or your conduct was unethical.

93. Apologizing to a Client for Your Own Mistake

Icebreaker: I've made a miscalculation that has created a problem for you. I have what I believe is a solution, but first I need to apologize to you. When I was scheduling your project, I failed to take into account that there were two religious holidays that fell during the time I'd set aside for printing. We're not going to be able to meet the schedule I laid out for you.

Accepting: *I'm not happy about this, but I admire your candor. I want you to know I expect special help from you. Now what's your plan?*

Angry: *I can't believe you could have been so stupid and negligent. What were you thinking? Weren't you paying attention? What's wrong with you?*

Offer plan: Thanks for your continued confidence in me. I won't let you down. I suggest we start by contacting another, larger printer I've lined up to find out if he can get the job done in time.

Outright apology: My relationship with you is very important to me. I feel horrible about what has happened. All I can do is apologize. I don't expect you to just pass this off, but I'd like a chance to earn your confidence back.

Offers another chance: *All right. Everyone can make a mistake. How do you plan on working this out?*

Still angry: *I can't afford to give you another chance. Not after the screwup you just made.*

Ask what can be done: Our relationship is important to me. Since an apology won't suffice, what can I do that would make up for this mistake? If I can do it, I will.

Issues threat: *You've done quite enough already. There's nothing more you can do for me. The only people that can help me now are [your professional association, the Better Business Bureau, or a consumer protection agency].*

Lower your fees: *You want to know what you can do? I'll tell you. You can lower your fees. They're too high, especially considering what just happened.*

Pick up the costs: *You want to know what you can do? I'll tell you. You can pick up the costs of this fiasco. That's what you can do.*

Be careful: If you think punishing me will help your situation, so be it. But I'd urge you to consider such steps carefully.

Can't do that: I'm afraid that would only affect the quality of what I do and that wouldn't help either of us. What if I help to absorb some of the cost of this problem?

Want to keep client: I simply can't afford to pick up all the costs, but I would be willing to pick up 50 percent of them.

Willing to lose client: I wish I could pick up the costs . . . I really do. But I simply can't do that. I'm sorry.

ADAPTATIONS

This script can be modified to:

- Explain a material disappointment or injury, created unintentionally by you, to a family member or friend.

KEY POINTS

- Be direct, frank, and contrite. Offer an explanation but not an excuse.
- If the client accepts your apology, immediately describe your plan.
- If the client gets angry, offer an outright, humble, and candid apology.
- If the client remains angry, ask what else you can do.
- If the client issues an unjustified threat, urge him to be cautious.
- If the client asks you to lower your fees, suggest absorbing some costs instead.
- If the client asks you to pick up the costs, say you'll absorb a share of them.

Pressing a Client
to Pay the Bill

STRATEGY

With companies and individuals all now working to hold on to money for as long as possible, pressing a client for payment is a challenge you're likely to face more and more often. Fortunately, this task is rarely as awkward as you imagine it might be; frequently there has been just a clerical mistake, or the client will at least pretend that there has been one. This often means you will have to let the client look into—or pretend to look into—the matter and schedule a second call. The attitude to take in the first call is that, since you are, in effect, partners, the client's failure to pay promptly is probably an oversight that can be swiftly corrected. In the second call, you should push for performance. Do not let the situation become confrontational unless the client signals a complete unwillingness to pay and you are willing to jeopardize your relationship with the client.

TACTICS

- **Attitude:** You have performed a service or delivered a product, and it is only reasonable that you be paid promptly. You value this client, and you know he values your services in return. By checking on payment, you are merely following normal business practices.
- **Preparation:** Have the invoices in question in front of you. Know the total amount due, and your client's payment history, including any advanced payments. Also, have all the particulars of the job or jobs in question in front of you: the day the project started, the day of delivery, any positive response it received, any problems or delays that occurred, and any special agreements that were made about payment terms.
- **Timing:** Call during business hours, so the client does not have the excuse that accounting personnel are not available. Call the day after you expected payment.

94. Pressing a Client to Pay the Bill

Icebreaker: Hi. I'm calling to check on the status of invoice number 1234, for the self-sharpening razors, that was due yesterday.

Mild apology: *Oh that. It got hung up on my desk for a few days. I'll check on it.*

Attempts pass off: *You'll have to call accounting about that.*

Pleads poverty: *I'm having some cash-flow problems. You'll have to wait awhile.*

Reject pass off: Clients' accounting departments aren't generally responsive to out-side suppliers. It's better if you follow up with them. I'll call you again at the end of the day to see what you've found out. I will be at your offices on Friday. I'd like to pick up the check then, if at all possible.

Stress urgency: I'd appreciate your giving it immediate attention. As you know, cash flow is the lifeblood of an operation like ours. I will be at your offices on Friday. Will it be possible for me to pick up the check then?

Call back: I'm following up on our conversation of this morning about invoice number 1234. Will the check be ready on Friday?

Accept, but except: Naturally, I'm sorry to hear you're having cash-flow problems and will have to ask some vendors to wait awhile. But I can't be one of those vendors. I will be at your offices on Friday. Will it be possible for me to pick up the check then?

Agrees to pay: *I found a way to get a check cut on Thursday. I'll see you Friday—but come by early. I have a two o'clock tee time.*

Pleads policy: *I checked with accounting. Our new company policy is to require three approvals and to hold on to everything for 120 days.*

Cite implied contract: I understand that some companies are going in that direction, and I can adjust my future pricing to reflect the change. But those aren't the terms under which we have been doing business or under which we agreed to this project.

Express thanks: I really appreciate this. I knew I could count on your help.

Agrees: *Okay, I'll send it over today. By the way, are you guys hiring?*

Won't commit: *No. I can't even do that.*

Negotiate partial payment: I need to get at least some payment from you so I can avoid turning the account over to collection. Is there some way to pay this out of discretionary funds? Can you at least pay us half now and the rest later?

Still cites policy: *There's no point in that. The bean counters are in control, and I can't get them to budge.*

Negotiate definite date: It's not going to do either of us any good if I have to turn the account over to collection. I can stall for two weeks if you fax me a commitment, in writing, to pay in full within two weeks. Can you do that?

Again pleads poverty: *You don't understand. We are in a real crunch. We may be fine in a while, but right now, no one gets paid a cent.*

- **Behavior:** Have this conversation over the phone, so it's less confrontational—but be ready to ask when you can come over and get a check in person. This will emphasize your sense of urgency. Keep things on a business-to-business level. Let the client know the call is standard procedure, not personal.

ADAPTATIONS

This script can be modified to:

- Press for alimony or child support.
- Collect on a charitable pledge.
- Collect condo or co-op dues.

KEY POINTS

- Reject pass-offs. You have no real leverage or relationship with his accounting department, and they are paid to maximize cash flow. Your agreement is with your client contact, and it's his job to get you paid.
- Resist the suggestion that he doesn't have the power to do so.
- Present this as a shared problem. If you or your client is at a big company, refer to accounting as "them," and you and your client as "us." Otherwise, refer to your accountants or lawyers (other than yourself) as "them."
- Sympathize with him, but press your demands.
- Do not get drawn into a discussion of his situation.

95

Telling a Client You've Increased Your Fees

STRATEGY

Increasing fees is one of the easiest ways for a business to increase its income. But doing so means you'll need to tell your existing clients that their bills will be going up. The best approach is to stress that the increase is absolutely necessary for the company to keep giving the client the level of professional service and attention she demands and has come to expect from you. You'll be surprised how many of your company's clients acquiesce.

TACTICS

- **Attitude:** This is an announcement, not a request. Don't treat it as a major event: raising fees periodically is part of the normal course of business; all businesses do it.
- **Preparation:** Determine how long it has been since your company last raised its fees and what services or capabilities have been added in the interim. Learn whether the client has recently increased her own fees or prices, or if any of the other businesses servicing the client have increased their fees. Know where your fees stand relative to your competitors, and have documentation. Be able to cite any increases in productivity or profitability you've helped the client attain. Finally, review your contract to see if it contains any specific procedures for raising rates.
- **Timing:** It's best to have this conversation shortly after the client has had a business success to which you contributed. But don't wait for that to happen. You need to get the higher fee accepted before your next budgeting and planning cycle.
- **Behavior:** Have this conversation face-to-face during regular business hours. Don't wear your Armani suit or your Rolex watch that day. Take charge of the conversation. It's your job to get this increase; no one else is going to do it for you. Stop the moment you have agreement and go on to other business.

95. Telling a Client You've Increased Your Fees

Icebreaker: For the past year the company has been paying so much attention to our clients' needs, including your own, that we haven't paid enough attention to our own business.

Pitch: The finance department has said we need to raise our fees so I can still serve you profitably. So, starting next month, our hourly rate will be $100. I think you'll agree that's fair and reflects the value we deliver to you.

Out of line: *Look, we'd all like to make more, but don't you think you're making quite enough already?*

Give me a deal: *I understand why you want to charge new clients a rate like that, if you can get it. But I think you should give us a break. We helped build your business. In a very real way, we paid the tuition for your education in our industry.*

Agree: *Sure, I understand. Besides, you'll still be getting less than the mechanic who fixes my Jaguar . . . and you're more reliable.*

Fees are gross: You have to remember expenses and all the costs of doing business have gone up. When you consider that, I think it's clear $100 an hour is more than reasonable.

New fee includes break: The price I quoted you is one we are offering only to you. We are charging new clients $125 an hour. I quoted you the lower fee because I value our relationship, and I don't want there to be any impediment to our continuing to work together.

Competitor threat: *I know you value our relationship. But I also know that if you raise your fees I'll have to choose a new vendor. I got a proposal just last week from another company who charges only $85 an hour. I've still got it on file.*

Caution: That sounds like a bargain—but please think carefully before you do anything like that. Check their references. We work very hard for you, and we're very productive. We know your plants, your customers, your sales force, and your intranet system. You'd lose a lot of momentum if you had to bring someone else up that learning curve.

Still unsure: *I don't know. I need some time to think.*

Make appointment: That's a good idea. Let's make an appointment for three days from now, and in the meantime I'll prepare a more complete presentation about the justification for this increase.

Express thanks: Thanks. We enjoy serving you and this increase will let us keep at it.

ADAPTATIONS

This script can be modified to:

- Tell a business partner that you're increasing your draw.
- Tell an investor that you're increasing your salary.

KEY POINTS

- Keep bringing the discussion back to the idea that the increase is reasonable.
- If she compares the fee to a salary, stress that the fee is a gross number.
- If she asks for a special deal, respond that the fee you quoted already represents a special deal.
- If she remains angry, schedule a meeting for a few days later to make a fuller presentation. Do not indicate that there is any room for negotiation.

Justifying Increased Fees to a Critical Client

96

STRATEGY

Encountering criticism when you tell a client about a fee increase can actually be a good sign—it generally means he wants to keep working with your company; now it's just an issue of price. What you need to do is convince your client he is getting a good deal and is actually benefiting by agreeing to the increased fees. Take the position that you and your client are strategic allies, part of a working team, so the client should care about your success as much as you care about his.

TACTICS

- **Attitude:** This is a business matter. You're doing what you always do—giving your client the background data he needs to make a wise decision.
- **Preparation:** Know how long it has been since your company last raised its fees and what services or capabilities have been added in the interim. Know how your company's profitability has changed during that period. If possible, find out what the normal profit margins are for your industry. Make a list of everything you provide for your client, and note everything your company doesn't charge for that competitors might, such as telephone calls, travel costs, photocopying, and the like. Note any concessions or special breaks you've given the client. Pull any complimentary memos you've received from the client. Be prepared to cite any increases in his productivity or profitability that resulted from your efforts. Know where your fees stand relative to your competitors, and have documentation. Review the client's mission statement and speeches to see if there are any statements about wanting strategic partners to be profitable.
- **Timing:** Give an angry client a couple of days to cool off and use that time to prepare. Consider having this meeting before or after regular business hours to make the point that you're busy attending to his needs during your regular hours.

96. Justifying Increased Fees to a Critical Client

Icebreaker: I appreciate that you need to understand the context for a fee increase. I'm sure that by the time I've given you all the facts, you'll see that paying us the increased fee is not only fair, it's also a good investment on your part.

Out of line: *Cut the sales pitch. I'm disappointed in you guys. This increase is totally out of line. You know we're cutting costs and have to cut staff, but you're going to the other way and asking for more.*

For your benefit:
I'm aware of your staff reductions. That's why I need to be sure that I'd be here for you when you need me for some of the functions you're going to outsource. We're increasing our fees so our operation will stay healthy and available to you.

Unfair to employees:
All that's irrelevant. The point is I can't give my employees raises right now, so I can't very well give you the increase you asked for.

Not an employee: We're not employees. You may be controlling your costs, but you're certainly not controlling your income—we're working like crazy together to increase it. Our efforts are aimed at contributing to your revenue stream. We think it's appropriate for you to invest a small amount in the continuing vitality of our part of your team.

Too big an increase:
I could sign off on a small increase, but this is too big. Your expenses haven't gone up that much. I don't see how you can justify this.

Brings me to market value: We're charging you the same rate we charged before we got cell phones and beepers so you could reach us twenty-four hours a day. We're charging well below our market value. We've paid closer attention to your business than our own. We will be charging you less than we would a new client. I think that kind of loyalty deserves some support.

Blames bosses: *This kind of nonsense could get me into all sorts of trouble with my management. I've already put in for my budget for the year, and I'm supposed to trim it 10 percent and it's already down to the bone.*

Offer solution: Not having us on your team would cause a greater shortfall in your budget than paying the increase. We've helped you raise revenues and control costs, and it's a lot less expensive to pay us as a vendor than as employees. I'd be happy to go over your budget in detail with you and see if I can help you find a way to generate the savings you need to cover our fee.

Agrees: *Okay, I'll pay it. But I still think it's steep. At those prices you'd better talk quickly on the telephone, and I'm sure not going to pay for you to attend our sales meeting.*

Thanks: I'm glad we have that matter settled because I'm eager to keep my focus on your business needs.

Competitor threat: *Haven't you been listening? I said no. Your old fee is what I have in the budget, and that's what I'm willing to pay. Either work for that or I'll find someone else.*

Leave door open: We've already worked for you for below market rates and we're offering you a discount. As much as we want to keep working with you, we can't work for less. But I want you to know that we'll be here if you find that our new rate was a good deal after all.

Better use of time: Our new fee is at or below the market for the quality and service we deliver. If you go to someone else, you may not get the same kind of intense attention that we give you. I think it would be better to pay us what we're worth and devote your valuable time to your core business.

Stays angry: *I'll tell you what a bad use of time is—this meeting. You know my position: no fee increase. Take it or leave it.*

- **Behavior:** Have the meeting in whatever space you normally use for strategic planning sessions. Remain cool and confident of the logic of your position. Don't get defensive or angry. Don't plead. Above all, don't negotiate.

ADAPTATIONS

This script can be modified to:

- Renegotiate a contract at renewal.

KEY POINTS

- Focus the discussion on the value your company brings him, positioning it as a contributor of revenue, not an expense.
- After you answer each objection, push for agreement.
- If he mentions cutbacks, tell him that's why he needs you to remain a viable outside resource.
- If he raises the issue of fairness to his employees, answer that you're not one of his employees.
- If he objects to the size of the increase, show that you're just bringing your fee up to market level.
- If you're unable to get agreement, leave the door open by showing that there are no hard feelings and indicating your willingness to come back on board—at the new fee.

Closing a Deal with a Client

97

STRATEGY

Most salespeople know that in order to make a sale you actually have to ask for a decision. But by directly asking potential customers, you're putting them on the spot. Some will opt to buy. A few will be equally direct and give you a flat-out no. But most will equivocate or stall, either because they're still unsure, they're afraid to say no, or they need a little bit more convincing. This script differs from most of the others in this book in that, rather than going through a complete dialogue, it concentrates on one part of the conversation, offering a series of responses to particular stalls.

TACTICS

- **Attitude:** It's better to push beyond a stall and either force a direct no or get more information so you can close more effectively.
- **Preparation:** In this case, preparation is more a matter of memorizing the responses you feel are most appropriate to your business.
- **Timing:** Ask for a decision as soon as you've finished your pitch.
- **Behavior:** Even though the language may seem a bit confrontational, if delivered in a caring, friendly tone it will simply be taken as a sign of persistence and concern.

97. Closing a Deal with a Client

I'd like to add your name to our client list. Shall we move ahead and fill out the order form?

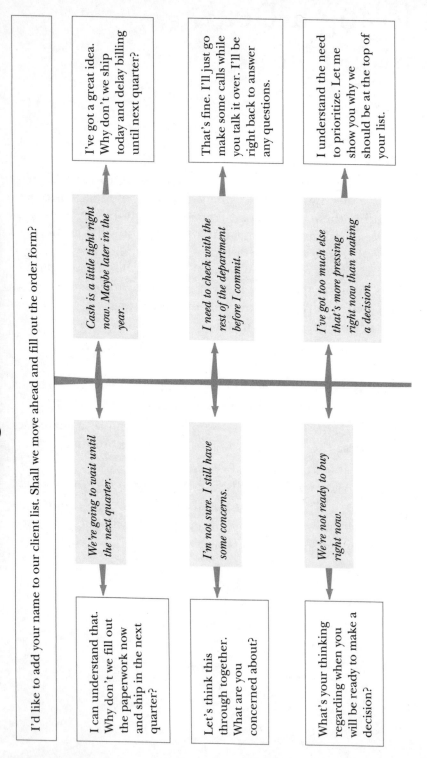

Cash is a little tight right now. Maybe later in the year.

I've got a great idea. Why don't we ship today and delay billing until next quarter?

We're going to wait until the next quarter.

I can understand that. Why don't we fill out the paperwork now and ship in the next quarter?

I need to check with the rest of the department before I commit.

That's fine. I'll just go make some calls while you talk it over. I'll be right back to answer any questions.

I'm not sure. I still have some concerns.

Let's think this through together. What are you concerned about?

I've got too much else that's more pressing right now than making a decision.

I understand the need to prioritize. Let me show you why we should be at the top of your list.

We're not ready to buy right now.

What's your thinking regarding when you will be ready to make a decision?

The way to turn a business around is to take positive steps. Let me show you how we can . . .

We just don't have the money for this right now.

I need to speak with my manager first.

Great. Why don't you introduce him to me and let me do the work? That's my job, after all.

ADAPTATIONS

This script can be modified to:

- Force a client to take an important step that he is delaying.

KEY POINTS

- Be caring and friendly and your effort to close won't sound confrontational.
- If the customer asks for more time, try to find out what the time is needed for.
- If the customer implies he'll buy later, push for a commitment now and either delivery or payment in the future.
- If the customer has to get approval, offer to help.
- If the customer isn't ready to buy, find out what would make him ready.
- If the customer cites poor business, either make the offer more affordable or show how it can boost business.

Overcoming a Gatekeeper

98

STRATEGY

Getting past a personal assistant who serves as a gatekeeper requires a unique combination of subtlety and brashness. Implying a close personal connection, without explicitly saying so, can ensure that you're put right through. Alternatively, if you openly state that you're calling about an emergency or a confidential matter, you might push your way past the barrier. If all else fails, extreme patience and persistence can pay off.

TACTICS

- **Attitude:** Assume you'll be put right through when you call and convey that to the gatekeeper. Acting surprised at being blocked will be more effective than anger.
- **Preparation:** Know and use both the first and the last name of the person you're calling. Learn his or her title and responsibilities so you can make it clear you're calling the correct person.
- **Timing:** Calling before or after normal business hours offers you the best chance of having the individual answer his or her own telephone or of appearing to have a personal connection.
- **Behavior:** Be friendly but insistent; direct but not pushy. Being rude and abrasive will reduce your chances of getting through.

98. Overcoming a Gatekeeper

Icebreaker: Hello. This is Charles Levin. I'm calling to speak with Matt Strauss.

Probes: *Can I tell him what this is in reference to?*

Block #1: *He's in a meeting* [or] *on another call. I'll tell him you called.*

Imply connection: He'll know what it's about.

Emergency: It's an urgent matter and I can only speak with him.

Personal: He may consider it confidential.

Relents: *I'll put you right through.*

Block #2: *I'll let him know you called.*

Still emergency: Please let him know it's an emergency and that I'll be calling back.

Patient: I don't mind holding. Please let him know I'm on the line.

ADAPTATIONS

This script can be modified to:

- Get past an assistant to speak with a manager.

KEY POINTS

- Use the other party's first and last names.
- Explain the call is either confidential or an emergency.
- Maintain control by saying you'll hold or will call back.

Asking a Vendor to Reduce a Price

99

STRATEGY

The secret to getting a price reduction from a vendor is to have an external reason for the request. It can't simply be that you want a higher profit at her expense. The external reason can be anything from a difficult client to an outside auditor or an unfair competitor. Obviously, the more important you are to this supplier, the more likely you are to get a reduction. Similarly, it will be easier if this is a one-time reduction. You can make longer-term reductions more palatable by making them temporary, agreeing to have another discussion at a specific point in the future. Make sure you're speaking with someone who has the power to make such a decision. Also, make sure this request is truly essential for your bottom line. This isn't something you can do regularly when your cash flow gets tight.

TACTICS

- **Attitude:** You're not asking the vendor to take a loss, simply to lower her profits temporarily in order to keep your business.
- **Preparation:** The more you know about the vendor's profit margins the better, so do some research. If you find out she has given price concessions to others, your case is strengthened. Also, make sure you have targeted someone with the power to make this decision.
- **Timing:** The best time to do this is either just after you have paid your most recent bill or just after placing a large order at your regular price. The idea is that there will be fresh evidence of your importance to the vendor.
- **Behavior:** It's okay to have this conversation on the telephone. Don't start out with a threat to shift your business. Instead, present it as a favor from one businessperson to another. If that doesn't work, ratchet up the pressure incrementally until you finally say

99. Asking a Vendor to Reduce a Price

Icebreaker: I consider you to be much more than a vendor [or] supplier. That's why I know I can take you into my confidence.

One-shot reduction: I'm doing a project for Acme Cable. They're very tough, as you may have heard. I'm working on a very tight margin on this one and I need your help. I need you to reduce your profit on this one and charge me [desired price].

Ongoing reduction: Accounting has been reviewing my margins. They've told me I have to improve my profitability. To do that, I'm going to need your help.

Agrees: I hate to do it, but if this job is that important to you I'll do it. But it's just this once, and you owe me one.

Won't do it: When I deal with you, it's always straight. I've always given you my best price.

Can't do it: I've always given you my preferred price. To do any more will only hurt me. I don't think I can help you.

Agrees: You're really killing me, but I don't want to be the one who puts you under. This can't go on forever. In three months we've got to return to normal.

Extraordinary situation: I've never questioned that. But right now I'm involved in an extraordinary situation. I want to stay with you, but I'm going to need your help.

Temporary situation: Look, I really want to keep on working with you. I value our relationship, but I need your help. Once accounting is off my back we can have another conversation.

Agrees: *Okay. If you put it that way, I really have no choice. Remember, though, what goes around comes around.*

Express thanks: You've got it. Thanks for your help. I'm glad we'll still be working together.

Can't do it: *I might be out of business by then. I just can't do it. I'm sorry.*

Reconsider: Look, do me a favor. Think about it overnight. I really want to continue working with you. You can get back to me tomorrow.

Can't do it: *I'd like to help you but I can't commit suicide. I have to sell it to you for the current price. That's the best I can do.*

Reconsider: That means I won't be able to use you for my deal with Acme. Please reconsider. You can get back to me tomorrow.

Agrees: *Okay. If you put it that way, I really have no choice. Remember, though, what goes around comes around.*

Express thanks: You've got it. Thanks for your help. I'm glad we'll be working together on this project.

directly that you'll have to shift your business unless the vendor agrees. Agree to any vague request for a quid pro quo. It's more of a face-saving gesture than a real request.

ADAPTATIONS

This script can be modified to:

- Make an unusually large purchase from an often-used retailer.

KEY POINTS

- Be direct and unambiguous. If possible, make a specific request.
- Make it clear whether this will be a one-time reduction or an ongoing reduction.
- If the vendor agrees right away, however grudgingly, immediately express your thanks.
- If the vendor balks, stress that the situation is either extraordinary or temporary, and that you want to continue to use her services.
- If the vendor continues to balk, ask her to reconsider and make it clear that otherwise you'll have to take your business elsewhere.
- If the vendor asks for a vague quid pro quo, agree immediately.

Complaining to a Vendor about Service

100

STRATEGY

It's not uncommon for vendors to run way behind schedule or to have problems getting things right. Whatever the reason for the unsatisfactory service, it's essential you get the results you're paying for as quickly as possible. You don't need the vendor to become a permanent staff member or to get paid for making mistakes. The secret to getting better service is to have a concise discussion that first, says you have a problem with the service, and second, probes for a reason. Your goal in this dialogue is to get better service, so be prepared to call any bluffs the vendor makes about your staff, to absorb any criticisms she offers, and even to eat a little crow if need be.

TACTICS

- **Attitude:** Be direct and clear. The service is unsatisfactory. You want to know why.
- **Preparation:** Go back to the original plans or proposal the vendor is working from and see if there's been a deviation. Interview anyone assigned to interface with the vendor to find out if there's a problem in-house. Finally, prepare a memo that reiterates your goals and needs.
- **Timing:** Call the vendor to set up a meeting, at your convenience.
- **Behavior:** Hold this meeting in your office. Make sure it's entirely private and confidential. Speak quietly. Make it clear you care about one thing only—getting the job done. Force the vendor to give a reason for the problem, address the reason directly, and tell the vendor to get on with the job.

100. Complaining to a Vendor about Service

Telephone teaser

Icebreaker #1: We need to have a meeting about the computer system in the office. I'd like you to come in Tuesday afternoon.

Face-to-face dialogue

Icebreaker #2: I'm very concerned about the length of time it's taking to get the system operational. I need to get it up and running. If there's been a problem with one of my people, tell me right now. If you're having a problem then I need you to do something about it, even if it means going out and hiring your own consultant.

Blames your staff: *I know it's taking longer than anticipated. But Joan keeps giving me conflicting directions. I don't think that she's fully familiar with your requirements or if she has enough time to put into this.*

Acquiesces: *I had no idea that you were having more than the average problems. I'll redouble my efforts and if I need any help I'll bring it in.*

Blames you: *Listen. Rome wasn't built in a day. This is a complicated system. You've barely been involved in the process, and you have no idea of the problems I've had on this job.*

Remove problem: Okay. If you believe her uncertainty is the reason for the delay, I will totally remove her from any responsibility. I'll sit with her and fill her in on exactly what I want. Or if you think you can repair your relationship with her I will free up more of her time.

Backs down: *I think I can work with her if she has the time to give me and if she's clear on your needs.*

Provide memo: I'm glad to hear you say that. Just to make sure there's no further misunderstanding, here's a memo spelling out exactly what I want from you. I don't care about egos . . . I just care about getting results.

Take responsibility: If the problem has been my lack of clarity or involvement, I'll accept responsibility. I will no longer be an obstacle to your completing this job as we contracted for in the

Backs down: *Thank you. Now I feel like we're getting somewhere. I don't think I'll have any further problems.*

ADAPTATIONS

This script can be modified to:

- Complain to a service provider working with your child.
- Complain to a service provider working with your parent.

KEY POINTS

- Be direct and very concise. The meeting should have no digressions—just as the vendor should have no digressions from getting the job done.
- If the vendor blames one of your staff, say you'll either remove the person or take the authority yourself, and insist on getting the job done now.
- If the vendor blames you, accept responsibility, say you won't be a problem anymore, and insist that the job get done now.
- If the vendor backs off or acquiesces, thank her, and offer a memo reiterating your goals and needs.

Getting a Vendor to Come in with a Very Low Bid

101

STRATEGY

This is probably the shortest script in this book. Yet it's one of the most important for businesspeople. Very often, faced with having to bid on a very competitive, potentially lucrative project, businesspeople are limited by the profitability of their own subcontractors. One way of landing that big project is to put the pressure on your own vendors to, in effect, become partners with you in the project. The only way this is going to work, however, is if you can hold out the opportunity of a big, profitable payoff down the road. Farsighted vendors with the ability to take a chance will be willing to do some initial work at their cost, or even at a loss, if it results in a long-term profitable relationship. The secret here is to ask for bids on both parts of the project so the vendor can see that you're not just pushing for a low price. By the way, keeping the name of your own client under wraps could help.

TACTICS

- **Attitude:** Be completely honest and clear about what you need. Don't feel guilty: he's helping you in a marketing effort that will be of long-term benefit to him as well.

- **Preparation:** If this is a new relationship, make sure the vendor comes highly recommended and is established enough to be able to "invest" with you in a major project. Find out who the decision maker is and speak with him directly.

- **Timing:** This dialogue can be held at your own convenience.

- **Behavior:** Have the conversation over the telephone. Be upfront about exactly what you need. Let the vendor make his usual statements about how good he is at what he does. Close by reiterating exactly what you expect from him.

101. Getting a Vendor to Come in with a Very Low Bid

Icebreaker and pitch: This is Mr. Carter of the Carter Agency. You were recommended to me by Sylvia Chartling of Acme & Zenith. I'd like you to bid on a printing order. However, before I send you the specs there are a few things you should know about the job. The initial press run on this job is only 5,000 because our client is testing the market. If the test is successful, the press run will be 500,000 . . . monthly. I need a bid on both the test and the full runs. Our client is a large multinational that measures risk very carefully. They want to limit their investment in this testing period to the bare minimum. We're willing to run with them and invest in the concept. We need our subcontractors to make the same kind of investment.

We're competitive: *As I'm sure you heard from Sylvia, we're as competitive as anyone in the business . . . and we provide better, more reliable service than any of our competitors. I'm sure you'll be happy with our bid and our work.*

Reiterate: That's why we're calling you to put in a bid. I just need to stress that your bid on the initial run cannot have profit built into it. As for your bid on the rest of the run, we just need it to be competitive. I'll send the specs along. If you have any questions, call me. I look forward to seeing your bid.

ADAPTATIONS

This script can be modified to:

- Ask for any kind of help from a vendor with whom you have had a good relationship.

KEY POINTS

- Be very clear about what you need.
- Consider keeping the name of your client from the subcontractor.
- Offer a long-term, sizable, profitable relationship in exchange for a bare-bones initial bid.
- Suggest the subcontractor submit simultaneous bids for both elements: the loss leader and the profit maker.
- Close by reiterating your needs.

Asking a Vendor to Accelerate Work

102

STRATEGY

Every service you buy from a vendor has four elements to it: speed, quality, scope, and cost. If you're going to request speedier service, you have got to accept that at least one of the other elements must change. In general, it's a mistake to accept a reduction in quality. Therefore you must be willing either to narrow the scope of the assignment or to increase the amount of money you're paying for it. Be aware that the more advance warning you can give, the less you'll have to reduce the scope or increase the price. Your best leverage in this dialogue is the potential you have to offer additional work, so save that as reward for agreement. Similarly, your biggest stick is taking the assignment away from the vendor, so save that as your final pitch. Avoid getting into detail about why the work has to be accelerated. The more details you offer, the more opportunity the vendor has to look for another solution. You've already made that analysis, so there's no point in getting the vendor involved.

TACTICS

- **Attitude:** Be clear and concise. Do not apologize—that just lays the groundwork for a price increase. As long as you're willing to increase your payment or reduce the scope of the project, you're not asking for anything unreasonable.
- **Preparation:** Exhaust all your other options before going to your vendor. Then, go over the details of the project carefully, looking for ways the scope can be reduced. If you don't find any, be prepared to increase the fee.
- **Timing:** Do this as far in advance of the deadline as possible. The more advance warning you give, the less you'll have to pay as a bonus, the less you'll have to reduce the scope of the project, and the more willing the vendor will be to make changes.

102. Asking a Vendor to Accelerate Work

Icebreaker: I need to speak with you about the project you're working on for me. We're facing a different situation now, and I need you to adjust the schedule. I need it to be completed by the fifteenth . . . and it's urgent.

Can't be changed: *I'm sorry, but my schedule is very tight this time of year, and I simply can't get it done by then.*

Sympathetic response: *What happened? What's the matter?*

Sees dollar signs: *Anything is possible. You know that. But it's going to cost. You're talking about lots of overtime.*

You're resourceful: I appreciate your problem. But one of the reasons I hired you was your resourcefulness.

Vague but firm: Unanticipated outside factors have come up forcing us to move the date up, and there's no option. But I think we can work this out.

You're professional: I knew you'd be able to deal with this. I didn't hire you solely on price but on your professionalism too. I think we can work this out.

Suggest reduced scope: I don't think we need to include all original art. Canned images would be sufficient. That should cut down on the amount of time and minimize the impact on your schedule.

Suggest increased budget: I would have no objection to picking up the cost of your bringing in a part-timer who, under your supervision, could help complete the job on time.

Afraid about quality: *That might work, but I don't think I'll be able to guarantee the same quality.*

Subtle threat: When I hired you for this job it was with the idea this would be the start of a long-term relationship. If going the extra mile means you'll be forced to lower your standards, let me know and I'll explore other options.

Agrees: *I'm not crazy about it, but I'll do the best I can.*

Hint of future work: I know you never expected this to happen—neither did I. I hope I'll be in a position to make this up to you with more work in the future.

Afraid of costs: *That might work, but how can I be sure this job won't end up costing me money?*

Subtle threat: When I hired you for this job it was with the idea this would be the start of a long-term relationship. If going the extra mile means you'll be hurt financially, let me know and I'll explore other options.

- **Behavior:** You can have this conversation over the telephone. Be single-minded. There should be no hint of the new deadline being negotiable. Deflect initial objections and launch right into your suggestion. Mitigate fears by hinting at additional work or make the threat to take the project elsewhere.

ADAPTATIONS

This script can be modified to:

- Accelerate the work of professionals.
- Broaden the scope of an assignment without significant additional costs.

KEY POINTS

- Be single-minded about the new deadline but flexible on scope and cost.
- If the vendor reflexively says it can't be done, praise her resourcefulness and launch into your suggestion.
- If the vendor reflexively sees dollar signs, show that you're open to negotiation.
- If the vendor probes for details, offer vague answers and launch into your suggestion.
- If the vendor is fearful of costs or quality, subtly threaten to take the project elsewhere.
- If the vendor agrees, offer the vague hope of future projects.

Returning a Meal in a Restaurant

103

STRATEGY

Very rarely should you have trouble returning a meal in a restaurant. Remember, these are service businesses that succeed by pleasing customers. If you're not happy with your experience, you won't be coming back. If you don't like a dish, call the waiter over and quietly give a specific reason for returning it (so the waiter can tell the chef and/or suggest something else for you), and you should have no problem. Obviously, you shouldn't eat half the dish before deciding you don't like it. Try to give a reason that's subjective, not objective. "Too spicy for me" is better than "overly spiced." That said, some restaurants don't empower the waiters to accept returns, so you may need to make the same presentation to the maître d'. However, if the maître d' doesn't immediately respond, you can make your dissatisfaction clear in a voice loud enough for diners at nearby tables (but not the whole room) to hear.

TACTICS

- **Attitude:** Don't hesitate to return a meal you're not happy with. You're the customer, and the restaurant's business is to please you.
- **Preparation:** Don't order something you know you're apt to dislike.
- **Timing:** Call the waiter over as soon as you know you're not happy with the meal.
- **Behavior:** Whisper to make it clear that you don't want to make a scene but know how to if need be. Give a specific reason for your dissatisfaction with the meal. Raise your voice only if both the waiter and the maître d' resist.

103. Returning a Meal in a Restaurant

Icebreaker and pitch: [Speaking quietly] I'm afraid I find this dish much too spicy for my taste. I'd appreciate it if you could take this back and bring me something else.

Agrees instantly: I'm terribly sorry, sir. What can I bring you instead? May I suggest the prime rib?

Can't do it: I'm sorry, sir, I'm not allowed to return dishes once they've been tasted.

You're the first: You're the first person who's ever complained about this.

Push the up button: I understand. In that case can you please have the maître d' come over to the table?

First today: You mean I'm the first today. Can you please have the maître d' come over to the table?

What's the problem?: Is something wrong, sir?

Repeat complaint: [Still whispering] Yes. As I said to your waiter, this dish is much too spicy for my taste. I'd appreciate it if you could take this back and bring me something else.

Agrees immediately: *I'm terribly sorry, sir. What can I bring you instead? May I suggest the prime rib?*

Won't do it: *I'm sorry, sir. Our policy is not to take dishes back once they've been tasted.*

Rejection: *[No longer whispering]* I'm sorry too, because my policy is not to pay for dishes I cannot eat, not to ever return to restaurants that treat their customers rudely, and to warn everyone I know about restaurants that provide poor service.

KEY POINTS

- Be discreet, yet direct and specific with your waiter.
- If your waiter hesitates, ask to speak with the maître d'.
- Be equally discreet, direct, and specific with the maître d'.
- If you still meet resistance, make it clear you won't be paying or returning.

Suggesting an Overcharge Took Place

104

STRATEGY

Whether or not you think an overcharge was deliberate, you should always act as if it was an honest mistake. That way you keep from getting into a debate over honesty and allow the other party to save face if it was intentional. Your goal, after all, is simply to correct the bill, not to make a citizen's arrest. Even if you have documentation that there was an overcharge, this isn't a simple matter since an item of yours may be held hostage. You'll have to accept that if the other party has got your property and you don't want to go to court, you may need to compromise. Your best tactic is to repeat over and over again that you probably wouldn't have had the work done if you knew the cost would be this high. The other party, if he's a savvy businessperson, will relent and eat the cost. If he's antagonistic, the best you'll be able to do is come up with a workable compromise.

TACTICS

- **Attitude:** You have an edge if the other party isn't holding your property hostage. But if he is, accept that you have no more leverage than he does—if you want to get your item back without a day in small claims court.
- **Preparation:** Have evidence of the original estimate available, but also have in your mind an agreeable compromise figure.
- **Timing:** The timing will be dictated by the other party since he'll either be sending or presenting you with a bill.
- **Behavior:** Don't get angry. That will lead to an argument over motivation and possible wrongdoing. Instead, be forthright and determined, yet flexible enough to compromise.

104. Suggesting an Overcharge Took Place

Icebreaker and pitch: There's a mistake in my bill that needs to be corrected. The price I agreed to for the repairs to my lawnmower was $100, but this bill says $150.

Quote was wrong: *I don't know who told you it would only be $100— but they were wrong.*

It's your staff: That may well be, but whoever it was works for you, not me. I wouldn't have left the mower here to be fixed if I knew that would be the price. I want to continue doing business with you, but I can't assume the cost for your staff's mistakes.

Customer is always right: *I'm terribly sorry. I'll take care of it. [Corrects bill.] Sorry for the inconvenience.*

Offer thanks: Thanks so much for your help. Your customer-friendly attitude is one of the reasons I always bring all my work here and tell my friends to do the same.

Job was more complex: *That's because once we had the mower disassembled we saw it needed some additional repairs.*

It's your problem: I never received a call telling me there were more problems and asking if I wanted to spend more to fix the mower. If I had received such a call, I probably wouldn't have authorized the repairs. I want to continue doing business with you in the future, but I can't assume the cost for your staff's mistakes.

Pay me for my work: *Look, I just want to be paid for what I did. Your machine needed these repairs. I can't release the machine unless I'm paid.*

Offer compromise: I'm sure you did what you thought you had to do. If the situation had been explained to me in advance perhaps I would have considered investing another $25 in the mower. But I wouldn't have wanted to spend another $50. After all, it's ten years old and a brand-new machine would cost me just a little bit more than this bill.

Accepts compromise: *Fair enough. That will cover my costs. I'm sorry we had a problem.*

Won't compromise: *That's less than it cost me. I'll be losing money on the deal.*

So am I: So am I. I'm not sure I would have left the mower here if I knew it would cost me that much. This is a case where I'm afraid we both have to pay because we didn't communicate with each other.

ADAPTATIONS

This script can be modified to:

- Renegotiate the price of a home repair or improvement.

KEY POINTS

- Assume an honest error was made, but insist it's not your responsibility.
- If the other party tries to rationalize the higher fee, insist that's his problem.
- If the other party backs down immediately, thank him and indicate you'll be a repeat customer.
- If the other party blames his staff, insist that's his problem, not yours.
- If the other party asks to be paid his costs, offer a compromise.
- If the compromise isn't accepted at first, stick to your guns.

Requesting Better Service from a Professional

105

STRATEGY

Far too many professionals forget that they are working for their clients. Whatever the poor service involves—whether they're being condescending to you, are rude, or aren't returning your calls promptly—you should put them on notice that it's not acceptable. Be prepared for them either to launch an attack of their own to regain control of the relationship or to offer a half-hearted and meaningless apology. You have all the leverage here since you're the one paying the bills. Don't let them forget it; insist that either their behavior changes or you'll change professionals.

TACTICS

- **Attitude:** If you're paying the bills, you're the boss, regardless of how much more the professional may know about his field.
- **Preparation:** Have examples of the offending behavior in mind before the meeting.
- **Timing:** Do this as soon as possible after poor service. The best time is when you've just received, but haven't yet paid, a bill for services.
- **Behavior:** If possible, have this conversation face to face in your office or home so his status is clear. If that's impossible, have the dialogue over the telephone. *Do not* go to his office or place of business. That will just reaffirm his sense of mastery.

105. Requesting Better Service from a Professional

Icebreaker: Our relationship is important to me, and something disquieting has happened that I need to speak to you about.

Open to conversation: *Our relationship is important to me too. What do you think is wrong with it?*

Stonewalls: *I can't imagine what you mean. Everything we've worked on has turned out very well, I thought.*

Attacks: *I've been meaning to speak with you, too. Your checks have been coming late, and you've built up quite an outstanding balance. I need you to pay more promptly.*

Regain control: What you've just said is indicative of the problem: your attitude.

Voice complaint: I think sometimes you forget that you're working for me and are supposed to be responsive to my needs and wants. For example, it took you three days to return the telephone call to set up this meeting.

Offers half apology: *I'm sorry you feel that way. That isn't my intent. But honestly, I'm doing the best I can. I'm very busy and sometimes it takes time to get back to people.*

Accepts criticism: *I'm so glad you called this to my attention. You're one of my most important clients. I value our relationship. I promise you it won't happen again.*

Won't back down: *I'm afraid I'm very busy, and my time is much in demand. You're expecting too much from me.*

Issue challenge: If the level of service you've been providing is the best you can offer, it simply isn't good enough. I want to continue working with you, but you'll need to improve the service you're providing.

Reaffirm relationship: Your response reaffirms my confidence in you and my choice of you as my [profession]. I'm glad we could work this out.

Threaten shift: What I'm asking of you is the minimum I expect from one of my professionals. If you can't provide that level of service, I'll find someone else who can. Good day.

See script 106: "Terminating a Relationship with a Professional"

ADAPTATIONS

This script can be modified to:

- Speak with higher-ups at an organization or bureaucracy after you've worked your way up the ladder.

KEY POINTS

- Be clear from the beginning that the relationship is in jeopardy.
- If the professional is open to conversation, voice your complaint.
- If the professional stonewalls or counterattacks, reassert your control by indicating that what just occurred is the problem, and then voicing your complaint.
- If the professional refuses to back down, say you'll be looking for another professional and end the dialogue.
- If the professional offers a half apology, put him on notice that his behavior must improve for the relationship to continue.
- If the professional accepts your criticism, reaffirm your relationship with him.

Terminating a Relationship with a Professional

106

STRATEGY

Terminating a professional is more difficult than firing an employee. That's because your relationship with a professional is more intimate. He knows a great deal about your legal and financial life. It's possible you have developed a personal bond as well. If this termination isn't handled well, your former professional can make life difficult for you by holding onto your records and papers and procrastinating about any pending issues. The best strategy in this situation is to try to separate your personal and professional relationships. By saying you want to maintain your personal relationship, you keep from attacking the professional as a person and you also maintain some leverage, increasing the chance of a smooth transition. You also may want to drop the name of your spouse or partner during the dialogue, demonstrating that she or he isn't an avenue for an appeal.

TACTICS

- **Attitude:** Realize this will be awkward and uncomfortable for both of you, but the sooner it's done, the better off for all.
- **Preparation:** Have another professional already lined up so there's no turning back. Discuss the issue with your spouse or partner so she or he can't be approached with appeals.
- **Timing:** Hold this conversation as soon as you have lined up a replacement. Do this before office hours if possible. If not, do it as early in the day as you can.
- **Behavior:** This conversation is best done over the telephone. Just make sure you call the professional's place of business rather than his home. That will support your contention that this is strictly a business matter.

106. Terminating a Relationship with a Professional

Icebreaker and pitch: I have two important things to discuss with you. First, I need to end our professional relationship. Second, but equally important, I need to continue our personal relationship.

Seeks clarification: *What have I done wrong? You're one of my most important clients.*

Antagonistic: *I'm not really surprised. But how do you expect us to remain friends when you're basically taking food out of my child's mouth?*

Seeks confrontation: *Are you firing me?*

Aren't we friends?: I never thought our relationship was dependent on my paying you money. It simply would be better for me if I have someone else handling my account. *[Spouse or partner]* and I have found someone else to take the job on. You'll be getting a call from him in the next couple of days.

Let's stay friends: Let me make myself clear. I want to continue our relationship but on a nonprofessional level. It would be better for me if I have someone else handling my account. *[Spouse or partner]* and I have found someone else to take the job on. You'll be getting a call from him in the next couple of days.

Poor chemistry: It's not a question of right and wrong. It's a question of chemistry. Our professional relationship isn't working out for me. *[Spouse or partner]* and I have found someone else to take the job on. You'll be getting a call from him in the next couple of days.

Assigns blame: *Is this [spouse or partner]'s idea?*

Second chance: *Isn't there something I can do to get you to reconsider?*

No blame: I can't say it's any one person's idea. However, I can tell you we're both in accord.

Not rash: We've been thinking about this for the past month and weighing all our options. So I'm afraid the answer is no.

Gets angry: *After pandering to your whims, after working at night and over the weekends, after doing everything I could to help you, this is the thanks I get?*

Express thanks: Everything you say you've done for me is true, and I'm grateful. I hope we can continue our personal relationship because that's what's most important to me right now.

ADAPTATIONS

This script can be modified to:

- Terminate household help to whom your children are attached.

KEY POINTS

- Be straightforward and clear, separating personal and business issues and taking the onus on yourself, not the professional.
- If the professional asks for clarification, offer generalities and note that you have someone else lined up already—you don't want to get into a debate.
- If the professional seems to be looking for a confrontation, repeat your pitch and note that you have someone else lined up already.
- If the professional seems antagonistic, stress the separation between personal and business issues and note that you have someone else lined up already.
- If the professional looks to assign blame or asks for a second chance, stress that there's no avenue for appeal and the decision is final.
- If the professional gets angry, express thanks for his past efforts, restate your wishes, and end the conversation.

107

Asking a Creditor for More Time

STRATEGY

The key to getting more time from a creditor is to beat her to the punch. If you call her before there's a problem, you're demonstrating that you're aware of your obligations and are concerned. Most lending and credit organizations have standard procedures that allow for partial payments and skipped payments. However, expect that you will be pushed for total payment. Fend off such efforts, explain that your problem is temporary, demonstrate your willingness to eventually pay off the total debt, and indicate that you'll keep the creditor abreast of your changing circumstances—and you'll be able to reach a compromise.

TACTICS

- **Attitude:** Be contrite yet adamant about your inability to pay at this time.
- **Preparation:** Before you call, make sure you have your account number, balance, date of your last payment, and an idea of when you'll be able to resume normal payments.
- **Timing:** Call as soon as you know you'll have a problem paying the bill. The more warning you give, the more flexible the creditor will be.
- **Behavior:** Be as cordial as possible under the circumstances and insist on being treated the same way. When you feel you're being treated improperly, push the up button.

107. Asking a Creditor for More Time

Icebreaker: I need to speak with you about my account. The number is 3939393. I'm calling to tell you that I will not be able to make the payment due next week nor the payments for the next two months.

Party line: *That's a violation of the terms of your agreement with us. According to the agreement you signed, you must make your payments on time. However, there is a five-day grace period you can take advantage of.*

Ignore party line: I've had a serious problem in my family, and I'm not able to make the payments until the problem has been resolved. I expect the matter will be cleared up by March 10. I understand my obligations to the company, and I regret having to ask for additional time, but it's either that or throw in the towel.

Gets aggressive: *In that case, I need you to send your card back to us. You'll then be hearing from our collection department.*

Agrees: *Why don't you skip this month's payment and give me a call ten days before the next payment is due so we can work something out again?*

Wants partial payment: *I probably can arrange to help you somewhat. Why don't you just pay the interest?*

Refuse: I'm sorry. I won't be able to make any payment this month.

Express thanks: Thank you. I won't be using the card until we clear this matter up. I will keep you abreast of my financial situation.

Push the up button: I'd like to speak with your supervisor, please. I think it's unfair for you to react this way when I have a reasonable basis to ask for an extension.

Passes you on: *I'm going to connect you to Mr. Heep, my supervisor. His extension is 2525.*

ADAPTATIONS

This script can be modified to:

- Speak to your landlord about late rent payments.

KEY POINTS

- State the facts of your case and say that you won't be making a payment.
- Ignore recitations of the party line and instead restate your case, stressing your willingness to meet your obligations when you can.
- If you're offered a month's grace period as a compromise, accept and agree to remain in touch.
- If you're asked to make a partial payment, refuse, restating that you'll be unable to make any payment this month.
- If you're offered no alternatives, push the up button until you reach someone with an open mind.

108

Renegotiating a Price with a Client

STRATEGY

At times your original estimate of what an assignment will cost turns out to have been mistaken. If you will end up with less of a profit than you hoped or you will break even, it's best to simply accept the situation as is, and learn from it. However, if you will end up losing money, it's worth trying to renegotiate your fee. The secret to doing this successfully is demonstrating that the project is more complex than you'd originally thought, and that in order for you to do the quality of work you'd promised, you'll need to increase your fee. By admitting you have made a mistake but linking the quality of the job to the increased fee, you may be able to get by with only a minimal amount of anger or annoyance from the client. However, be aware that you're putting your long-term relationship with the client or customer at risk.

TACTICS

- **Attitude:** Realize that you're going to have to admit an error of judgment and that you'll be placing your long-term relationship at risk.
- **Preparation:** Have an explanation for your miscalculation and a plan for moving forward ready before the conversation. In addition, have an answer ready if the client tries to negotiate the amount of the increase.
- **Timing:** Do this as soon as you realize your original estimate was wrong.
- **Behavior:** You can have this conversation over the telephone. Absorb any anger or resentment, but impress that the quality of service is contingent on an increase in the fee. Indicate that you're only looking to break even. Don't press for a final answer in this conversation.

108. Renegotiating a Price with a Client

Icebreaker and pitch: Monica, this is Victor. You're not only one of my most important clients, you've also become a close friend. That's why I have to share with you a problem I have with the marketing study you asked us to prepare for you. In order for us to do an effective job we've got to bring in a media expert. Of course, I'm not going to mark up his cost, but it will increase the price another $5,000.

How did this happen: *I don't understand how this could happen. A month ago you said the price would be $10,000. Nothing has changed. Why has the price gone up?*

Eat it: *You can't make that my responsibility. I relied on your price to get my manager to agree to this project. You're a businessman. When I make a mistake, I have to eat it. This is your problem, not mine.*

You said you could do it: *I thought you were experts in this field. That's what you told me. If you had told me I needed an expert, I would have gone to one in the first place.*

Forget it: *I can't afford that. Maybe we should just forget about it and continue another time when I have the money.*

Not extraordinary: I understand your confusion. What happened isn't that extraordinary. We've just discovered that you're a potentially larger player than you thought. That means we need to bring in another specialist.

Quality at risk: Look, the whole issue here is that we want to do the best job possible for you. I can, if you wish, stick to the original price. But I have to warn you that we're taking a risk. The decision is yours.

I can but . . . : We are experts. Our reputation is important to us and so is the quality of what we do. That's why I'm recommending we get a second opinion. Besides, you couldn't go directly to this kind of expert.

I've already done work: That would be extremely difficult for us. We've already invested over 100 hours of our time in this project.

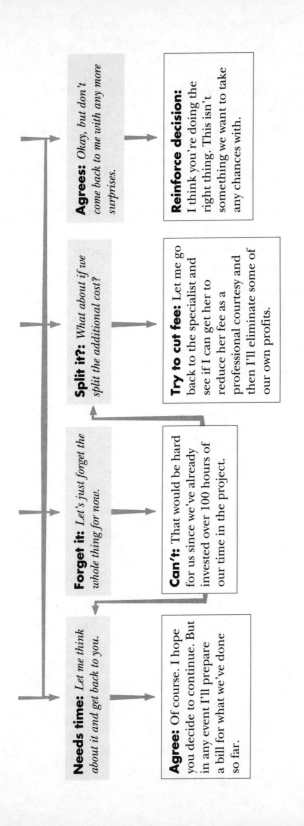

Needs time: *Let me think about it and get back to you.*

Agree: Of course. I hope you decide to continue. But in any event I'll prepare a bill for what we've done so far.

Forget it: *Let's just forget the whole thing for now.*

Can't: That would be hard for us since we've already invested over 100 hours of our time in the project.

Split it?: *What about if we split the additional cost?*

Try to cut fee: Let me go back to the specialist and see if I can get her to reduce her fee as a professional courtesy and then I'll eliminate some of our own profits.

Agrees: *Okay, but don't come back to me with any more surprises.*

Reinforce decision: I think you're doing the right thing. This isn't something we want to take any chances with.

KEY POINTS

- Stress the importance of the relationship, personally and professionally, as well as the need to provide top quality.
- If the client wants to abandon the project, note that you'll need payment for what you've already done.
- If the client asks you how this could have happened, stress the increased complexity.
- If the client asks you to absorb the cost, suggest that would lead to lower quality.
- If the client questions your professionalism, explain that that's exactly why you've spotted the need for additional work.
- If the client suggests splitting the added cost, respond with a proposal of your own.

Explaining a Delay to a Client

STRATEGY

Delays are a fact of life in business. But explaining them to an anxious client isn't easy. Whether the delay was caused by your own miscalculation about your capacity or by an objective circumstance doesn't matter at this point. Since delay is now unavoidable, there's nothing to be gained by going into detailed explanations of what went wrong. In any case, the client is probably not interested in the reason. The secret here is to do whatever you can to accommodate the client. If that means cutting into your profits, so be it. To make the delay tolerable, you have to offer something on the promised date. While it may not be all the client wants, at least she won't be empty-handed.

TACTICS

- **Attitude:** Realize you're going to take some heat for this and risk losing the client.
- **Preparation:** Have ready a very brief and vague explanation of the problem, and prepare a plan that will offer the client something on the promised date of delivery.
- **Timing:** Do this as soon as you realize the scheduled delivery is impossible.
- **Behavior:** Have this dialogue over the telephone—you don't want it going on too long. Absorb any anger and accept full and total responsibility, even while noting that the situation was beyond your control. Then offer your partial product or service and explain how this might be sufficient for the time being. Finally, let the client have the last word—it will help her save face since she really has no alternative but to accept the situation.

109. Explaining a Delay to a Client

Icebreaker and pitch: I'm calling to let you know the brochure will not be ready in time for your sales meeting before the trade show in Las Vegas. We've had a technical problem at the printer. I'll be able to get them to you the morning of the day the trade show opens.

You're responsible: *How do you plan on dealing with this? What are you going to do?*

Take responsibility: The delay is unavoidable and beyond our control, but I take full responsibility for it. I think I have a solution, however.

Angry: *You've had more than enough time to get this done. If I can't count on you for this, I can't count on you for anything.*

Anger won't help: Please don't prejudice our relationship over something that was unavoidable and beyond our control. If you calm down, I can tell you my solution to this problem.

Fearful: *How could you do this to me? You know I've got to have that brochure before the show to prep the sales staff.*

Don't worry: There's no reason to panic. The delay was unavoidable and beyond our control. I think I have a solution to your problem.

Offer solution: I can have working drafts of the brochure, without the edited copy, retouched photos, and four-color graphics, for all of your salespeople by the end of the week. That way you'll be able to go over the brochures with them before the trade show.

Takes parting shot: *Well, I've got no choice, have I, so I suppose that will have to do. But you'd better come through this time . . . understand?*

ADAPTATIONS

This script can be modified to:

- Counter any frustrations you expect from a third party who isn't going to receive what he anticipated.

KEY POINTS

- Be businesslike, direct, and concise. State explicitly that there will be a delay and that there's no way to avoid it.
- If the client expresses fears, explain that panic isn't necessary and offer your plan.
- If the client holds you responsible, accept responsibility and offer your plan.
- If the client gets angry, absorb the anger and offer your plan.
- Let the client have the last word.